W9-BNE-120

GEORGE II
John Shackleton

Fr.   *Photo W. F. Mansell and Co.*

ENGLAND IN THE EIGHTEENTH CENTURY

BY

R. B. MOWAT

PROFESSOR OF HISTORY IN THE UNIVERSITY OF
BRISTOL
FORMERLY FELLOW AND TUTOR OF CORPUS
CHRISTI COLLEGE OXFORD

SEMPER
PARATVS

NEW YORK
ROBERT M. McBRIDE & COMPANY

PREFACE

LECKY, in the preface to his great history, drew attention to the fact that Lord Mahon had already written a fine *History of England in the Eighteenth Century* which appeared to cover the same ground as did Lecky himself. The later historian, however, defended his work by saying that he and Mahon dealt with much the same subject-matter, yet in different ways, and that they did not compete with each other, but rather jointly contributed to the understanding of a great epoch.

In the same way I desire modestly (without in the remotest degree measuring my efforts with the magnificent achievement of Lecky) to draw attention to a recent work which to some extent covers the same ground as I do in this book; I mean Mr. Turberville's admirable *English Men and Manners in the Eighteenth Century*, published by the Oxford University Press. It is reasonable to claim that the subject-matter of the history of England in the eighteenth century is so infinite and so varied that no single interpretation can ever do really more than whet the appetite of a discerning public for knowledge. Every scholar builds upon those before him, and acknowledges his debt, yet is in no way robbed of his opportunity of creating new work, and of setting forth his individual interpretation.

. . . .

The quarterly journal of the Historical Association, *History*, has in recent years been producing a highly interesting series of articles under the title of 'Historical Revisions.' It is surprising how many judgments, hitherto accepted without question, have now to be altered, sometimes because new material has been discovered, but in other cases simply because it has occurred to somebody to think out an old situation anew. Historians, like everybody else, have something of the nature of sheep, and are apt to go on repeating, generation after generation, the views that they have learned in their youth.

In this book I have not precisely undertaken a work of historical revision; but in the process of setting down an interpretation of the eighteenth century, and in re-reading familiar authorities and reconsidering old facts, different conclusions have been occasionally suggested from what I had previously been led to regard as accepted. Thus, for instance, there is some reason to hold that much of the social ill often ascribed to the Industrial Revolution was really caused by the great wars. The British Empire in India may have been in a sense, as Seeley says, accidental, but it was also founded through a deliberate imitation of French methods. The result of the English rule in eighteenth-century Ireland was in most respects deplorable, yet in certain (though very limited) respects was admirable, particularly in regard to intellectual culture. The secession of the American Colonies was not inevitable (unless all things are predestined), but was almost accidental, for the principles of colonial government, which, apparently, would have satisfied the Americans, were known to the English Governments of that time, and on various occasions were officially put into practice, but not consistently. The famous Party System, the original Whigs and Tories, according to Mr. Namier's investigations and conclusions, became practically unrecognisable at one period of the eighteenth century.

A great part of British foreign affairs in the eighteenth century concerns colonial or commercial disputes with Spain. It is usual for British historians to defend Great Britain by pointing to the rigid monopoly of trade which Spain maintained over her colonies; but as a matter of fact Great Britain was quite as jealous as was Spain, and quite as determined to exclude foreign nations from the benefits of trade with the British Isles or with the British Empire overseas. The war made by Great Britain upon Spain in 1739 because Spain stopped British trade with Spanish colonies had absolutely no moral justification. It was a war of pure aggression, with the object of forcing Spain to give up a policy of economic Protection which Great Britain in her own dominions enforced against Spain and every other foreign country.

History, which, justly pursued, is one of the most beneficent studies, can also be made—has often been made—one of the most evil. I venture to say that it has been the greatest breeder of prejudice, the greatest *misleader* of mankind. Yet an intelligent reading of the past, instead of fortifying prejudice, ought surely to make every people modest, tolerant, and broadminded. For it emerges clearly out of history that no people or party in any controversy or in any policy has ever been wholly in the right or ever completely in possession of the truth. As we learn to read the past tolerantly we shall come to regard the present tolerantly too ; and future historians will have the pleasant task of chronicling peace, not wars.

.   .   .   .   .

I am indebted to Sir G. M. Trevelyan and to the Delegates of the Clarendon Press, Oxford, for permission to quote a passage from *The Two-party System in English Political History*.

R. B. MOWAT

THE UNIVERSITY
BRISTOL

CONTENTS

ILLUSTRATIONS

MAPS

ENGLAND IN THE EIGHTEENTH CENTURY

CHAPTER I

THE UNITY OF CIVILISATION

THERE was a time when there was only one type of civilisation over Central and Western Europe. This civilisation was drawn chiefly from Latin literature, Roman law, and the Christian religion. Its common language was Latin. In the sixteenth century, however, Latin began to lose its position as a universal language, and thus a blow was struck at the unity of Western civilisation. In the same century, the sixteenth, the Reformation destroyed the unity of the Western Church. To complete the international chaos, the theory of the absolute sovereignty of monarchs or states was universally adopted, so that every monarchy became a law to itself, acknowledging no superior control, and claiming the right to settle every dispute with its neighbour by the lawless method of war.

During the course of the sixteenth century, in place of the common mediæval civilisation, there grew up distinctly national cultures—Italian, Spanish, French, German, English, Scandinavian. Systems of law and education, which had been similar throughout all Central and Western Europe in the Middle Ages, became different in every separate country. Religious divisions made people suspicious of strangers. John Milton, travelling in Italy after leaving Cambridge, ran a risk of imprisonment at the hands of the Papal Inquisition. Shorthouse's novel, *John Inglesant*, gives an imaginative yet true picture of the life of an intellectual and sensitive Englishman in seventeenth-century Italy ; it was not a country in which an Englishman could take root, however sympathetic he might happen to be.

By the time, however, that the eighteenth century opened, some approach had again been made towards a unity of Western civilisation, although this approach was, and still is, very far from complete. One thing which greatly helped to restore the balance towards a unity of civilisation was the growth of toleration. The age of religious wars was over. Men could travel freely in every country without fear of religious persecution.

As in the Middle Ages, the universities were recognised as centres of a knowledge which was common to all, and of methods of instruction which were universally familiar. When Dr. Johnson was an undergraduate at Pembroke College, Oxford (1729), Dr. Panting, the Master, heard him through the door saying : ' Well, I have a mind to see what is done in other places of learning. I'll go and visit the universities abroad. I'll go to France and Italy. I'll go to Padua.' [1] But this design was never carried out. Oliver Goldsmith, however, who was about the same age as Johnson, did carry out such a design. He toured—walked, it is said—through France, Italy, and Holland, stopping at the universities, and, being without means, earned his board by ' disputing ' before other scholars, presumably in the Latin tongue. The result of this journey, about which very little is known, combined with Goldsmith's later studies, was his book on *The Present State of Polite Learning in Europe* (1759). In this work he passed in review all the chief countries of the Continent, and estimated the degree and the kind of culture—literary, scientific, classical—which they possessed.

Goldsmith recognised in Europe a ' Commonwealth of literature,' which had existed since the time of Virgil and Horace. He went so far as to say that it was by a nation's position in this commonwealth that it would be judged

[1] Boswell's *Life of Johnson,* sub anno 1729.

throughout all time : ' Whatever the skill of any country may be in sciences, it is from its excellence in polite learning alone that it must expect a character from posterity.' [1] The springs of this culture were all classical. ' In running over Europe, we shall find that wherever learning has been cultivated, it has flourished by the same advantages as in Greece and Rome ; and that, wherever it has declined, it sinks by the same causes of decay.' [2]   The Germans were backward in regard to polite learning, because they continued, at least many of them, to write in Latin ; but 'the society established by the King of Prussia at Berlin is one of the finest literary institutions that any age or nation has produced ' ; this refers to the great Academy of Berlin, founded, on the advice of Leibniz, by Frederick I of Prussia.   In Holland men had the fault of relying on their memory rather than their judgment.   Spain, ' whose genius is naturally fine,' was now ' behind the rest of Europe.' Denmark had one man of letters of European standing, Baron Holberg, ' the son of a private sentinel,' who toured Europe on foot, spent two years at Oxford, earning his living by teaching French and music, and writing a universal history.   He returned to Copenhagen and wrote eighteen comedies; and ' a life begun in contempt and penury ended in opulence and esteem.' [3]   The French had of late ' fallen into a method of considering every part of art and science as arising from simple principles ' ; and from ' contracting a science into a system ' they were proceeding to draw up ' a system of all the sciences united '—hence ' those monsters of learning,' the Encyclopædias and *Bibliothèques* of the age.   Finally Goldsmith turns to Great Britain, eminent among its Continental peers : ' To acquire a character for learning amongst the English at present, it is necessary to know much more than is either important or useful.'

For the purposes of learning Europe was a unit ; a student could choose any university he liked.

[1] *Present State of Polite Learning*, chap. 2.
[2] *Ibid.*, chap. 34.   [3] *Ibid.*, chap. 6.

' The universities of Europe may be divided into three classes. Those upon the old scholastic establishment, where the pupils are immured, talk nothing but Latin, and support every day syllogistical disputations in school philosophy. Would not one be apt to imagine this was the proper education to make man a fool ? Such are the universities of Prague, Louvain, and Padua. The second is where the pupils are under few restrictions, where all scholastic jargon is banished, where they take a degree when they think proper, and live not in the college, but the city. Such are Edinburgh, Leyden, Göttingen, Geneva. The third is a mixture of the two former, where the pupils are restrained but not confined, where many, though not all, of the absurdities of scholastic philosophy are suppressed, and where the first degree is taken after four years' matriculation. Such are Oxford, Cambridge, and Dublin.' [1]

Although this was a tolerant age, Protestant families, as they still do, tended to send their sons to Protestant universities. Outside Oxford and Cambridge, where the university degrees were strictly limited to men who would sign the articles of the Church of England, Leyden was the favoured institution. When Alexander Carlyle, a distinguished Scottish student, went to Leyden in 1745, he found twenty-two young Scotsmen or Englishmen there, including Charles Townshend, later Chancellor of the Exchequer, and John Wilkes, later the notorious champion of liberty. [2] Carlyle lived in Madame Vandertasse's lodging-house.

' Our house was in high repute for the best coffee, so that our friends were pleased when they were invited to partake with us of that delicious beverage. We had no company to dinner; but in the evenings about a

[1] *Present State of Polite Learning*, chap. 13.
[2] *The Autobiography of the Rev. Dr. Alexander Carlyle, Minister of Inveresk* (1910 ed.), p. 175.

dozen of us met at one another's rooms in turn three times a week, and drank coffee, and smoked tobacco, and chatted about politics, and drank claret, and supped on bukkam (Dutch red-herrings), and eggs, and salad, and never sat later than twelve o'clock.' [1]

The unity of Western civilisation, however, which Goldsmith both assumes and demonstrates, stopped at the Vistula. The Russians were outside it, without literature, without scholarship, unvisited by travellers from the West, although Peter the Great had broken through his country's barriers in his famous visits to ' Europe ' in 1697 and 1716. Even ' high life,' which in most countries is cosmopolitan, was not cosmopolitan in Russia. The aristocracy of the neighbouring state, Poland, was well known in the rest of Europe for its wealth and culture, and for libraries and galleries of pictures collected in the great Polish *châteaux*; but the Russian *boyars* were still nothing but big landowners, interested in hunting and country-life, but without any of the amenities which distinguished country-life in the rest of Europe.

In the armies and navies of Europe there was a large element of cosmopolitanism. Armies were not then, as they are now, nations in arms, with the whole male citizen body being passed through the ranks. In the eighteenth century the army was professional. People—officers as well as privates—took to soldiering for their livelihood. The tradition of the mercenary soldier still lingered in Europe. In every army on the Continent there were large numbers of foreigners. In the Dutch service there were whole regiments of Scots. In the French army there were Swiss regiments; their faithfulness at the time of the Revolution is commemorated by the Lion of Lucerne. The Papal troops were, as they still are, almost wholly foreign. An Irishman, Richard Wall (1694–1778), became an ambassador, and later Minister of Foreign Affairs, of Spain.

---

[1] *The Autobiography of Alexander Carlyle of Inveresk*, p. 175.

B

A Scotsman, James Keith (1696–1758), became a Prussian Field-Marshal. He was killed at the battle of Hochkirch in the Seven Years War and is buried at Berlin. Sir John Acton (1736–1811) was chief Minister to the King of Naples. In England, Luke Schaub, a Swiss, rose to the rank of ambassador. He was particularly active in the complicated negotiations of the years 1715–18.

England in the eighteenth century had the largest share in this cosmopolitan stream, perhaps because, as the only free country in Europe, she attracted foreigners who found conditions at home too restricted. The German philosopher Leibniz visited and had friends in England, including Sir Isaac Newton; and before the accession of George I to the English throne, he did much by his correspondence to prepare the way for that event. Leibniz died at Hanover in 1716. Voltaire, who came to England in 1726 and stayed about three years, was practically an exile. He had been shut up in the Bastille because, after the Duke of Rohan had him whipped by lackeys, he wanted to challenge the duke to a duel. When released, he was ordered by the Government to leave Paris. Voltaire always had a little money of his own, and he knew how to take care of it and increase it by judicious investment. He lived in England comfortably enough, and found society very much to his taste. Men of letters were held in high estimation, and—as never happened in France—they were admitted freely into politics. ' The poet who had been thrown into prison for resenting a whipping from a nobleman's lackeys, found himself in a land where Newton and Locke were rewarded with lucrative posts in the administration of the country, where Prior and Gay acted in important embassies, and where Addison was a Secretary of State.' [1] Like the men of letters in France, the English writers had views about the government of the country, and, unlike the Frenchmen, they had unrestricted liberty to express those views as they pleased. ' From Bolingbroke and

---

[1] Morley, *Voltaire* (1891), pp. 59–60.

Swift down to the author of the *Golden Rump*, every writer who chose to consider himself in opposition treated the Minister [Walpole] with a violence and ferocity which neither irritated nor daunted that sage head, but which would in France have crowded the lowest dungeons of the Bastille with victims of Fleury's anger and fright.' [1]

Voltaire admired the country-life which he found in England. He noticed that the peasant did not have his feet bruised by being shod in wooden shoes, that he ate white bread, was decently clad, and was not afraid to increase his stock of cattle, or to repair the roof of his cottage, lest his taxes should be increased next year. Nor was the substantial yeoman fleeing to the towns. Voltaire observed a large number of farmers in England, ' with five or six hundred pounds sterling a year,' who did not think it beneath them to cultivate the earth and to work with their own hands.[2] In France every countryman who could accumulate a little capital was eager to quit the country and to buy a place in a town.[3]

Voltaire was not the only eminent Frenchman who came to England, not simply on a visit, but to make a long stay. Montesquieu, who was a friend of Lord Chesterfield, lived and studied in England from 1729 to 1731 : Rousseau found a home for eighteen months at Wootton, in Staffordshire (1766–67). A Corsican, General Paoli, the defender of Corsica against the French, made his home in London, with a pension from George III, from the year 1769 to his death in 1807. He formed one of Dr. Johnson's circle ; Boswell stayed with him in London. Obviously English

---

[1] Morley, *Voltaire*, p. 62. The *Golden Rump* was a manuscript farce attacking Walpole, and attributed to the authorship of Fielding, 1735. It came into Walpole's hands. The Prime Minister read objectionable passages from it in the House of Commons. It was in consequence of this that the Act of 1737 was passed making the licence of the Lord Chamberlain necessary for dramatic performances.

[2] Voltaire's *Lettres*, X (*Œuvres*, XXXV, p. 81, *apud* Morley).

[3] Tocqueville, *L'Ancien Régime et la Révolution*, LIV, ii, chap. 9.

Society was something with which a gentleman even from distant Corsica could become intimately familiar.

Men passed with surprising ease from country to country, and gained a living in each. Casanova, the author of celebrated memoirs, is a type of many adventurers who were to be found in every capital in Europe. Born in Venice in 1725, he received a poor education. Becoming a clergyman in minor orders, he went on to be a soldier, a violinist, a worker of magic. Living by his wits, he visited all the great cities of Europe, including, of course, London, sometimes in prison, sometimes fleeing from creditors, always observing men, women, and manners with a keen eye and considerable humour. He ended his long life in peace, after thirteen years' residence in Dux, the castle of the great Waldstein family in Bohemia, where he wrote the *Mémoires*, the record of a thoroughly loose and cynical character. He died at Dux in 1798.

It was not in Western or Central Europe only that social conditions were similar. European civilisation had been transplanted to the New World, and, by the opening of the eighteenth century, was flourishing there. In South and Central America there was a Spanish society, highly aristocratic, a society of landowners and officials. In the Southern States of the United States there was also a European society, a slave-owning class of great landed proprietors. Their homes were like the homes of English squires, but the existence of slavery constituted an essential difference between, for instance, the squires of Virginia, in America, and Norfolk, in England.

In the New England States, however, a society which was English and European from top to bottom had grown up since the Pilgrim Fathers landed on Cape Cod in 1620. It was a society of farmers, fishermen, and merchants. There was no slave-labour, no coloured population except for some scattered tribes of Indians, steadily receding into the backwoods. Local government and State government were conducted according to English traditions ; there were printing-presses and newspapers ; and ' Latin schools ' and colleges for the education of the people in the scholarship which is common to Western civilisation.

Harvard College in Cambridge, Massachusetts, was founded in 1636, and by the opening of the eighteenth century was a firmly established college producing scholars, clergy, and men of affairs in New England. The New England clergymen were, as a rule, hardworking men with good libraries. One of them, Jonathan Edwards, was a philosopher of distinction. He was born at East Windsor, Connecticut, in 1703. At the age of seventeen he graduated at Yale College, and for two years was a tutor there. In 1727 he was ordained a Congregational minister, and for the next seventeen years worked with devotion in his charge at Northampton, Massachusetts. In 1758 he died of small-pox, a short time after he had been installed as President of Princeton College. He had written works on metaphysics, one of which—*The Freedom of the Will*—is still a standard treatise.

The unity of civilisation as between the old country and the new can be realised by a reading of Benjamin Franklin's *Autobiography*. It is such a career as, *mutatis mutandis*, might have been made in the Old World, though in some ways against greater obstacles than in the New. A young Philadelphian printer makes a competence by his business and at the same time engages in mechanical studies and in local politics. Society was not *stratified* in America as it was in eighteenth-century England, so that it was easier for Franklin to rise in politics in the colonies than it would have been in London. There was a ' governing class ' in England, and the landed aristocracy, which had grasped . power at the Revolution of 1688, held it in a fairly close monopoly down to the other and more far-reaching, the Industrial Revolution. Outside politics, however, conditions were not so different between the American colonies on the one hand and old England on the other. When Benjamin Franklin came to London in 1757, he conversed with people as one who was already familiar with their affairs.

A great humanitarian and religious movement was begun in England when John Wesley, after reading William Law's *Serious Call to a Devout and Holy Life*, took up his evangelical work. Wesley's *Journal* is the record of this lifelong mission, of his travels and labours in the British Isles and on the Continent. In the American colonies John Woolman of Burlington, in New Jersey (1720–72), was undertaking similar labours, in a life of continual travel and self-sacrifice. His *Journal* is a plain and impressive record of this, the first of the ' abolitionists.' He opposed negro slavery, and preached the gospel without ceasing. In 1772 Woolman visited England, and died there of smallpox.

The evangelical and humanitarian movement was not confined to England and America. On the continent of Europe the Moravian Brethren, an earnest body of German Protestants, were labouring against scepticism, worldliness, and ill-faith. John Wesley visited one of their leaders, Count Zinzendorf, at Marienborn, near Frankfort, in 1738. The Marquis Beccaria was studying law and the systems of punishment. His great book *On Crimes and Punishments* was published at Monaco in 1764.

An Englishman, John Howard, was, like Beccaria, a student of the European systems of justice, chiefly from the point of view of prison-reform. Having inherited a considerable fortune, Howard resolved to devote his life to improving the conditions of prisons, where men, women, and children were herded together in indescribable stench and filth. He began his travels at the age of thirty in 1756. His tours took him through the British Isles and most of the Continental countries. No danger deterred him. He made a passage in a ship which had plague in it in order to see how the sufferers fared. He died of camp-fever (typhus) at Kherson, in South Russia, in 1790, having gone to visit Russian military hospitals during the Russo-Turkish War. His great books, containing faithful and frightful disclosures, were *The State of the Prisons in England and Wales*, published in 1777, and *An Account of the Principal Lazarettos in Europe*, published in 1789.

Another noble life among these eighteenth-century philanthropists was that of Johann Friedrich Oberlin, who was Protestant pastor of Steinthal, in Alsace, from 1767 (when he was twenty-seven years old) to his death in 1826. Oberlin made the rude, desolate valley with the miserable inhabitants into one of the most prosperous districts in Europe. The children were educated in the schools which he started ; the peasants were taught new methods of cultivating the soil ; a library was established ; roads and bridges were constructed ; manufactures grew up. The moral and religious welfare of the inhabitants, besides their increasing material prosperity, made Oberlin's work in the Steinthal celebrated throughout Europe. In another valley, in the neighbouring country of Switzerland, the Swiss Pestalozzi was in the last quarter of the eighteenth century showing how education could be given to rich and poor children together in the same schools, and how the children could be trained in moral virtues as well as intellectual by methods of freedom. All Western and Central Europe was awaking to humanitarian and educational zeal.

FOR FURTHER STUDY

Sir J. E. SANDYS, *A History of Classical Scholarship* (3rd ed., 1921).

G. DESNOIRESTERRES, *Voltaire et la Société Française au 18me siècle* (8 vols., 1867–76).

EDWARD CHANNING, *History of the United States* (1905), vols. i–iii.

CASANOVA, *Mémoires* (6 vols., 1912).

R. B. MOWAT, *A History of European Diplomacy*, 1451–1789 (1928), chaps. 21, 26.

J. CHURTON COLLINS, *Bolingbroke* and *Voltaire in England* (1886).

CHAPTER II

POLITICS

EIGHTEENTH-CENTURY politics in England were peculiar. Disraeli in *Coningsby* has compared the ruling politicians to the ' Venetian Oligarchy.' The Venetian aristocrats, however, were secured in their power by the laws and constitution of the State. The English governing class was not. It is rather to be compared with the governing class of ancient Rome in the last two centuries of the Republic. There, a number of families of political experience, which had produced Senators for several generations, managed to have their members elected to all the chief offices; and, justifying their position by their administrative ability, they guided the State successfully through the period of the Punic Wars and converted Rome into a world-wide empire.

The English governing class of the eighteenth century was not a closed aristocracy, a caste, like the contemporary Venetian aristocracy. In Venice the name of every noble family had been inscribed in 1297 in the Golden Book, which was thereupon closed ; no new family-names were admitted to the Golden Book, except rarely by special decree on account of exceptional services to the State. In England there was no such *Serrata del Consiglio*, no such closure of the governing body of the State, although Sunderland's Peerage Bill of 1719 was an attempt to establish something like it.

The Peerage Bill, introduced by Charles Spencer, 3rd Earl of Sunderland, into the House of Lords and passed in that House, would have practically closed the peerage, the class which since the Revolution had supplied most of the Ministers of State. The Crown was only to be permitted to add six new names in all to the existing peerage unless a noble family had become extinct; in this case, another family could be ennobled to fill the vacancy. The number of peers in 1719 was (without the bishops) 178. Had the Bill been passed into law the number, even counting the Scottish and Irish peers, would never have been more than 200; whereas the number now is about 700—an increase less than the growth of population and the wealth of the country could justify. Throughout the eighteenth century the great majority of Cabinet Ministers (although not of Prime Ministers [1]) were peers. The Peerage Bill of 1719 would probably have made the Cabinet almost a monopoly of the peers. Even without the Peerage Bill, their political power, on account of their control of pocket boroughs and of the social esteem in which they were held, was enormous. The Bill was rejected in the House of Commons, after a strong speech made against it by Robert Walpole, who was Member for King's Lynn.

The Scottish peerage was closed by the Act of Union of 1707. The closure, however, was of no social or political significance, because the king could make new peers *in* Scotland although not peers *of* Scotland; he could make Scotsmen peers of the United Kingdom. In any case the Scottish peers did not exercise a monopoly of political power in Scotland, for in addition to the noble ' lairds ' were the numerous untitled lairds, like the English squires, who were very powerful.

Since the Revolution of 1688 politics had been directed through the party system. This was a feature peculiar to Great Britain in the eighteenth century, where there were only two parties, the Whig and Tory. The system can scarcely be said to exist in perfection anywhere now; in twentieth-century Great Britain there are three parties.

[1] This title was not legally recognised till 1907, nor commonly used till about 1800.

The United States and Japan are perhaps the only two countries where not more than two parties control the politics of the nation.

The essence of the party system is that each party should claim to represent the whole people and assume the task of governing the country in the interest of the community and not of any particular class. A party must aim at becoming the Government by convincing a majority of the people that its policy is the best for the country. Thus, after a General Election it will have a majority of votes in the House of Commons, and so will control both legislation and seats in the Cabinet; and so it will become the Government of the day. When it ceases to have the support of a majority of the people it will at the ensuing General Election fail to obtain a majority of votes, and will give place to the other party, who will then become the Government of the day. Any attempt of a party or body of men by force to make themselves the Government or to compel the Government to act in a certain way is obviously a confession that they have not the approval of a majority of the people; for if they had, they could become the Government or command the Government simply through exercising their votes.

In the eighteenth century after 1714 the two parties did not differ from each other in so marked a degree as in the reigns of William III and Anne. Lord Hervey, who was a Whig and a supporter of Walpole, wrote:

' The two chief characteristics of the Tories originally were the maintenance of the prerogatives of the Crown and the dignity of the Church; both which they pretended were now become, if not by profession, at least by practice, much more the care of the Whigs. Nor were the Whigs quite innocent of this imputation: long service and favour had gradually taught them a much greater complaisance to the Crown than they had formerly paid to it, and the power of the Crown being an engine at present in their

own hands, they were not very reluctant to keep up an authority they exercised, and support the prerogative which was their own present though precarious possession. The assistance likewise which the Whigs in power had received from the bench of bishops in parliamentary affairs had made them show their gratitude in return, by supporting both them and the inferior clergy in all ecclesiastical concerns (except the suffering the Convocation to sit, with as much vigour and firmness as the most zealous of those who are called the Church party could have done).' [1]

The Whig Party was almost continuously in power, formed the majority in the House of Commons, and supplied nearly all the Cabinet Ministers, from the Revolution down to the tenth year of the reign of George III. The adherents of the party were chiefly townspeople (especially the growing class of rich merchants), and a number of squires—not so much the smaller or medium squires, who were for the most part Tory, but certain big ' Houses,' powerful and wealthy families like the Grenvilles (Earls Temple), the Russells (Dukes of Bedford), the Cavendishes (Dukes of Devonshire), the Pelhams (Dukes of Newcastle). Their political principles might be summarised under the terms ' Revolution of 1688,' ' Limited Monarchy,' ' Parliamentary Government through the Cabinet,' and ' Religious Toleration.' The Tories differed from the Whigs through having less reverence for the Revolution of 1688, being more favourable to the exercise of the Royal Prerogative, relying rather upon the electors than on the elected Members of Parliament, and supporting the Church of England with Penal Acts against nonconformists. The Whigs also tried to make out that the Tories were Jacobites, secret opponents of the House of Hanover; but, although many Tories, like Dr. Johnson, professed a sentimental regard for the exiled

----

[1] *Memoirs of the Reign of George II*, by John, Lord Hervey (1884), p. 5.

House of Stewart, very few of them were prepared to be active Jacobites.

It is very difficult for a party to remain hopeful and strong, zealous and well disciplined, if it is continuously in Opposition, and for years sees little prospect of becoming the Government. Yet the Tory Party never looked like dying out at any time in the eighteenth century. Tory candidates stood at the elections; there was a considerable body of Tories in Parliament; the Tories were always ready to form a Government whenever a majority of the electorate should vote in their favour; and when their time came in 1770 they did form a powerful and capable, although, for certain reasons, not a successful Government.

How the Tories kept their organisation in life and strength during the long and apparently hopeless years in Opposition is not known. A modern historian has approached this question, but has not solved it:

'Toryism from 1714 to 1760 may be said to be hibernating. "It is not dead but sleepeth," dreaming, in old manor houses and colleges and cathedral cloisters, of Charles the Martyr and the days of the Merry Monarch "when loyalty no harm meant." The history of the long Tory hibernation has yet to be written. How far, and by whom, was the Tory electoral machine kept going in those barren years? How many candidates did they "run" at elections, and on what issues, with what success? We need good books on the subject, based on research that has still to be done. The corresponding "hibernation" of the Whig party from 1793 to 1830 is better known to us all, from the picturesque records of Holland House, the interesting personalities of Fox and his followers, and the better reporting of Parliamentary debates and electoral contests at that later period.

But the Toryism of the period from 1714 to 1760, though its political activities remain somewhat obscure to us through the deficiencies of history, is known to us all as a personal creed through the merits of literature. Squire Western represents to us the more old-fashioned rural squirearchy, and Dr. Johnson, the Church, the two pillars of the Tory temple which stood firm under water during the forty years when the Whig deluge covered the earth, to reappear strong as ever when the waves subsided.

Johnson, a man of the people from a cathedral town, is the typical High Churchman as Highchurchmanship was understood in that day. His religion, which underlay all he did, was by him identified with his ideal system of politics. Squire Western, a more comic character, drawn of course with all the exaggeration of humorous fiction, is not a man of much religion; we may say that landowning is his religion, for it is his sincere and earnest rule of life. He identifies landowning, illogically perhaps, with Tory politics and a dislike of Dissenters, who were probably small freeholders or even suspected poachers of his partridges.

Fielding's imaginary squire and Boswell's very real doctor have in common a traditional view of politics: a strong dislike of Dissenters and of their patrons the Whig lords; an attachment to the Anglican traditions of the earlier kings of the House of Stuart, rendered inoperative in the present by the fear felt by all true Tories of again putting a Roman Catholic prince on the throne, and by their innate respect for law and order even when administered by their political rivals. Politically, Toryism was rather a futile creed under the first two Georges. Its adherents were in an impasse, from which they were delivered by the accession to the throne of a particularly strong Protestant with their own Tory sympathies, in the person of George III.

From 1761 to 1782 the Tory party came out of its long hibernation and helped the King to rule the land. It did so in the first instance not as a Parliamentary but as a Royalist party, as the " King's Friends," supporters of George III's personal rule. When this failed them, just as the personal rule of the later Stuarts had failed them, they again became a Parliamentary party—a transformation rapidly and easily accomplished under the able leadership of the younger Pitt. Thenceforward till 1830 the Tory party governed the Empire. The reaction against Jacobinism and the Napoleonic wars gave them an advantage over their rivals analogous to the advantage which the fear of Jacobitism and the ambitions of Louis XIV had given to the Whigs.' [1]

The Whig and Tory Parties both made use of pocket boroughs—small towns or even villages which had the right of returning one or two members to Parliament and where the local landowner could direct the votes. Yet although both parties commanded a considerable number of pocket boroughs, and even some county constituencies, public opinion, in times of crisis or excitement, was able to assert itself, and to change the balance of parties. This happened in 1701, when the General Election went against the Tories, who had a majority in the previous Parliament, and who were averse from opposing Louis XIV by war in the question of the Spanish Succession ; in 1742, when all the borough influence of the Walpole Government could not prevent it from losing constituencies ; and in 1784, when a General Election resulted in the utter defeat of Fox and North, who were then at the head of the Government of the day and held a large majority of votes in the Parliament of 1783.

Nevertheless, although constituencies, particularly county constituencies, could, and frequently did, assert their independence, it is true that almost any man, by buying a borough, was able in normal times to make sure of his return to Parliament. It was by this means that home-coming ' Indian Nabobs '—Englishmen who had made a fortune in India—bought their way into political life. This facility of entrance into Parliament was not necessarily

---

[1] G. M. Trevelyan, *The Two-party System in English Political History* (1926), pp. 20–22.

contrary to the public interest. It enabled ' keen ' young
men, like the Pitts, father and son, to become members of
the House of Commons as soon as they attained the legal
age (21) or as soon afterwards as they were finished with
the university and the ' Grand Tour.' It enabled men of
experience in the public service, like Clive, when he came
back in 1760 after performing a great work in India, to stand
for Parliament without loss of time or effort, and with the
practical certainty of election. There may have been keen
young politicians who had neither the wealth nor the connections (relatives, friends, interested parties) necessary for
obtaining a pocket borough; yet such instances have not
been noted frequently in the history of the eighteenth
century. The leaders of the two great parties were usually
observant of political talent wherever it could be found, and
were quick to recruit able young men into their party and
to help them to a constituency. The truth appears to be
that at this time political aspirations were not common
outside the class of men of birth and of at least some wealth
—the ' governing class ' of England. It was probably only
after the Industrial Revolution came upon the land that an
intellectual ferment was set up which penetrated to the
hitherto ' unpolitical ' classes of people and caused them to
aspire to Parliament. In the eighteenth century the members of the House of Commons were not all squires or rich
merchants, but most of them were ' well-connected ' and
either had a small ' competence ' of their own, or were
provided with a sinecure public office. The circumstances
of William Pitt in the early part of his career are probably
typical of the entry of many other men into politics. Pitt
was the younger son of a Cornish squire. His grandfather
had been Governor of Madras; his grandmother was Vis-
countess Grandison; his mother was Lady Harriet Villiers.
He received the best education of the time, at Eton and
Trinity, Oxford, and he made the Grand Tour of France
and Italy. His income, however, was only about £100 a
year, so that he cannot be said to have owed his advance

PITT THE ELDER

Thomas Gainsborough

Photo W. F. Mansell and Co.

32

to wealth. Nevertheless, it was through a pocket borough which belonged to his father, Old Sarum, that he entered politics (1735). From this moment he became well known as an orator. Although for long very unpopular with the parliamentary chiefs, he could never be suppressed; for, once he had secured his entry into politics, he soon discovered the power of the public, so that he taught even George II ' to look for the opinion of his people outside the walls of the house.' The political vicissitudes of Wilkes show that in the eighteenth century, even when the Court and Parliament were determined in one direction, the electors, if determined in another, could have their way.

John Wilkes was the son of a distiller and was born at Clerkenwell in 1727. He received a good education, including some terms at the University of Leyden. On returning from the Continent he married an heiress and became a man about town. He knew all the rakes, but also the literary men, like Dr. Johnson, and the great politicians, like Pitt. As Member of Parliament for Aylesbury he opposed Lord Bute, and was unsuccessfully prosecuted by the Government for his writings in Number 45 of his paper, the *North Briton* (1763). In 1764 he was expelled from the House of Commons by vote for being the author of Number 45. He went abroad for four years. Returning in 1768, he stood for Parliament in the election for the City of London, and failed, but was elected for the county of Middlesex. The Government majority refused to admit him to the House of Commons, and he was re-elected by the freeholders of Middlesex three times. In 1774 he was elected again and this time was permitted to take his seat. Wilkes died in 1797. With all the forces of Government and privilege against him, he had triumphed simply by reason of his popular appeal.

One of the chief differences between modern and mediaeval history is that since the early fifteenth century people have been strongly interested in politics; during the Middle Ages they were not. The number of people

c

interested in politics, the size of the ' political nation,' has varied from age to age, increasing with the growth of population, the advance of education, and in general with the expansion of what may be called democratic sentiment. In the eighteenth century, or at any rate in the first three-quarters of it, the political nation was the people who had the right of voting; nobody else had much influence on politics or, probably, thought very much about political affairs. The number of people entitled to vote can be calculated only approximately. There may have been about 160,000 voters in the counties and about 85,000 in boroughs.

Not all the voters wanted to be Members of Parliament, and only a portion of them had any chance of being nominated and elected. Yet it is probable that almost everybody who seriously wanted to be a member of the House of Commons in the eighteenth century could, with moderate luck and ability, achieve this ambition. The number of members of the House of Commons in the eighteenth century was 558. The yearly average number of new members was about 50. About 70,000 men annually became twenty-one years of age. Of these only a small percentage was educated and likely to aspire to Parliament, and of that percentage many were clergy and therefore ineligible. Therefore, ' it is hardly astonishing to find how very few among those who desired to enter the House of Commons failed to get a chance.' The fact that the House was open to all who could reasonably aspire to it ' had a wonderfully unifying and stimulating influence on the nation.' [1]

It was a generally accepted idea that the politically active part of the nation, those people who were in Parliament and their friends, had a claim on the purse of the State. They expected to receive places of profit or pensions from the Government. These emoluments they considered to be

[1] L. B. Namier, *The Structure of Politics at the Accession of George III* (1929), p. 4.

a return for public service; not to receive them was regarded as censure or neglect of their services; to receive them was the mark of official approval, the certificate of good service. Thus the giving and receiving was not necessarily corrupt; in most cases it was not corrupt at all in the ordinary sense of the word. Ministers were, however, being constantly plagued by Members of Parliament for favours, not merely for offices or pensions, but for steps of promotion in the Army or Navy. A wise mother, however, in 1760, in recommending her son, a candidate for Parliament, to the Duke of Newcastle, was careful to point out that the young man would bear all his own expenses and that he had ' no relations to sollicit favours for.' [1] This must have been a rare experience for the Duke. Anson, who was a most excellent Lord of the Admiralty, remonstrated with Newcastle, who was urging the advancement in the Navy of certain officer Members of Parliament. ' I must now beg your Grace will seriously consider what must be the condition of your Fleet if these borough recommendations, which must be frequent, are to be complied with.'

The composition of the House of Commons in the eighteenth century may be gauged from the information adduced chiefly from the Newcastle Papers relating to the Parliament of 1761. At the General Election of that year sixty-four serving officers of the Army were elected, ' including the best-known generals of the time,' such as Lord Ligonier, Lord Granby (who had Irish peerages and could therefore sit in the Commons), and Robert Clive. Admirals and other high naval officers also became Members of Parliament; a material result of this was that debates on the Navy were capably conducted, although it also brought politics into the Navy. Admiral Rodney declared that some of his officers were such partisans ' as almost to wish for a defeat if it would produce the dismission of Ministers.' [2] He

---

[1] Namier, *op. cit.*, p. 30 (quoting British Museum Add. MSS. 32902, f. 141).

[2] Namier, *op. cit.*, p. 41.

himself longed for a seat in Parliament. ' I hope my rank and long services will entitle me to an Admiralty borough,' he wrote in 1780.

The higher civil servants regularly sat in the House of Commons. In 1760 the Civil Service had not yet ' acquired its present corporate structure, independence, and aloofness.' Barristers were numerous in the House, as they are now; in 1760 there were some forty. The great mercantile class was represented by fewer members than might be expected, the number being only about fifty.

Voting in the counties, under the Act of 1430, was according to the ' forty-shilling freehold franchise ' which, however, was interpreted to include leaseholds for life. The County elections were fairly, perhaps almost completely, independent of Government influence; the big landowners, naturally, wielded considerable influence. It was in the boroughs that Government had its opportunities. There were in 1760 224 boroughs. Of these twenty-four had an electorate of over 1000 (Westminster had 9000 electors, the City of London 6000). Some twenty-two boroughs had electorates of 500–1000 voters. Most of the rest of the boroughs might be called ' pocket ' or ' rotten.' Where the franchise depended upon the possession of certain lands or houses, the man who already owned, or could purchase, a majority of these burgages could return the borough member. England was really ruled by the region south of the Thames, where 130 boroughs returned 261 members; in all England north of the Thames there were only 74 boroughs, returning 144 members. Some Government departments owned sufficient burgages to secure the return of a number of members. The Treasury, the Admiralty, the Ordnance, each had a few boroughs. The total number of seats which the Government could thus directly control was in 1761 thirty-two.[1]

The ' structure of politics,' as viewed from the House of Commons, would not show the whole field. The famous

[1] Namier, *op. cit.*, p. 174.

debates were, as a rule, in 'the House.' Parliamentary
strategy meant the management of the Commons. The
fate of Cabinets hinged upon the divisions there. Divisions
in the House of Lords were seldom critical, although the
division on Fox's India Bill in 1783 had the issues of fate
in it. In that quiet and unimpassioned assemblage the
Whigs had a large majority throughout the greater part of
the eighteenth century. Whether one Cabinet or another
had the confidence of the House of Commons, the Cabinets
were always filled with peers; and peers held most of the
high places in the Navy, Army, and diplomatic service: ' in
those days an industrious duke, or even one like Grafton
who was not industrious, could have almost what he chose.' [1]
Although the Prime Ministers might be commoners, the
administration was predominantly an administration of
peers.

' Their *régime* was safe, but it was not inspiring; if it
was not entirely selfish, it was very limited in vision. . . .
It bungled the Colonial question and the Irish question:
it did not even recognise that the Industrial Revolution
involved the birth of a social problem. On the other
hand there was yet no class antagonism in Great Britain,
and the dangers that must attend the dominance of one
class, whenever it is suspected and hated by others, did
not exist. The permanence of the system undoubtedly
gave stability to government and continuity to national
policy. Such benefits the aristocracy was able to bestow
on the State in the eighteenth century. Still more valuable was the habit of public service. Whatever its short-
comings, the House of Lords at least maintained that
great tradition.' [2]

[1] Lord Rosebery, *Chatham : his Early Life and Connections*
(1910), p. 264, quoted by A. S. Turberville, *The House of Lords
in the Eighteenth Century* (1929), p. 483.
[2] Turberville, *op. cit.*, p. 497.

FOR FURTHER STUDY

K. FEILING, *A History of the Tory Party*, 1640–1714 (1924).

A. S. TURBERVILLE, *The House of Lords in the Eighteenth Century* (1927).

LORD ROSEBERY, *Chatham : his Early Life and Connections* (1910).

—— *Pitt* ("Twelve English Statesmen" series) (1891).

COXE'S *Memoirs of Walpole* (1800).

D. A. WINSTANLEY, *Lord Chatham and the Whig Opposition* (1912).

CHARLES GRANT ROBERTSON, *England under the Hanoverians* (1912).

CHAPTER III

THE CLERGY

O F pastors,' wrote George Herbert, in *A Priest to the Temple*, ' some live in the universities, some in Noble houses, some in Parishes residing on their cures.' This description done in 1634 was still true for the eighteenth century. The university clergy were Fellows or Heads of the Colleges of Oxford and Cambridge. Nearly every Fellowship involved with respect to its holder an obligation to enter into Holy Orders in the Church of England. A majority of the Fellows probably entered into Holy Orders as an inevitable, though not unacceptable, incident in their academic careers. As clergymen they were not careless, but they were not zealous. They went regularly to college chapel and performed their duty as they saw it, which did not amount to very much. The most zealous of them as clergymen would find college life without sufficient scope, and would accept a living in town or country, as George Herbert (who was a Fellow of Trinity, Cambridge) did in the previous century, and as John Wesley, who was a Fellow of Lincoln College, did in the eighteenth. Those who remained in their colleges or returned to them, became known, if they were to be known at all, as scholars. Of such, Richard Bentley is the acknowledged chief. Born in 1662, educated at Wakefield Grammar School and St. John's College, Cambridge, Bentley was appointed Master of Trinity, which is a Crown nomination, in 1700. Continually at war with the Fellows of Trinity, and indeed with the whole university, Bentley remained unconquered to the end. He found time to edit Horace, Terence, and other classical authors, and to perform the duties of Regius Professor of Divinity. He died in 1742.

In Oxford, Thomas Warton, Dr. Johnson's friend, was a good example of the eighteenth-century scholar-clergyman of the university type. He was born in 1728, the son of the Rev. Thomas Warton, vicar of Basingstoke, and was educated at Basingstoke and at Trinity College, Oxford. Obtaining a Fellowship in 1751, he became a college tutor. In 1767 he accepted a country living, but still spent much of his time at the University, writing his great *History of English Poetry*. It is a work of immense learning, as well as of critical power. As a clergyman, however, Warton took his duties very easily, for he found the society and the good food and wine of the Trinity common-room and of Dr. Johnson's Club in London preferable to what he could obtain in a country parish.

Bentley, Warton, and others whose portraits in oils look down from the walls of stately college halls, were good and worthy men, but they were scholars first, and clergymen afterwards; notwithstanding this, if any of them were preferred to bishoprics, they made quite good bishops. ' Greek Play bishops,' they were sometimes called, because they had edited one of the Attic dramas or other classics.

The second class mentioned by George Herbert, the chaplains in noble houses, may be called perhaps the failures of the university scholars. Having failed to gain Fellowships at their colleges, feeling no serious call to the humdrum labours of a parish, they accepted the career of chaplain to a rich family, where easy circumstances and the pleasures of country-life could be secured so long as the chaplain was complaisant and did not quarrel with his employer. George Herbert long ago warned these men: ' They are not to be over-submissive and base, but to keep up with the Lord and Lady of the house, and to preserve a boldness with them and all, even so far as reproof to their very face when occasion calls, but seasonably and discreetly.' Obviously the position of domestic chaplain was difficult for an earnest and independently minded man to fill; and few there were that rose to eminence from that condition.

Jonathan Swift is perhaps the only exception; he was in Holy Orders when he resided, for the second time, at Moor Park, Sir William Temple's house, in 1698–99, but he appears to have held more of the position of secretary and librarian than that of domestic chaplain. He spent much time in the library, and wrote the *Tale of a Tub* and the *Battle of the Books*. After Temple's death in 1699 Swift had a stormy life, writing passionate Tory pamphlets which may be said to have established the power of the Press in politics. In 1713 he was rewarded by the Government with the position of Dean of St. Patrick's, Dublin; he remained a political force, spending half his time in London and half in Ireland down to his last years, which were clouded by mental failure. He died in 1745.

The parish clergyman, especially in the country parish, was a beloved figure in the eighteenth century, and numerous are the contemporary descriptions of him. There is Fielding's Parson Adams, Goldsmith's Vicar of Wakefield, and there is the Reverend James Woodforde's naïve and detailed account of himself and his work, in the long *Diary* recently published.[1] Fielding's description is as follows :

' Mr. Abraham Adams was an excellent scholar. He was a perfect master of the Greek and Latin Languages; to which he added a great share of knowledge in the Oriental tongues; and could read and translate French, Italian and Spanish. He had applied many years to the most severe study, and had treasured up a fund of learning rarely to be met with in a university. He was, besides, a man of good sense, good parts, and good nature; but was at the same time as entirely ignorant of the ways of this world as an infant just entered into it could possibly be. . . .

[1] *The Diary of a Country Parson : The Reverend James Woodforde*, 1758–96 (four vols., 1924–29).

' His virtue and his other qualifications, as they rendered him equal to his office, so they made him an agreeable and valuable companion, and had so much endeared and well recommended him to a bishop, that at the age of fifty he was provided with a handsome income of twenty-three pounds a year; which, however, he could not make any great figure with, because he lived in a dear country, and was a little encumbered with a wife and six children.'

The original of Oliver Goldsmith's good Vicar was undoubtedly his own brother Henry, who was the parish clergyman at Kilkenny, in Ireland. Oliver, a youthful and dejected traveller—

> Remote, unfriended, melancholy, slow—

passes in review one after another the great geographical features of Europe, the Rhine, the Scheldt, the Alps, the Danube.

> Where'er I roam, whatever realms to see,
> My heart untravell'd fondly turns to thee;
> Still to my brother turns, with ceaseless pain,
> And drags at each remove a lengthening chain.

Oliver Goldsmith lovingly describes the brother in *The Deserted Village* :

> A man he was to all the country dear,
> And passing rich with forty pounds a year. . . .
>
> His house was known to all the vagrant train;
> He chid their wanderings, but relieved their pain. . . .
>
> The broken soldier, kindly bade to stay,
> Sat by his fire, and talked the night away;
> Wept o'er his wounds, or, tales of sorrow done,
> Shouldered his crutch, and showed how fields were won.
> Pleased with his guests, the good man learned to glow,
> And quite forgot their vices in their woe. . . .
>
> At church, with meek and unaffected grace,
> His looks adorned the venerable place;
> Truth from his lips prevailed with double sway,
> And fools, who came to scoff, remained to pray.

In *The Vicar of Wakefield* the picture is elaborately developed. The Reverend Dr. Primrose is a good, single-minded man. He is a scholar, with a theological problem to solve and an important pamphlet to write. He is careful about the spiritual needs of his parishioners, and his heart is full of a large charity. He has a good wife and large family. His means are narrow, and his household is outwardly like that of a small yeoman. His stipend is only £15 a year.

'Our little habitation was situated at the foot of a sloping hill, sheltered with a beautiful underwood behind, and a prattling river before: on one side a meadow, on the other a green. My farm consisted of about twenty acres of excellent land, having given an hundred pound for my predecessor's good-will. Nothing could exceed the neatness of my little enclosures, the elms and hedgerows appearing with inexpressible beauty. My house consisted of but one story, and was covered with thatch, which gave it an air of great snugness. The walls on the inside were nicely whitewashed, and my daughters undertook to adorn them with pictures of their own designing. Though the same room served us for parlour and kitchen, that only made it the warmer. Besides, as it was kept with the utmost neatness—the dishes, plates and coppers being well scoured, and all disposed in bright rows on the shelves—the eye was agreeably relieved, and did not want richer furniture. There were three other apartments— one for my wife and me ; another for our two daughters, within our own ; and the third, with two beds, for the rest of the children.'

This is a picture of the household of a very poor clerical family; but probably such were not the majority of the clergy. The writer of the *Diary* of the Reverend James Woodforde lived on a higher plane of comfort, in a good house, with servants, and amidst frequent entertaining and being entertained.

The parish clergy were in intellect and education well above the level of their parishioners, and probably above the level of most professional men of the time. They were all, practically without exception, university men, graduates of Oxford or Cambridge (in Ireland, of Trinity College, Dublin). Many of them had been Fellows of their colleges who felt the call to parish work and so left the university, or who desired to marry (all Fellowships were ' celibate ' in those days and until the middle of the nineteenth century), and therefore accepted a college living. All colleges possessed, as part of their estate, a number of advowsons— that is to say, they had the patronage of certain rectories or vicarates, and could therefore nominate the incumbent. It was customary when a vacancy occurred in a living for the college which possessed the advowson to nominate one of its own members, a Fellow if one were available; and thus the parish received a man of good education, and, not infrequently, of spiritual character. Of such a type was the author of *Selborne*.

Gilbert White was born at Selborne, in Hampshire, in 1720. At the age of nineteen he became an undergraduate at Oriel College, Oxford. In 1744 he was elected to a Fellowship at his college, and remained in residence until 1752. He was ordained a clergyman, and retired to his home in Selborne, until his death in 1793.

Gilbert White never held a cure of souls, but he frequently helped in the parish church, and took the service for the vicar. For forty years he lived in the rambling old house with his nieces, spending much of each day out of doors, observing the trees and flowers, the birds, the skies, and the seasons. In the winter evenings he would sit by a big fire of logs in the large dining-room, talking with his nieces, listening to music, or writing the letters which in their published form are known as *The Natural History of Selborne*. They were written to the Honourable Daines Barrington, a lawyer and naturalist, and were probably meant to form a book. A charming piece of literature, a valuable record of the things of natural history at a time when people were little observant of such things, a faithful although not detailed picture of village life in a typical rural community of old England, White's *Selborne* is the most graceful and one of the most precious products of the eighteenth-century scholar-clergyman.

The Reverend James Woodforde was born at Ansford, in Somerset. His father was rector in the village. He was educated at Winchester and New College, Oxford, and was elected to a Fellowship in 1761. He was ordained priest, and, after serving for ten years as a curate in Somerset, he was presented to the living of Weston, in Norfolk, and lived there until his death in 1803. From the age of eighteen he kept a diary of his life, his friends, his journeys, his dinners, his duties, his purchases of books, his expenses, and his charities. He dines frequently with the squire. He entertains generously in his own house. He is unmarried ; his father, sister, and a scapegrace brother who takes to drink, live with him. He himself likes good fare, though not excessively, and when there is a particularly good chicken or turkey for dinner, he writes this fact, with the price, in his journal, and also the wine which is drunk and the number of bottles. He is a good parson, and attentive to his duties; he comforts his parishioners when they are sick, marries them when they are in love, relieves them when they are in want, and buries them when they are dead. There was perhaps no great spiritual earnestness about the Reverend James Woodforde, and he certainly would never have frightened any of his parishioners away from church by the intensity with which he conducted the services. He was just a worthy, respectable, amiable gentleman, scholarly withal, friendly, charitable, and religious, but not at all sacerdotal ; his parishioners addressed him as ' sir,' but if one of them had called him ' father,' he would probably have been shocked, and certainly would have severely discouraged them from addressing him in this way again.

There is a common idea prevalent to-day that the

eighteenth-century church was dull and apathetic. A contrary impression, however, is obtained from an inspection of the communicant registers of the country parishes. The number of communicants every Sunday seems as high as could reasonably be expected in the villages, and is as high as in villages of the same size at the present day.

The bishops were seldom drawn from the parish clergy. They had usually been heads of colleges in Oxford or Cambridge, chaplains at Court, tutors to some great noblemen, or perhaps vicar of some historic church in the City of London. One of them, Dr. John Robinson, Bishop of Bristol from 1710 to 1713, and of London from 1713 to 1723, had been a hardworking and successful diplomatist, who took part in Marlborough's negotiations with Charles XII of Sweden in 1707, and also in making the Peace of Utrecht in 1713.

The career of Dr. John Robinson, however, was not typical of the English episcopate. The eighteenth-century bishops were, as a rule, not very political. They were cultured, many of them learned, men, who had the interests of the Church at heart, and who attended to their duties. There was certainly, in the Church of England as a whole, an absence of ' enthusiasm,' even of earnestness; yet there was, in general, a steady progress made from the worldliness which characterised the Church at the opening of the century—progress caused largely by the rising Evangelical movement, and later by the influence of Wesleyanism. On the other hand, the corporate life of the Church suffered from the fact that its representative body was suspended. Convocation was prorogued in 1717, and did not meet again for one hundred and thirty-five years.

The adjective evangelical is defined in Johnson's *Dictionary* as ' agreeable to the Gospel.' The Evangelical clergy were therefore an instance of a continually recurring movement in Church history, the movement to go back to the original simplicity of the Church as it was in the time of Christ, before tradition and custom had added to its ritual, customs, and beliefs. The return to Gospel simplicity cannot be completely effected, but the tendency towards this is a distinct and practical movement, obviously different from that inaugurated by William Laud which has become known as the High Church movement.

The Evangelicals of the eighteenth century drew their inspiration partly from the writings of William Law, a nonjuring [1] clergyman who lived on his small property at King's Cliffe, Northamptonshire. He had been tutor and religious guide to the father of Edward Gibbon, the historian. From 1740 to his death in 1761, Law and Miss Hester Gibbon, the aunt of the historian, and Mrs. Hutcheson, a widow, formed by themselves a sort of religious community at King's Cliffe wholly devoted to meditation, study, and charity. His best-known work, *The Serious Call to a Devout and Holy Life* (1728), had a profound influence on Wesley.

Law, who in later life was a mystic, never associated himself with the Evangelical clergy, although he is one of the founders of their simple and earnest school. Their great supporter was Selina Hastings, Countess of Huntingdon (1707-91), who protected them against the bishops by appointing them her chaplains. She maintained at her own expense a college at Trevecca, in North Wales, for training men, who would later be ordained in the Church of England or in any other Protestant body. Among her friends in the English Church was Augustus Toplady, vicar of Broadhembury, Devonshire, the writer of the *Rock of Ages*.

Some of the associates of the Countess of Huntingdon were Methodists. The rise of this great religious community is one of the successes of modern history, and is simply the story of John Wesley, which has been often told.

---

[1] The non-juring clergy were originally those who, having sworn allegiance to James II, refused to take the oaths to William and Mary. They continued to ordain clergymen throughout a great part of the eighteenth century. The last non-juring Bishop, Robert Gordon, died in 1779.

John Wesley was a son of a clergyman of the Church of England; received a splendid education at Charterhouse and Christ Church, Oxford; became a Fellow and Tutor of Lincoln College and was ordained a clergyman of the Church of England. In 1729 he founded a ' Methodist ' society at Oxford, a group of earnest young men who met together in each other's rooms to pray and study the gospels. This is the beginning of Methodism and also of Wesley's wonderful career as a missionary (he left Oxford in 1735) in Georgia, and in England and Wales, Ireland, and Scotland. It was not until 1784 that he began to ordain clergy himself, finding that he could not obtain a sufficient number of qualified missioners with Anglican orders.

The Methodist revival had an immense effect upon the social life of England, and was particularly strong in the parts of the country where, under the Industrial Revolution, the people were increasing in number and where, therefore, the ordinary parish organisation was not sufficient to deal with them. The function of Methodism was not to displace the Church of England, nor even to compete with it in old centres of population, but to supplement it in the new industrial areas where the Church was ' behind the times.'

FOR FURTHER STUDY

J. H. OVERTON and F. RELTON, *A History of the English Church*, vol. vii (1714–1800).

G. R. BALLEINE, *A History of the Evangelical Party in the Church of England* (1911).

John Wesley's Journals (Standard edition, 8 vols., 1909).

S. TYTLER, *The Countess of Huntingdon and her Circle* (1907).

SIR L. STEPHEN, 'William Law,' article in *Dictionary of National Biography*.

Chapter IV

COUNTRY-HOUSE LIFE

THE eighteenth century is the age of the squires.
They were the bulk of the members of the House of
Commons, for although there were many more boroughs
than county constituencies, the squires secured their own
election not merely as knights of the shire, but also as
members for 'pocket boroughs.' Squires or their sons
throughout the eighteenth century shared the positions in
the Cabinet with the great nobles; they were, with very
few exceptions, the generals of the Army and—to a somewhat less extent—the admirals of the Navy; they filled
nearly all the diplomatic posts, the embassies and legations.
In addition to all this, the machinery of local government
and poor law depended entirely upon them.

A squire is defined in Johnson's *Dictionary* simply as
' a gentleman next in rank to a knight.' This definition,
which may have satisfied feudal law, will hardly do for the
eighteenth century. Sir Roger de Coverley is both baronet
and squire; he is the ideal squire too, the complete representative. Addison uses the word squire in the sense of
country gentleman.

' The fair understanding between Sir Roger and his
chaplain, and their mutual concurrence in doing good,
is the more remarkable, because the very next village is
famous for the differences and contentions that rise between the parson and the squire, who live in a state of
perpetual war. The parson is always at the squire, and
the squire, to be revenged on the parson, never comes
to church.'

D
49

This was written in 1711 (*Spectator*, No. 112). In 1718 Lady Mary Wortley Montagu, whose husband was British Ambassador to the Sublime Porte, returned to England after about two and a half years' absence. She writes to a friend :

' I cannot help looking with partial eyes on my native land. That partiality was certainly given us by nature, to prevent rambling, the effect of an ambitious thirst after knowledge, which we are not formed to enjoy. All we get by it is a fruitless desire of mixing the different pleasures and conveniences which are given to different parts of the world, and cannot meet in any of them. . . . And after having seen part of Asia and Africa, and almost made the tour of Europe, I think the honest English squire more happy, who verily believes the Greek wines less delicious than March beer; that the African fruits have not so fine a flavour as golden-pippins; and the becafiguas of Italy are not so well tasted as a rump of beef; and that, in short, there is no perfect enjoyment in this life out of Old England.'

The squires as an element in English society undoubtedly originated in the ' lesser barons ' of the Middle Ages who are mentioned in Article 14 of Magna Carta: ' And for holding a common council of the realm . . . we shall cause to be summoned the archbishops, bishops, abbots, earls, and major barons singly by our letters; and besides we shall cause to be summoned, in general through our sheriffs and bailiffs, all those who hold from us in chief (*in capite*).' These latter are the lesser or minor barons, the smaller country gentry or ' squires,' as contrasted with the greater or major barons who later formed the peerage.

These minor barons differed from the major barons, as far as is known, merely by possessing smaller estates. They were ' landed gentry,' but not great landed gentry. When Edward I created the modern Parliament in 1295, the great barons became the Lords of Parliament; and the minor barons went on as the class out of which the knights of the shire—the parliamentary representatives of the counties—were elected. Almost everyone of them was lord of a manor; and their dwelling-houses were fortified like little castles.

In the course of the fifteenth century feudalism decayed, and the influence of the great lords grew less. The countryside became safer, and instead of castles and keeps dwellings of a more domestic character were being constructed. The former barons, major and minor, became, on the whole, peaceful country gentry. The dissolution of the monasteries, and the increase in land values that came with the rise of modern capitalism, enriched the country gentry. The Tudor monarchs employed them upon every sort of business, and made them the agents for carrying into effect the numerous Acts of Parliament and ordinances of the Privy Council. Every squire became a representative of the central government in his own locality. His duties were heavy, but his personal influence and the influence of his class were increased. The Civil War which ended with victory for the nonconformist townspeople (though led by squires like Hampden and Cromwell) shook the squires' power for a time; but they regained it—at any rate the great landed gentry regained it—at the Revolution of 1688; and in the eighteenth century the whole body of squires was more powerful than ever before in central and local government.

Although considerably enriched since the close of the Middle Ages, the income of the ordinary squire about the end of the seventeenth century and the opening of the eighteenth was still not large, although the great nobility were becoming very wealthy. An ordinary squire had an income of something under £500 a year from rents and from the sale of his own produce. The Public School had not become fashionable, and he only sent his sons there if it were near; otherwise they went to the local grammar school. He was not, as a rule, a cultured man. In the

famous third chapter of the *History of England*, Macaulay
has described the household of the ordinary squire: ' The
litter of a farmyard gathered under the windows of his
bed-chamber, and the cabbages and gooseberry bushes
grew close to his hall door.' He could not afford to travel
on the Continent, or to maintain an establishment in
London, or even to visit the Metropolis frequently. ' His
chief serious employment was the care of his property.
He examined samples of grain, handled pigs, and, on
market days, made bargains over a tankard with drovers
and hop-merchants. His chief pleasures were commonly
derived from field sports, and from an unrefined sensuality.'

Inevitably there was a ' country ' atmosphere and aspect
of things inside the squire's house; and, if allowance be
made for the greater orderliness and refinement of modern
conditions, the internal economy of the house of an old
country family of those days might be recognised in that
of a similar family to-day. If you stepped into the house
of a certain squire Hastings, son, brother, and uncle to the
Earl of Huntingdon (described in Shaftesbury's autobiography), you found a noble yet not extravagant or luxurious
profusion. His house, which was in Dorsetshire, stood in
the midst of a large, timbered park. Deer-parks and rabbit-
warrens supplied meat for the household. The timber
and wood from coppices provided fuel. Near the house
was a bowling-green, with a summer-house or ' banqueting-
house,' as it was called, built around a tree. There were
fish-ponds and great kennels. Any neighbour, rich or
poor, could visit the house at any time, and find plentiful
beef, pudding, and light beer. In the great hall of the house
the floor was always littered with marrow-bones for the
dogs, or with little sticks, called perches, which were used
for hawks to alight on. Hounds and spaniels lay in front
of the hearth, or nosed among the bones. The great arm-
chairs were nearly always occupied by a litter of cats. The
squire had his meals at a table in this hall with his dogs
and cats beside him. He would throw them pieces of

meat; he always had a little round stick beside his plate,
and he used this to beat down the dogs when they tried
to snatch his food. All around on the walls of the hall
were hung the skins of foxes and polecats. On the ledges
of the windows, which were deeply set back, lay numerous
arrows, cross-bows, and stone-bows or large catapults. At
the lower end of the hall was a table for oysters; the squire
never failed to eat a dish of oysters every day before dinner
and supper: they came from the neighbouring fishing-
township of Poole. At the other end of the room was a
table on which were a large Bible and Fox's *Book of Martyrs*.
The huge room had many other tables, strewn with various
things: old felt hats with the crowns turned inwards, holding each ten or a dozen pheasant's eggs; dice and cards and
boxes for games. A store of tobacco pipes was kept in a
desk. The old chapel, leading out of the hall, was now
disused, but the pulpit, being out of reach of the dogs, was
full of cold beef, venison, bacon, and apple-pie. All this
lavish housekeeping cost very little, for most of the food
came from the estate. There was little drinking: beer and
wine were served in small glasses. The squire never drank
too much and would allow nobody else to exceed. He lived
to be a hundred, and to the end could read without spectacles
and mount his horse without help.[1]

Such is Shaftesbury's picture of a wealthy, unambitious
country squire in the last half of the seventeenth century;
his condition in the eighteenth century would have been
much the same.

There are two contemporary descriptions of an eighteenth-
century squire, the one considerably idealised, the other
more realistic. The idealised description is that of Sir
Roger de Coverley; the realistic is that of Squire Western.

    'The first of our society (the Spectator Club) is a
gentleman of Worcestershire, of ancient descent, a
baronet, his name, Sir Roger de Coverley. His great-

---

[1] See *Shaftesbury*, by H. D. Traill (1886), pp. 13-15.

grandfather was inventor of that famous country-dance which is called after him. . . . He is a gentleman that is very singular in his behaviour, but his singularities proceed from his good sense, and are contradictions to the manners of the world, only as he thinks the world is in the wrong. . . . When he is in town, he lives in Soho Square. It is said he keeps himself a bachelor by reason he was crossed in love by a perverse beautiful widow of the next county to him. Before this disappointment, Sir Roger was what you call a fine gentleman, had often supped with Lord Rochester and Sir George Etherege, fought a duel upon his first coming to town, and kicked Bully Dawson in a public coffee-house for calling him youngster. . . . He is now in his fifty-sixth year, cheerful, gay and hearty; keeps a good house both in town and country; a great lover of mankind; but there is such a mirthful cast in his behaviour, that he is rather beloved than esteemed; his tenants grow rich, his servants look satisfied. . . . I must not omit, that Sir Roger is a justice of the quorum; that he fills the chair at a quarter-session with great abilities, and three months ago gained universal applause by explaining a passage in the game act.'[1]

Defoe wrote about ten or fifteen years later a work called *The Compleat English Gentleman* which, however, lay in manuscript until its publication in 1890. It is a highly uncomplimentary description, an attack upon the idea of noble or gentle birth, and upon this exalted creature of our own forming. Defoe held the gentry of his age to be almost wholly uneducated. 'To me,' he writes, 'an untaught, unpolish'd gentleman is one of the most deplorable objects in the world.' By reason of their wealth and of the resources of civilisation which were at their disposal, the English gentry were 'qualified to be the most compleatly happy of any people in the world'; and instead of this, they were 'attended with the unhappiness of a voluntary and affected stupidity and ignorance.'

[1] *Spectator*, No. 2, Friday, March 2, 1711.

' How carefull (writes Defoe) are the gentlemen of their parks, their woods, their lands, that their wasts be enclosed, the timber preserv'd, their farms well tenanted, the tennants bound up to rules of husbandry, to lay the ploug'd lands fallow at due times, to preserv the pastures and break them up with the plow, and, in a word, to practise good husbandry for improving the estate, to commit no wast, make no trespass, keep the farm-houses in due repair: how carefull, I say, are our gentry in all these things.

' In a word, nothing is forgotten to improv the estate, nothing entirely neglected but the heir, as if his estate was to be improv'd but not his head, and his land to be duly cultivated, but not his brains.' [1]

Evidently, there was much extravagance among the gentry of the early eighteenth century. They lived ' above themselves.' The rich, with great estates, could recover their fortunes by economy, for they had a large margin of wealth to work upon; but the mass of the gentry, ' of £400 to £500 a year estate,' could not recoup themselves easily. Yet, in Defoe's eyes, there was no excuse for a gentleman, even one of this middling rank, falling into debt.

' His first advantage is that he pays no rent, that his park having some meadow grounds within the pale, few parks are without it, affords him grass and hay for his coach horses and saddle horses, which goes also a great way in the expense of the family; besides that, he has venison perhaps in his park, sufficient for his own table at least, and rabbits in his own warren adjoining, pigeons from a dove house in the yard, fish from his own ponds or in some small river adjoining and within his own royalty, and milk with all the needful addenda to his kitchen, which a small dairy of four or five cow yields to him.

[1] Defoe, *The Compleat English Gentleman* (1890 ed.), p. 106.

'All these are vast helps in housekeeping to a frugal family and give my lady, his Major Domo, opportunity to keep a good house upon very reasonable terms, and which, if the gentleman was inclined to manage with prudence, would go a great way towards living comfortably.'

The small squire, however, is not comfortable, for his eldest son, on becoming a man, has to have a servant and couple of hunters; his younger son has to be bought a commission in the Army for £1000; his ' four daughters' (evidently families were large in Defoe's day) must have £800 each ' to marry as well as they can.' Thus, by the time the eldest son succeeds his father, the estate is heavily mortgaged; and besides, ' his mother, during her life, keeps £200 a year from him, which was her joynture, and must be out of his hands while she lives.' Defoe's picture of the half-insolvent and isolated conditions of the small country gentry in the ' seventeen-twenties ' is like that given by Alexis de Tocqueville of the numerous small French nobility before the Revolution. The English gentry, however, more fortunate than the French, had to face no Revolution at home; also their rent-roll soon began to swell under the effects of the ' Agricultural Revolution ' of which there were already signs in the ' seventeen-twenties.'

Although it might be true to say that the small country gentry were not well educated in the first half of the eighteenth century, this certainly could not be said of the wealthier members of the class. Robert Harley, Earl of Oxford, the friend of Swift and of other men of letters, founded the great Harleian Collection of books and manuscripts which is in the British Museum; Henry St. John, Viscount Bolingbroke, was the friend of Pope, and himself the author of the *Patriot King* and many other works; Philip Dormer Stanhope, Earl of Chesterfield, was a wit, a patron of literature, and the author of the famous *Letters to his Son*; John Carteret, Earl Granville, was noted for his knowledge of the classics, and repeated a speech from the *Iliad* to the friend who visited him on his deathbed.

By the end of the eighteenth century the standard of living and culture of the country gentry had risen enormously as compared with conditions at the time of the Revolution of 1688.

'The modern country gentleman generally receives a liberal education, passes from a distinguished school to a distinguished college, and has ample opportunity to become an excellent scholar. He has generally seen something of foreign countries. A considerable part of his life has generally been passed in the Capital; and the refinements of the Capital follow him into the country. There is perhaps no class of dwellings so pleasing as the rural seats of the English gentry. In the parks and pleasure grounds, nature, dressed yet not disguised by art, wears her most alluring form. In the buildings, good sense and good taste combine to produce a happy union of the comfortable and the graceful. The pictures, the musical instruments, the library would in any other country be considered as proving the owner to be an eminently polished and accomplished man.'[1]

The eighteenth century was the period of the ennobling of the squires. Those who rose high in politics, like St. John, Harley, Walpole, Carteret, Pulteney, Robinson, the Grenvilles, the elder Pitt, were almost sure to be made peers at some time or other in their careers. The younger Pitt seems to have had a fixed policy of securing peerages for squires, not only for such as rose high in politics, but for any who were noted for public services, and who were wealthy enough to support the dignity of a peerage. As the 'Agricultural Revolution' was greatly increasing the incomes of the squires, opportunities for rising to the peerage were frequent. The increase of the peerage under

[1] Macaulay, *History of England*, chap. III.

George I was three, under George II two, and under George III one hundred and forty-three. With the exception of some lawyers and Army and Navy men, practically all these were squires or their sons. The younger Pitt created his banker Baron Carrington in 1797; but this was exceptional promotion for a business man in the eighteenth century.

Coke of Norfolk was a type of the great squire, enriched by his ability, taking advantage of the Agricultural Revolution, and ennobled for public, although not political, services.

Thomas William Coke, of Holkham, in Norfolk, was born in 1752. His father was rich and a landowner. Young Coke was educated at Eton, and then went on the Grand Tour magnificently and was called in Rome ' the Handsome Englishman.' In 1776, at the age of twenty-five, he was elected without a contest to the constituency of the county of Norfolk, which his father had just vacated by death. From this time, until 1832 (with the exception of the years 1784–90) he was member for Norfolk, in the Whig interest. His ennoblement did not come actually until 1837, when he was created Earl of Leicester.

Coke's great work as a landowner and developer of the resources of his estate dates from the moment when he came into his property in 1776. At that time Norfolk, now so rich and fertile, was a bare, unenclosed region, with almost no agriculture, no cows, and only a few miserable sheep. Coke at once began farming for himself, and did it with skill, foresight, enterprise, and generosity. By the application of brains and capital to his land he increased his rent-roll, and raised the standard of living and the profits of all his tenants and of the neighbouring farmers. He held a great agricultural ' show ' every year in his grounds, so that Holkham, during his lifetime, became an agricultural centre for England, and attracted visitors even from the Continent of Europe.

Midway between the squires on the one hand and the farmers (whether owners or tenants) on the other were a number of gentry who lived in the country yet scarcely had their roots in it. These were the sons of professional or business men, or were themselves retired professional or business men. Having made or inherited a small fortune, they chose to have their home in the country with their wife and family. They lived not in a ' great house ' like the squires, but in a substantial house in the village. Their refined, domestic circle was a pleasant feature in village life; and if they did not play a very vigorous or effective part in the national life, they were amiable, friendly, and charitable towards their neighbours. Jane Austen, who as the daughter of a country rector knew families of this kind, has described several of them. Such were the Bennets of *Pride and Prejudice*. Mr. Bennet with his wife and daughters lived comfortably and quietly in a nice house with a garden in Hertfordshire. He was not a hunting man, nor were his friends. ' With a book he was regardless of time.' The Bennets were not exactly ' county people '; their friends had landed property, but had made their money in trade or had inherited it from a father in trade or in the Law. Mr. Bennet, however, had entailed property, worth £2000 a year, though how he had come into this, the authoress does not disclose. The pleasant and comfortably situated families in *Emma* are of the same kind of gentlefolk living in the country, but not country gentry. They have houses in Esher, make picnics on Box Hill, and enjoy the picturesque aspects of village life. It is not an unduly idealised picture, and with very little alteration might be applied to many villages in the more opulent and pictorial parts of England to-day.

FOR FURTHER STUDY

A. M. W. STIRLING, *Coke of Norfolk and his Friends* (1912).
SUSAN EMILY CHRISTIAN, *A Cotswold Family: Hicks and Hicks-Beach* (1909).
P. H. DITCHFIELD, *The Old English Country Squire* (1912).

CHAPTER V

LITERARY DICTATORSHIPS

IN the eighteenth century it was remarkable how great was the respect in which certain literary men were held, and the frequency with which men of letters met together. As a result of these two things, some of the most outstanding men of letters acquired a position of undisputed pre-eminence among their fellows, and held positions of almost dictatorial authority. In the literary circle to which they belonged, and which usually met once or twice each week in a coffee-house or inn, the dictator's word was law. Outside this circle, among other writers and with the general public of readers, the dictator's name carried great weight; his approval was sought by all literary aspirants; his remarks were quoted everywhere, passed from mouth to mouth, made and unmade reputations. In France a type of these potentates of the world of letters was Voltaire between 1746 and 1778. In England the position was held undisputed by Dryden from about 1670 to 1700; by Addison (not altogether unchallenged) from 1709 to 1719; by Pope after Addison; and by Johnson after Pope. Here the series of dictators stopped. There were powerful personalities in literary circles in the Romantic Era and throughout the first three-quarters of the nineteenth century; but nobody after the death of Dr. Johnson in 1784 ever wielded universally acknowledged authority in the English world of letters.

John Dryden was one of the most eminent men of letters— perhaps the most eminent (after Milton)—of the Restoration and Revolution period. Although one writer might equal him in drama, another in lyrical verse, a third in prose, no other was great like him in all three. He was also a man of established family and the owner of a small estate in Northamptonshire. He had influence at Court. He had a strong will and a capacity for forcible expression. He liked company, and delighted to meet his friends and other guests in one of the coffee-houses, which were becoming a prominent feature of London life.

For all these reasons Dryden, who had many years of established reputation before his death in 1700, was eminently fitted to be a literary dictator. Readers of Sir Walter Scott's *Pirate* will remember the reverence with which the remarks of ' Glorious John ' were repeated by the Shetland poet who had been fortunate enough to see this mighty man of letters in his heyday, laying down the law to an admiring circle, from his chair at Wills's Coffee House in Russell Street, Covent Garden.

All Dryden's life except the very last year was passed in the seventeenth century; and it was to that century that he definitely belonged. His terrible literary battles, his fierce personal satires, his plays—not much more decent than other Restoration dramas—attach him closely to his age. In the eighteenth century people were more refined, or at any rate less unpolished, than were the men of the seventeenth. On the whole the men of the eighteenth century had less strength and grandeur, for they lived in less stirring times. They lacked the impulse of Puritanism, and the agonising stimulus that comes with domestic upheaval and calamity, and with conflicts for the deepest issues. Swift, though he did practically all his writing in the eighteenth century, seems by his tremendous power, his capacity for suffering and emotion, his savage satire, and his frequent coarseness, to belong to the seventeenth. He had a circle of admirers in Dublin, but in London where literary dictatorships were made he had no following. Dryden's mantle of dictator at Wills's Coffee House fell to Congreve. This famous dramatist had ceased to write dramas by the time the eighteenth century opened. It was just as well, for Jeremy Collier's *Short View of the Immorality and Profaneness of the English Stage*, published in 1698, had started a reaction which gradually made plays in Congreve's style uncalled for. Congreve was a famous literary figure in his time, and had the reputation of a very fashionable gentleman. His personal ascendancy, however, in the literary world was less than that either of his predecessor, Dryden, or his successor, Addison.

Button's, like Wills's and Tom's (the third of the great coffee-houses), was in Russell Street. It was at Button's that Addison had his seat. Joseph Addison, 1672–1719, although not born precisely with a silver spoon in his mouth, may be said to have had an easy time all his life. His father, the Reverend Dr. Lancelot Addison, was in prosperous circumstances. Joseph received a good education at Charterhouse and at Queen's College, Oxford, from which he migrated to Magdalen College. He was a shy young man of refined manners, and of great industry, prolonging his hours of study deeply into the night. He was elected to a Fellowship; and in 1699, through the influence of Charles Montagu, Chancellor of the Exchequer, and Lord Somers, Lord Chancellor, he was assigned a pension of £300 a year. The two great Whig chiefs were anxious to recruit talented young men for their party. By their intervention Addison was able to retain his Fellowship (in addition to the pension) although he did not, as was normally required of Fellows of colleges, enter into Holy Orders.

Well supplied with money by college and Government, Addison went to the Continent to study French and to observe men and manners, with a view eventually to taking up diplomatic service. Like another John Inglesant, this shy, reflective, attractive young Englishman sojourned in Paris, Blois, Milan, Venice, Rome, and Naples. He paced, Virgil in hand, over scenes described by his beloved poet. By easy stages he travelled back to Geneva, and there learned that with the death of William III and certain changes in the Government he had lost his pension.   He found a post, however, as tutor to another young English traveller, and in this company wandered through Switzerland and France. Not until 1703 did he return to England. For a time Addison lived somewhat poorly. Not that he can have been really indigent.   He still had his Fellowship, which probably was worth about £100 a year.   He lived in a room described as a garret in Haymarket, but his friends introduced him to the Kit-Cat Club.   This delightful society contained men of political influence as well as men of letters.   When the battle of Blenheim was won, poems were composed in its praise and in praise of its victor. None was good enough to satisfy the Government, which naturally wanted to celebrate worthily its success.   Godolphin, the leader of the Ministry, consulted Charles Montagu, who by this time was Earl of Halifax.   Montagu mentioned his former *protégé*, Addison.   The result was a request from the Government for a poem.   The Chancellor of the Exchequer, Henry Boyle, came up the garret stairs in the Haymarket to convey the request.   Addison wrote *The Campaign* and was given a Commissionership in the Treasury, worth £200 a year (1704).

From this time Addison's career was happy, tranquil, and successful by every test except that of long life.   He published a graceful and appreciated account of his travels. He wrote the libretto of *Rosamond* for an opera.   In 1705 the Whig Government made him an Under-Secretary of State, although he was not in Parliament until 1708.   Then, without apparently ever opening his lips to speak, he was promoted from Under-Secretary to be Chief Secretary for Ireland, and finally to the position of Secretary of State (1717), ' the highest,' as Macaulay says, ' that Chatham or Fox ever reached.'   His rise was, at any rate, partly due to his services to the Whig Party, services which were probably done by writing, for the Press and the pamphlet were becoming potent literary instruments.   Addison was useful to the party.   He was also lovable.   Perhaps he was

the best-liked man of his time. At any rate he had very
few enemies; nobody had a grievance against Addison
(except Pope, who thought that Addison did not appreciate
his *Iliad*); and everybody who came in contact with him
felt his charm.

Addison resigned his Fellowship in 1710. He was in
no need of money now, for he had continuous employment
from the State, and his literary works brought him something extra. The Whig Government, however, was defeated
at the elections of 1710, and Addison was able to say in
his cheerful, philosophic way, that he had lost his Fellowship, his place in the Government, and his mistress; for
he had fallen in love with a great lady, who rejected his
advances when his party fell from power. Doubtless, it
was to make up for these losses that in 1711 he started the
Spectator, a periodical which in the course of its brief two
years of life established itself for ever in the hearts of his
countrymen.

In 1716 Addison married the Dowager Countess of
Warwick, probably the lady who had rejected him in 1710.
It is said that his wife did not prove congenial. If this
was so it may have increased his tendency to go to Wills's
Coffee House, to sit in the centre of a group of admiring and
warm-hearted friends, there, as Macaulay says, to talk
about Virgil and Boileau (the literary dictator of Addison's
Paris days) over a bottle of claret. For years this had been
his habit. The same friends would assemble at the same
time; some lucky stranger might secure an introduction;
and the great man, usually so shy and quiet, would expand
in response to the genial warmth of his friends, of the fire,
and of the wine. A word of commendation from Addison
would make a reputation. Nor did he misuse his power.
Addison had no conceit and no venom. He had no pleasure
in sarcasm and invective, and never indulged in it. He was
the real aristocrat; his superiority was recognised. He
basked in the approval of his fellows and gave them of the
sweetness of his ample and sympathetic nature. Addison

VISCOUNT BOLINGBROKE
French School
National Portrait Gallery

died in Holland House on June 17, 1719, at the age of forty-seven.

Pope, the next man whose ascendancy was almost unchallenged in the world of letters, was born in the year of the Revolution, 1688, and was therefore thirty-one when Addison died. For a time Pope had been at any rate an occasional member of Addison's circle, along with Steele, Ambrose Phillips, and others, at Button's Coffee House. About the year 1715, however, Pope made a quarrel with Addison, whose 'little Senate' he affected to despise. Nevertheless, Pope himself formed something like a little Senate at Twickenham, where he was settled in a pleasant villa by the side of the Thames from 1720 to his death in 1744. His health was too delicate for London coffee-house or club life, which involved long hours of sitting in ill-ventilated rooms, inhaling much tobacco smoke, drinking considerable quantities of claret or port, and supping late.

Twickenham is within an easy drive of Town. Most of the Englishmen of 'polite learning' of that time visited Pope. In his regular circle were Viscount Bolingbroke (St. John, the statesman, disfranchised for complicity in the Jacobite Rebellion of 1715); Jonathan Swift; the amiable Dr. Arbuthnot, physician to Queen Anne, a man of wit and of letters; young Horace Walpole, son of the statesman; Gay, the attractive but somewhat shiftless author of *The Beggar's Opera*. Together Pope's group wrote a series of satires on dullness called *The Works of Dr. Scriblerus*. Pope took his position as dictator in the world of letters seriously, and held it his duty to slay unworthy citizens. He was ready also to acknowledge young men of talent. When Samuel Johnson in 1738, then an unknown 'Grub Street' writer, published *London, a Satire*, Pope took notice of it and endeavoured, ineffectually, to procure a degree from the University of Dublin for the author. He died at Twickenham in 1744.

The succession to supremacy in the little world of letters

E

(little but steadily expanding throughout the eighteenth century) was not at once taken up. Samuel Johnson, who came up to London from Lichfield in 1737, was still struggling with spasmodic energy to make his way, reporting parliamentary speeches for the *Gentleman's Magazine*, and writing many fugitive pieces which are difficult to trace, although Boswell later did his very best to ascertain them. In 1747 Johnson began work on his projected *Dictionary*. In 1755 the *Dictionary* was published. It completed the author's title to fame. He established himself in a house in Gough Square with two widows of old acquaintances whom he charitably maintained (later he moved with them to Inner Temple Lane). In 1762 George III awarded him a pension of £300 a year. His house was always open to his friends; and their houses, especially Reynolds' and the Thrales', saw him often. It was at the Literary Club, however, that his presidency of the world of British letters was completely established.

The eighteenth century was a great age for clubs. These were not the ' co-operative palaces of luxury,' which exist now in Pall Mall or St. James's Street. They were simply groups of mutually congenial men who agreed to meet once a week or once a fortnight in a certain coffee-house or tavern. They met in order to enjoy the society and conversation of one another. Each member ordered what he pleased to eat or drink or smoke and paid his own reckoning. There were thousands of such clubs all over the country, arising, living, dying, according as a few like-minded men chose to associate or to separate. Johnson, who in spite of his obstinacy and love of contention and his impatience of opposition was particularly ' clubable ' (the word is his own invention[1]), had taken pleasure in such informal groupings ever since he came to London, and had

---

[1] Boswell's *Life of Johnson*, sub anno 1783, *note*. ' I was in Scotland when this club (Essex Head) was founded. . . . Johnson, however, declared I should be a member, and invented a word upon the occasion: " Boswell," said he, " is a very clubable man." '

SAMUEL JOHNSON
Sir Joshua Reynolds
National Portrait Gallery

66

founded a club himself in Ivy Street, Paternoster Row, at the time when he was at work on the *Dictionary*. Towards the end of his life he founded another at the Essex Head Tavern, Essex Street; one of the members was Daines Barrington, the gentleman to whom the letters known as White's *Selborne* were addressed.

But the most famous of all such societies was the Literary Club, started in 1764 and still in existence and flourishing. ' Sir Joshua Reynolds had the merit of being the first proposer of it, to which Johnson acceded, and the original members were Sir Joshua Reynolds, Dr. Johnson, Mr. Edmund Burke, Dr. Nugent, Mr. Beauclerk, Mr. Langton, Dr. Goldsmith, Mr. Chamier, and Sir John Hawkins. They met at the Turk's Head in Gerrard Street, Soho, one evening in every week at seven, and generally continued their conversation to a pretty late hour. This club has been gradually increased to its present number, thirty-five. After about ten years, instead of supping weekly, it was resolved to dine together once a fortnight during the meeting of Parliament. Their original tavern having been converted into a private house, they moved first to Prince's in Sackville Street, then to Le Telier's in Dover Street, and now meet at Parsloe's, St. James's Street.' [1] Other members who joined subsequently were Dunning (afterwards Lord Ashburton, the proposer of a famous motion of 1780 in the House of Commons), Adam Smith (author of *The Wealth of Nations*), Lord Charlemont (the Irish statesman), Dr. Percy, Bishop of Dromore (editor of the *Reliques*), Charles James Fox, Sir Joseph Banks (the scientist), Sheridan, Gibbon, Sir William Jones (a great authority on India and on Asia in general), Dr. Warton (the literary critic), Sir William Hamilton (the diplomatist), and Boswell himself. After Boswell wrote his account of the Club in 1791, Sir Walter Scott joined it, with other famous people. Johnson died in 1784. Boswell says that he was called ' The Great Cham of literature.' Certainly, if his

[1] Boswell's *Life of Johnson*, sub anno 1764.

words were received like oracles, this was not because
(as Pope charged Addison) he surrounded himself with
admiring nonentities. With men like Burke, Reynolds,
Adam Smith and Dr. Percy around him (not to mention
Boswell, who, if a flatterer, had plenty of talent) Johnson
could not have obtained supremacy, unless he deserved it.
Occasionally a small man challenged his ascendancy, but
the great men never. He was much made of, but he made
much of his friends in return. He had the capacity which
only the most lovable old people have of keeping his old
friends and making new friendships with young people.
In his last years he had a warm friendship with Fanny
Burney (' little Burney,' he called her), who leaped into
fame in the year 1778 with the publication of *Evelina*.

' Dictatorships of this kind are rare,' Carlyle wrote many
years later. Dr. Johnson's was really the last. In the first
twenty or thirty years of the eighteenth century the number
of men of letters, even the number of well-educated men,
in England was small. Almost all lived in London, which
was not then a large city. They all knew each other, could
meet and dine together frequently, and formed almost
a single group. Such a small society naturally has a leader
or head. A literary dictatorship becomes possible and
natural. It was fairly easy to establish one in Addison's time;
not quite so easy in Pope's; but in Johnson's time only a
very dominating personality who, in addition to writing
famously, was prepared to spend much of his time in literary
society, could achieve an ascendancy.

The number of educated people and of writers was
constantly growing. Of a book written in 1702 Johnson
remarked to Boswell: ' It is sad stuff, sir, miserably written,
as books in general then were '; but he added: ' There is
now an elegance of style universally diffused.'[1] The world
of letters, like the world of politics, was losing homogeneity,
and was divided into many groups or schools. After
Johnson's death no single man was acknowledged head of

[1] Boswell's *Life of Johnson*, sub anno 1778.

the world of letters. There were numerous great writers in the next twenty or thirty years—Scott, Wordsworth, Coleridge, Keats, Shelley, Byron, Lamb, Hazlitt—each one of whom was a star fitted to shine in a constellation of its own. Men of letters no longer all lived near each other in London, but wherever the fancy took them—in the Lake District, in Rome, by the side of Lake Geneva, in Edinburgh, or in a Somersetshire village. The place of the literary dictator was taken by the *Review* which could reach an increasingly wide public and which could speak with a sort of corporate magisterial authority.[1]

[1] The *Edinburgh Review* was founded in 1802, the *Quarterly Review* in 1809.

FOR FURTHER STUDY

Cambridge History of English Literature (vols. vii–x), (1911).

J. BAILEY, *Dr. Johnson and his Circle* (Home University Library, 1913).

SIR LESLIE STEPHEN, *Johnson* (1878).

—— *Pope* (1880).

Chapter VI

SPA LIFE

THE eighteenth century in England was an age of watering-places. There was a great deal of wine-drinking. Since the great French wars of Louis XIV the English had been taking to port instead of claret. The Methuen Treaty of 1703 gave preferential terms for the import of Portugal wines. The result of Englishmen's changing over from claret to port and of drinking too much was an access of gout which became chronic among the wealthier people. Because of this they frequented watering-places.

They drank deeply of the water, which was doubtless good for them; and they bathed in a covered pool, men and women together, as is told in Steele's essay from the *Guardian* (No. 174, September 30, 1713), *On the Humours of the Bath*. Physicians were numerous and flourished at these watering-places. Diversion and amusement was, however, probably as much sought as health. The spas with their leafy promenades (of which Cheltenham had and has perhaps the most beautiful) were places for showing off fine clothes and for light conversation. Literature was not neglected, and there was, according to the same essay of Steele, quite a race of ' water-poets.'

Bath was the first spa to become popular. Its springs had been greatly used by the Romans (the magnificent Roman swimming-pool is still there), perhaps even by the Britons previously to the Roman period. Before the end of the seventeenth century people were beginning to frequent the pretty little town in its sheltered cup among splendid wooded hills. In 1705 a stranger came to settle there.

Richard Nash was born at Swansea, the son of a poor Welsh gentleman, in 1674. He had a good education, at a school in Carmarthen and at Jesus College, Oxford. He then obtained a commission in the Army. Thence he passed on to the Middle Temple as a student of law. He made no money by this, however, yet he was always magnificently dressed, and was able to engage in polite dissipations. It was a mystery to everyone where this young man of no family, no property, and no apparent means of subsistence could obtain all the money which he spent. Some people thought that he must be a highwayman, who appeared in Society, well-groomed, point-device, with the latest fashion in clothes and the most elegant manners, after a midnight depredation of a stage-coach. Apparently, however, it was only by gambling and betting that Nash made good his livelihood; even this was wonderful and romantic enough, for only a very few people in the history of the world can have managed to do so.

It can, however, only have been chance, not foresight or gambler's skill, which led Nash to fix upon Bath as the place in which to make his abiding fortune; for the little town on the Avon, with the unpretentious houses, the poor inns, the narrow, dirty streets, had no special attractions as compared with other spas or possible spas—as compared, for instance, with Tunbridge Wells, so conveniently situated in one of the Home Counties, or with Brill, picturesquely perched on its sugar-loaf hill in Buckinghamshire. It is true that Queen Anne had visited Bath in 1702; this had certainly drawn particular attention to the waters of Bath; and perhaps Nash saw in this the means of future development. There must have been something forceful and persuasive beneath Nash's nonchalant mien and easy manner. For he did not simply wait upon chance; he thought out a policy for the development of the town as a spa, and he induced the townspeople to adopt his policy and to find the necessary funds.

Within a few years Bath became a new place. It provided itself with a fine band and a ball-room, a new pump-room, a theatre. The inns were improved. Private villas began to arise. The town began to take on its present stately, opulent appearance. In the eighteenth century means of communication and transportation were the key to material progress. Bath would never have had anything more than a summer season—and an uncertain season at that—unless the mud-road from London had been improved. Nash raised money to improve the ' Bath Road ' and others leading to the town. For forty years his reign was unchallenged. He was recognised as Master of the Ceremonies—some people called him the King of Bath—and he established rules of dress and deportment which visitors dared not disregard. He continued to dress magnificently, he lived splendidly, and, as usual, the sources of his income were unknown. Probably he had shares in some of the gaming-tables or other ventures in the spa. About the year 1745, however, luck failed him. He lost money and became poor, but the Bath town council gave him a small pension. He died at Bath in 1761, and was given a public burial in the Abbey there, where his memorial-tablet may still be seen. Although not a man of high character or ideals, he was generous, charitable, and good-natured, giving away freely the money which he so easily made. He had the best hotel-keeping sense, insisting upon cleanness, beauty, and spaciousness in his surroundings, and decency and decorum in the visitors. Under Beau Nash's *régime* Bath was a model spa.

Life at Bath was much like that at any other spa then or now. People bathed and drank the waters, with a great deal of conversation, before breakfast. They walked or rode or took carriage exercise; dined about three o'clock; strolled in the streets or gardens in their best clothes; took tea and then went to the theatre, cards, or dancing. According to Fanny Burney's *Memoirs*, there was a good deal of interesting conversation and of pleasant parties. Doubtless much of the social life of the place was insipid and dull; yet, as nearly all the talent of England in the eighteenth century went there some time or other, and some for periods of considerable length, there must have been brilliant society in Bath on occasion. One feature of the life there was probably unique. In Nash's time it was correct for the visitors to attend morning service in the Abbey, after they had drunk their waters and had breakfast.

On the outskirts of Bristol, immediately below the village or suburb of Clifton (which stands on high ground above the Avon), were the Hotwells, quite a celebrated little spa in the eighteenth century. Bristol itself was no more than a thriving commercial city, with some beautiful churches, particularly St. Mary Redcliff, still reckoned to be the finest parish church in England. Dr. Johnson and Boswell went down in 1776 to see if there were any authentic old poems such as Chatterton said that he had found in the muniments of St. Mary Redcliff. The two visitors put up at a very indifferent inn, so bad, indeed, that Boswell even wished he were back in Scotland. Clifton and the Hotwells must have had better accommodation, or visitors seeking pleasure as much as health would not have stayed there. Fanny Burney laid the scene of *Evelina* (published in 1778) at Clifton and the Hotwells. A guide-book published shortly before the end of the century describes life at the Hotwells. The visitors drank six half-pint glasses of water each day in the pump-room, and took the opportunity for conversation; they strolled in a shady walk by the river Avon; listened to a band and read newspapers in the public rooms of the spa; went for sails down the river; and attended public breakfasts on Mondays and Thursdays, and a ball on Tuesdays. There was a Master of Ceremonies who had a position of power, honour, and dignity, and of emolument as well, for each visitor was intended to pay him ' an acknowledgment ' for his services on leaving.

Cheltenham was a prosperous village of thatched cottages. The families there spun yarn for the clothiers of Stroud and also grew tobacco until William III stopped this for the sake of the growers in the American colonies.

In 1716 a Mr. Mason of Cheltenham observed that flocks of pigeons came every day to feed around a spring in his field. He came to the conclusion that the birds visited there for salt which they found deposited in particles near the spring. Thus he discovered the medicinal property of the waters.

The English medical profession was in high repute at this time; indeed, it had been so ever since Harvey discovered the circulation of the blood in 1628. In Queen Anne's reign Dr. Radcliffe made a large fortune and was able later to leave noble legacies to the University of Oxford. Among the numerous medical treatises produced by English physicians in the first half of the eighteenth century were many on mineral waters and their curative properties. Every ill had, according to these treatises, its appropriate curative water. ' Spas,' as the watering-places were called (from the famous watering-place, Spa, in the Austrian Netherlands), increased greatly in popularity. Bath was already in the middle eighteenth century becoming the height of fashion; a lovely new city of grey stone, in stately terraces, was arising to the designs of the Woods, father and son (between 1750 and 1769). It is a well-known fact in business that one popular shop brings custom also to its neighbour. People who went for the waters to Bath sometimes also went to Cheltenham. The village grew into a town. A pump-room, a paved court in which visitors could sip the waters, and shady walks and avenues where they could stroll, converse, and show their fine clothes were constructed. Cheltenham began to have quite a vogue. Its great fortune came to it when in 1788 the royal physicians prescribed Cheltenham to George III. The king, his wife and daughters, and all the large Court and numerous servants were soon occupying the best houses in the town. More visitors came, and the place went on prospering until the time of the Regency, when the present

crescents and terraces of magnificent pillared and colon-
naded houses were built in the style of John Nash, the architect, who according to an Austrian diplomatist had the
notions and style of a *grand seigneur*.[1]

In the latter half of the eighteenth century Harrogate
became popular and indeed fashionable, not only for
Scotsmen, to whom it was more accessible than Bath or
Cheltenham, but also for English aristocracy. Alexander
Carlyle, the minister of Inveresk and author of the lively
Autobiography, went to Harrogate in 1763, staying at the
Dragon Inn. He found this house to be a cheap place.
' Breakfast cost gentlemen only 2*d*. apiece for their muffins, as
it was the custom for ladies to furnish tea and sugar; dinner
1*s*. 0*d*.; supper 6*d*.; chambers nothing, wine and other
extras at the usual price, and as little as you please; horses
and servants at a reasonable rate. We had two haunches of
venison twice a week during the season. The ladies gave
afternoon's tea and coffee in their turns, which, coming but
once in four or five weeks, amounted to a trifle.' Although the
place was cheap the society was good; there were several
Members of Parliament, and ' baronets and great squires—
your Sir Thomas Claverings and Sir Harry Grays, and
Drummond of Blairdrummond.' Yet none of all these
gentry had the forethought to order a newspaper. They
would have been entirely without news of the outside
world, had not Andrew Millar, a celebrated Scottish book-
seller, who was taking the waters, given them the use of
two papers which arrived for him by every post (probably
only twice a week). While Carlyle was on this visit to
Harrogate, Clive arrived at the Dragon, travelling like the
greatest of noblemen with quite a ' train,' including two
secretaries, ' both jolly fellows who loved a good glass of
claret,' and numerous servants. Carlyle saw the great
man sitting before a pile of papers which had arrived for

---

[1] See *The Memoirs of Philipv on Neumann*, s.v. September 19,
1819. John Nash (1752–1835) was the architect of Regent Street
and the Brighton Pavilion.

him by that day's post. One of these dispatches contained the news that he had lost £25,000 a year through the seizure of certain territory in India on which he had a *jaghire*, or rent-charge. Clive read the bad news, but made not a sign; observers noticed ' no change in the muscles of his face which were well suited to bad news.' [1]

Mineral springs with more or less useful qualities exist in many different parts of England, so that numerous spas could be established, wherever there was, in addition to waters, something of the picturesque, as at Brill, the village on the steep little hill that rises like a sugar-loaf out of Otmoor, in Oxfordshire. Nearly all these little spas are now dead.

The Scots had a few ' Spaws ' (as they were called by Sir Walter Scott), of which the best known was at Innerleithen. This village in the quiet, pastoral Southern country, its half-fashionable society, its intrigues and its quarrels, are described in Scott's *St. Ronan's Well.* There is the honest old inn of Meg Dodds, still doing a fair business, but sharing in none of the sudden prosperity of the ' Spaw,' because it is some way off from the source. There are the new houses around the springs, with the aristocracy of doubtful title, the half-pay captain, the mysterious stranger, the ladies of rather faded beauty, none of them rich enough for Bath, Cheltenham, or even Harrogate, but enjoying something of the reflected glory of those places at the humbler St. Ronan's Well.

Sea-bathing and going to the seaside only became common and fashionable in the latter half of the eighteenth century. Attention was directed to the virtues of salt water by the book of Richard Russell, a physician of Lewes, on the subject, published in 1750. George III patronised Weymouth. Brighton or Brighthelmstone is frequently mentioned in Fanny Burney's *Memoirs.* She went there often with the Thrales, and bathed even in the month of November.

[1] *The Autobiography of Alexander Carlyle of Inveresk*, pp. 454–461.

' BRIGHTHELMSTONE, 1782, *Wednesday Nov. 20.* Mrs.
and the three Miss Thrales and myself all arose at six
o'clock in the morning, and " by the pale blink of the
moon " we went to the seaside, where we had bespoke the
bathing-woman to be ready for us, and into the ocean
we plunged. It was cold but pleasant. I have bathed
so often as to lose my dread of the operation, which now
gives me nothing but animation and vigour. We then
returned home, and dressed by candle-light.'

Scarborough was well enough known for Sheridan to
make it the scene of his amusing play, *A Trip to Scarborough.*
The popularity of Blackpool came later; it is a product of
the Industrial Revolution, the holiday recreation-ground of
the mill and factory workers of the north-west.

FOR FURTHER STUDY

L. MELVILLE, *Bath under Beau Nash* (1907).
A. S. TURBERVILLE, *English Men and Manners in the Eighteenth
Century* (1926).

CHAPTER VII

THE ARMY

THE ' Regular ' army—paid, permanent, professional—
may be dated from the New Model Army of the
Commonwealth. The New Model survived down to the
Restoration, and was taken over, or partly taken over, by
Charles II, and incorporated in his new regiments. The
numbers in peace-time were about 15,000 until 1698, when
Parliament, considering that the chances of peace were good
after the Treaty of Ryswick, reduced the Army in England
to seven thousand men. It expanded again during the War
of the Spanish Succession; and after the war it was maintained at a level of about 20,000 men (8000 in Great Britain
and about 12,000 overseas) until the War of the Austrian
Succession. A considerable number of the troops were
always engaged in foreign service—in Gibraltar, in the
North American colonies, the West Indies, and in India at
the charges of the East India Company.

There were not sufficient barracks for all the soldiers in
Great Britain until after the Peninsular War. Certain
castles could house their garrisons—Windsor, Edinburgh,
Stirling, and a few others. In some places where there
were troops the officers and men lived in private houses
or in lodgings. According to the terms of the Petition of
Right, 1628, soldiers could not be billeted by force in private
houses, but they were free to find lodgings, which they paid
for in an ordinary commercial way.

The uniforms adopted since the time of Charles II were
picturesque, but not always smart. In Hogarth's picture
called *The Roast Beef of Old England*, 1749, the two soldiers

are tall, upstanding men, but they look hungry and their uniforms are in rags. The men were generally young, and were engaged to serve for life; after release from service they retired to civil life as guards on coaches, ostlers, night-watchmen, or keepers of public-houses. Each regiment was recruited in a different part of the country. Most of the men were country lads. Occasionally a gentleman took the King's Shilling. Richard Steele was a trooper about the beginning of the century and Samuel Taylor Coleridge towards the end. William Cobbett, who came from agricultural stock, served as a private soldier from 1784 to 1791. The pay of the infantry was a shilling a day.

The officers were usually men of good birth and of some means. They obtained their commissions and their steps of promotion by purchase from officers who were vacating, except in time of war, when promotion went by merit as vacancies were created by death or wounds. Dr. Shipley, Bishop of St. Asaph, at a dinner-party with Sir Joshua Reynolds, at which Johnson and Boswell were present, said: ' I remember when I was with the army, after the battle of Lawfeldt, the officers seriously grumbled that no general was killed.' [1] The junior officers were all complaining of the small number of casualties, for they felt that they were being robbed of promotion. Not all of the officers had private means; poor officers, except in war-time, had no chance of promotion. The purchase price of commissions was fixed by the terms of a Royal Warrant of Charles II. The system had the advantage that it enabled keen young officers, if they could command money, to rise fairly rapidly to the rank of Colonel (above which rank no promotions were made by purchase). A wealthy officer who was not interested in his profession would not be likely to stay in the army at all. Thus the purchase system on the whole resulted in the promotion of men of efficiency and ability.

---

[1] Boswell's *Life of Johnson*, sub anno 1778. At Lawfeldt the Duke of Cumberland was defeated by Marshal Saxe in 1747. The site of the battle is near Maastricht.

Some never rose, perhaps because they married young and had no money to spare. Laurence Sterne's father was an Ensign Sterne who went on the expedition to Vigo in 1719, served in the defence of Gibraltar in 1727, and, after a somewhat shiftless, wandering life, died in 1729 of fever at Jamaica, while still only having the rank of Lieutenant. It was probably not merely lack of money which kept him back. His widow was left to bring up the family on a pension of £20 a year.

James Edward Oglethorpe was the type of officer of respectable parentage and moderate fortune. He was born in 1696, the son of General Theophilus Oglethorpe, M.P. for Haslemere, Surrey. At the age of fourteen he obtained a commission in the British Army, and in 1712 he served as a volunteer in Prince Eugène's army against the Turks. In 1714 he matriculated at Corpus Christi College, Oxford.

Oglethorpe was only intermittently in military service, for he was a Member of Parliament for many years. He was one of the earliest enquirers into the conditions of prisons and a reformer. In 1732 he went out to the region of the Savannah river and founded the colony of Georgia as a home for paupers and debtors where they could begin a new life. He returned from Georgia in 1734, and went out again in 1736, taking with him John and Charles Wesley. When the Wesleys went back to England, Oglethorpe brought out the great evangelical preacher, Whitefield, to the colony. But philanthropy was not his only work, for he had to undertake the defence of Georgia against the Spaniards of Florida, and had to engage in difficult war-like operations. In the War of Jenkins' Ear, 1739, which merged with the War of the Austrian Succession, Oglethorpe (now on his third prolonged stay in Georgia) had to conduct military operations almost on the grand scale. He returned to England in 1743, married an heiress, and settled down as a country gentleman at Cranham Hall, Essex. In 1745, however, the Jacobite Rebellion brought him again into active service; he raised a regiment and led it in the army of the Duke of Cumberland. After this he had no more connection with the Army.

Oglethorpe, who had the rank of General, lived until 1785, pursuing his philanthropic work, and engaging in social intercourse with Johnson, Goldsmith, Burke, and other serious-minded literary men. He was a member of Dr. Johnson's famous Club, and he frequently entertained Johnson, Boswell, and their circle. Although he was a professional soldier who had taken part in some of the hardest campaigns in history, he took a place in London literary society simply as a cultured gentleman, interested in letters, in charity, in politics and in the friendships of an age which loved serious conversation.

The *beau ideal* of a British officer was John Churchill, Duke of Marlborough. He was a handsome, sweet-faced man, tall, well-made, always faultlessly dressed, wearing his uniform with an air and grace that nobody could equal. He had a genius for strategy, for tactics, for detail; his eye was everywhere. With a record of almost unbroken success in the field, he is said never to have wasted the life of a soldier (although Malplaquet might be advanced as an instance to the contrary). His men loved him; and he was careful for their comfort as few commanders in those rough days were. At a time when discipline was harsh and often inhumanly cruel, he was kindly and long-suffering. Boswell tells a story, doubtless authentic, which had come down in eighteenth-century tradition:

'When the great Duke of Marlborough, accompanied by Lord Cadogan, was one day reconnoitring the army in Flanders, a heavy rain came on, and they both called for their cloaks. Lord Cadogan's servant, a good-humoured, alert lad, brought his lordship's in a minute. The Duke's servant, a lazy, sulky dog, was so sluggish, that his Grace, being wet to the skin, reproved him, and had for answer with a grunt, " I came as fast as I could ";

F

upon which the Duke calmly said,—" Cadogan, I would not for a thousand pounds have that fellow's temper." '[1]

A successful general might be voted a pension (perhaps even a hereditary pension), and ' compassionate allowances ' might be granted to widows, but there were not regularly pensions for the ordinary officers and men. In the University Galleries at Oxford there is a touching picture of Field-Marshal the Marquis of Granby being appealed to for charity by a discharged wounded soldier and his family. Those who, like Corporal Trim in *Tristram Shandy*, could find employment in civilian life as valets or coachmen with their old officers were fortunate.

The reminiscences in *Tristram Shandy* are probably not far from the truth if the reader bears in mind that, as always happens in military history, the blood and the filth, the discomforts, miseries, and agonies are omitted. Campaigning is not all sharp pain or dull misery; and for a strong man it was probably more tolerable in the eighteenth century than in any other age. Armies fought to win battles, one or two in a season. A battle itself was not wholly terrible; it was an affair of manœuvre and evolution. Nothing of course could mitigate the agonies of the actual struggle with bayonet or musketry fire at close range, which only supreme courage could face calmly. The story of the British column at Fontenoy which slowly advanced and slowly retired, in perfect line, under a murderous fire, is immortal. Warfare was not so absolutely desperate that it left no room for punctilio. ' *Messieurs les Gardes Français, tirez les premiers,*' said the courteous British officers at Fontenoy. ' *Non, Non, nous ne tirons jamais les premiers,*' answered the French.[2] While their kneeling men were aiming at the approaching enemy, the British officers could be seen through the smoke

---

[1] Boswell's *Life of Johnson*. Advertisement to the second edition.

[2] Fortescue (*History of the British Army*, ii, 115) considers this to be a legend, because, as a matter of fact, the French fired first.

walking along the line, gently tapping the muzzles of the muskets with their rattan canes, to prevent the fire going high. Opposing troops sometimes conversed friendly-wise across a stream on the evening before a battle was fought. But the inside of an eighteenth-century military hospital dims these bright scenes for a historian. There, such of the wounded men as were brought off the battlefield (many were left to die raving with thirst) were laid on straw, closely packed together, tended by a few men-orderlies and a small number of army surgeons, without anæsthetics or antiseptics, without even proper dressings or common physical comforts. Few severely wounded men survived a military hospital.

Southey has written a poem called *The Battle of Blenheim*, to show the meaninglessness of the eighteenth-century wars, perhaps of all wars, to the peasant who knew only that his house was in flames, and that his cow had been driven off by soldiery. Indeed, it is difficult for us now, looking back to those eighteenth-century wars, to realise that people were passionately convinced of the righteousness and necessity of the struggles. Yet it was just as true then as it is to-day that the soldier is seldom a mere mercenary; and many, if not all, believed then, just as fervently as did the soldiers of the Great War, that they were sacrificing their home, fortune, and life itself for the defence of their king and country.

' Those who are formed for command (wrote Richard Steele, who was himself a soldier), are such as have reasoned themselves, out of a consideration of greater good than length of days, into such a negligence of their being, as to make it their first position that it is one day to be resigned;—and since it is in the prosecution of worthy actions and service of mankind, they can put it to habitual hazard. The event of our designs, say they, as it relates to others, is uncertain; but as it relates to ourselves it must be prosperous, while we are in the pursuit of our duty, and within the terms upon which Providence has ensured our happiness, whether we die

or live. . . . Without a resignation to the necessity of
dying, there can be no capacity in man to attempt any
thing that is glorious: but when they have once attained
to that perfection, the pleasures of a life spent in martial
adventures are as great as any of which the human mind
is capable. The force of reason gives a certain beauty,
mixed with the consciousness of well-doing and thirst of
glory, to all which before was terrible and ghastly to the
imagination. Add to this that the fellowship of danger,
the common good of mankind, the general cause, and the
manifest virtue you may observe in so many men, who
made no figure until that day, are so many incentives to
destroy the little consideration of their own persons.'[1]

Here we have what a Dutch historian has called ' the very
core of courage '—man stepping out of his narrow egotism,
ready to die at what he knows will be the best moment of
his life when he gives himself for others.[2] The poet
Collins was an indolent, irresolute Oxford scholar who had
once thought of joining the Army, but actually was enjoying
literary life in London. He wrote an ode on Fontenoy:

> How sleep the brave, who sink to rest
> By all their country's wishes blest!
> When Spring, with dewy fingers cold,
> Returns to deck their hallowed mould,
> She there shall dress a sweeter sod
> Than Fancy's feet have ever trod.
> By fairy hands their knell is rung;
> By forms unseen their dirge is sung;
> There Honour comes, a pilgrim gray,
> To bless the turf that wraps their clay,
> And Freedom shall awhile repair,
> To dwell, a weeping hermit, there !

' Every man thinks meanly of himself for not having been
a soldier,' said Dr. Johnson.[3] Yet this remark was made

---

[1] *Spectator*, No. 152, August 24, 1711.
[2] See J. Huizinga, *The Waning of the Middle Ages* (1924), p. 65.
[3] Boswell's *Life of Johnson*, sub anno 1778.

at a time when the rank and file of the Army were not held particularly highly in popular esteem, when, indeed, the private soldier was looked upon as something of a ne'er-do-well who had not been able to settle down in civilian life. It was not a time like that of the last Great War when every able-bodied man was expected to serve in the necessities of the country. Nevertheless, Johnson expressed a universal feeling, the consciousness of inferiority which every citizen experiences alongside of the soldier, not at all because the soldier may kill people, but because he is prepared at any moment ' to put it to the touch,' and lay down his life. Self-forgetfulness is the one virtue, universally admired the world over. It is the supreme miracle, out of which all other miracles grow.[1]

[1] *Cp.* Emerson, essay on *Courage*, ad. init.

FOR FURTHER STUDY

Sir John Fortescue, *History of the British Army* (vols. i–iii) (1899).

Henry Bruce, *Life of General Oglethorpe* (New York, 1890).

G. Saintsbury, *Marlborough* (1885).

C. T. Atkinson, *Marlborough and the Rise of the British Army* (1921).

G. M. Trevelyan, *Blenheim* (1930).

CHAPTER VIII

THE NAVY

THE Royal Navy is much older than the British Army. There have been King's ships ever since the time of Alfred. The Tudor Navy was a substantial thing; the Anthony Roll preserved in Samuel Pepys' library at Magdalene College, Cambridge, shows how carefully it was organised in the reign of Henry VIII. In the Restoration period the Navy was, naturally, of great national importance, although the public were not greatly interested in it. During the eighteenth century, however, it steadily grew in strength and in public estimation.

In the time of Charles II and James II the men who joined the Navy as ordinary sailors were seamen already. They joined for the period of a ship's commission, and were paid off at the end of the commission. The officers were for the most part professional sailors, men who made their career at sea, and who were called ' tarpaulins '; but some were Court gentry or men with family influence who were given a ship or a high rank in a ship as a royal favour. These men were naturally not popular in the Service and disappeared after the bad times of Charles II and James II.

The officers, like the men, were usually engaged for the term of a ship's commission, and were generally paid off at the end. There was no regular half-pay until the wars of Nelson's time. There was not, however, any difficulty on the part of the Admiralty in finding good officers; the same men gladly offered themselves for ship after ship. The common seamen, however, were not attracted to the Service. The pay was poor, discipline was harsh, and the conditions of life were terrible on board ship. The ' press ' was freely used by a ship's company which was not complete. This brutal system, so alien to the notions of freedom which were commonly ascribed to England, was quite legal, and had judicial decisions in its favour. When Voltaire was in London he met a boatman on the Thames,

' who, seeing that he was a Frenchman, with a too charac-teristic kind of courtesy, took the opportunity of bawling out, with the added emphasis of a round oath, that he would rather be a boatman on the Thames than an arch-bishop in France. The next day Voltaire saw this man in prison with irons on and praying an alms from the passers-by, and so asked him whether he still thought as scurvily of an archbishop in France. " Ah, sir," cried the man, " what an abominable government! I have been carried off by force to go and serve in one of the King's ships in Norway. They take me away from my wife and my children, and lay me up in prison with irons on my legs until the time for going on board for fear I should run away." A countryman of Voltaire's confessed that he felt a splenetic joy that a people, who were con-stantly taunting the French with their servitude, were in sooth just as much slaves themselves; " but for my own part," says Voltaire, " I felt a humaner sentiment. I was afflicted at there being no liberty on the earth." ' [1]

Dr. Johnson always expressed horror at the idea of a sailor's life; and indeed it was very terrible in the eighteenth century. The difference between the sailor's diet then and now is enormous; then there was on ships no fresh meat, not even canned, no vegetables; scarcely any fruit; no ice; no fresh water. The living quarters were low, narrow, dark, smelling. Smollett, who was a naval surgeon, has described them in *Humphrey Clinker*. Dr. Johnson said: ' When you look down from the quarter-deck to the space below, you see the utmost extremity of human misery: such

[1] Morley, *Voltaire*, p. 69.

crowding, such filth, such stench.' He added, however:
' The profession of soldiers and sailors has the dignity of
danger. Mankind reverence those who have got over fear,
which is so general a weakness.' [1]

The eighteenth century in Europe was comparatively
peaceful—that is, as compared with the previous centuries
since the fall of the Roman Empire. There were forty-four
years of large-scale war in the eighteenth century, against
sixty-three in the seventeenth and eighty-six in the sixteenth.

Great Britain was involved in all the great wars of the
eighteenth century except the War of the Polish Succession,
which went on from 1733 to 1738 nominally, but in which
hostilities for the most part stopped after 1735. The
British effort in the wars in which Great Britain was engaged
was both military and naval. Intense and often successful
as was the military effort, it could not have been made
without the Navy. On this all things depended.

Without the Navy troops could not have been transported
to the Continent; and, except for the Navy's unresting
vigilance, Continental troops would have landed on the
British Isles. The service of transporting British troops to
the Continent is passed over almost without notice by
historians. Yet it was a marvellous thing that armies could
be shipped from England to the Continent without loss in
the War of the Spanish Succession, and the other eighteenth-
century wars, as also in the Napoleonic War and the Great
War of 1914–18.

The most general principle of naval strategy has not
changed in the last three centuries. It is that the duty of
a fleet in war is to seek out the enemy fleet and destroy it.
This was the principle inculcated by the British Admiralty
upon its officers, and it was the spirit of the *Fighting Instructions* issued in 1665–66 by James, Duke of York, and
Prince Rupert. The insistence of the Admiralty upon this
principle and its observance by the commanders gave a dash
and spirit to the Royal Navy which often surprised its

[1] Boswell's *Life of Johnson*, sub anno 1778

enemies. During the Anglo-French wars the British Navy was usually the attacker. The initiative, and the habit of seizing the initiative, are valuable things in time of war. The French Navy, on the whole, adopted a defensive strategy. It regarded its work as auxiliary to the land forces. Therefore the French Navy tended to confine its efforts to defending colonies, especially the West Indian Islands, to convoying merchant-ships and troops, and to safeguarding the French coast from hostile landing.

The result of this difference in the attitudes of the two Navies, the one ' offensive,' and the other ' defensive,' was that the British ships in the eighteenth century were much more at sea than the French, searching for the French Navy or blockading French ports. The French Navy was often in the condition of being blockaded; its seamanship deteriorated in port. The British crews were stationed, in all sorts of bad weather at sea, outside the French ports, growing ever more skilful in handling ships, on the alert to pounce upon out-coming enemy.

Westerly winds appear to be, on the whole, more frequent than easterly winds. Most of the French ports look towards the west. The task of blockading the great French dock-yard of Brest, for instance, was facilitated by the prevailing westerly winds. The French ships, if they came out, had to tack against the wind; the British blockading squadron bore down upon them with the wind behind.

Another advantage lay with the British fleets. France has not many large and safe natural harbours, and in any case a navy cannot be kept in small sections scattered among a number of different ports. For all practical purposes, the French had to use two places as their great naval dock-yards: Brest for the Atlantic and Toulon for the Mediter-ranean. A strong British fleet could keep the French fleets of these two ports apart from each other; and if they came out to sea, one French fleet might be attacked and destroyed before the other could join it. The only thing that the British fleets badly wanted, in their task of keeping the

Brest and Toulon fleets apart, was a base, a station to which they could go for supplies and for refitting, at some point between the Mediterranean and the Atlantic. The capture of Gibraltar in 1704 provided them with such a station.

Throughout the eighteenth century the Royal Navy had, on the whole, a clear superiority over its only powerful adversary, the French, both in the Channel and in the Mediterranean. Command of the Mediterranean was not quite so important then as now, when communication has to be made through it with the Suez Canal, and the Indian Empire. Yet even in the eighteenth century, England could not afford to neglect the Mediterranean, on account of the rich commerce there, and also on account of maintaining touch with Southern Spain and the Italian states, especially with Savoy, Sardinia, and Tuscany. Even for naval operations off the western (Atlantic) coast of Spain a base away from England was necessary. When, at the opening of the Spanish Succession War, the Government proposed to the officials at the Admiralty that the fleet should be sent to Spain, ' they pointed out that Spain was a thousand miles away; and its Mediterranean coasts at least double the distance.' [1] Naval operations in these circumstances were of almost inconceivable difficulty; the problem of maintaining supplies was especially hard.

The Spanish Succession War began in 1702. Admiral Rooke was sent with a fleet to capture Cadiz, and to use this as the naval base needed for British operations in those waters. The expedition was a failure, but on the way home Rooke swooped into Vigo Bay and destroyed forty-one French and Spanish ships (1702). It was after this success that the British Minister of Lisbon, Paul Methuen, was able to negotiate the alliance which put Lisbon as a naval base at the disposal of the British. This fine harbour, however, did not prove as suitable for the purposes of the

---

[1] G. Callender, *The Naval Side of British History* (1925), pp. 133–134.

war as was expected. Admiral Rooke had it in his mind to find another base.

On November 17, 1703, the fleet, anchored in the Downs, met a terrible fate, not at the hands of the French, but from a tempest—' the storm which, according to Defoe, destroyed one million pounds' worth of property alone; the storm in which Addison discerned the figure of the destroying Angel executing judgment on a guilty land.'[1] Twelve battleships went down with their crews. Nevertheless the fleet, in good condition, was ready when the campaign of 1704 was opened.

In this year Rooke, with fifty English and fifty Dutch ships, sailed for the Mediterranean. He made for Gibraltar. Marines were landed on the sandy isthmus that connects the Rock with the mainland. While the attention of the garrison was occupied with this attack and with a bombardment from the ships, a party of sailors was landed on the Rock. They swarmed up, entered the fortress, and captured it and its garrison.

The Spanish and French were quite aware of the significance of the taking of Gibraltar, and they at once made a supreme effort to recapture it. The Rock was besieged by land and sea. Admiral Leake sailed from Lisbon to relieve it, and, meeting the French fleet off Marbella, ' had the satisfaction of destroying it, and then of listening to the tramp of thousands, as the armies of Lewis raised the siege and marched away in despair ' (1705).[2]

The capture of Barcelona in 1705 was considered to be as remarkable an achievement as the capture of Gibraltar. Macaulay in his dramatic essay on *The War of the Succession in Spain* has assigned the chief credit to the Earl of Peterborough. The soldiers on land, however, could have done nothing without the guns from Admiral Clowdisley Shovell's fleet.

' First he converted the guns of his fleet into a siege train, with handy men as gunners and engineers, then

---

[1] Callender, *op. cit.*, p. 136.　　[2] *Ibid.*, p. 139.

with marvellous ingenuity and resourcefulness he lifted his siege train from the sea level to the top of the cliffs, and finally placed his batteries, opened fire, and compelled the place to surrender.' [1]

Shovell performed further notable services in the Mediterranean until he was recalled by the Admiralty in the winter of 1706. His fleet was struck by a terrible storm. Shovell's flagship foundered with all hands, except the Admiral himself, a magnificent swimmer, who, ' after cleaving the icy waters and making land, was knocked on the head by a Scilly Islander, who coveted one of his rings.'

The last important success of the Navy in the War of the Spanish Succession was the capture of Minorca by Admiral Leake in 1708. The Peace of Utrecht in 1713 left Great Britain in possession of Gibraltar and Minorca, justly considered to be the keys of the Mediterranean.

While in politics the eighteenth century was an Age of Reason or Common Sense, in naval matters it was an Age of Iron. The men were swept into the ships by the brutal press-gang; they were fed on salt pork until their hair dropped off through scurvy; breaches of discipline were corrected with the lash, the terrible cat-o'-nine-tails. Nor were the officers, all things considered, treated much better. Their quarters on the ship were somewhat superior; their pay enabled them to have rather better food; they had more leave ashore (much more than they wanted, for they were left months, sometimes years, without a ship). If their lot was a little brighter in peace-time than that of the ordinary sailor, in war-time they had no privileges. When wounded, they suffered, as Nelson did, with the men in the dark and suffocating cockpit; when defeated (sometimes even when victors), they were tried by court-martial, dismissed the Service, branded with shame and ignominy. Admiral Rooke in 1704, after his brilliant capture of Gibraltar, fought a ' checking ' battle against the French off Malaga, and put

---

[1] Callender, *op. cit.*, p. 140.

them to flight. He was dismissed from the Service for not having destroyed them. Admiral Leake, after relieving Barcelona (besieged by the French) in 1706, was recalled owing to an adverse report from the Earl of Peterborough. He was, however, kept in the Service. In 1744, in the War of the Austrian Succession, Admiral Mathews made a very vigorous, if not perfectly skilful, attack on the Franco-Spanish fleet off Toulon, drove them into retreat, and prevented the transporting of a French army from Toulon to Italy. He was court-martialled for attacking the enemy fleet without dressing his line properly, and was dismissed the Service. The worst case was that of Admiral John Byng in 1756, at the opening of the Seven Years War. He failed to relieve Port Mahon (which was besieged by a French army on land as well as by a French fleet at sea). He was found guilty by a court-martial of not having done all that was humanly possible. This officer, who, though not a naval genius, was a real hero, was shot by a file of his marines on the quarterdeck of his flagship. All these men paid the penalty not so much for errors of their own, as for the inefficiency, carelessness, perhaps even the corruption, of the politicians and civil servants who had not provided them with good enough ships or enough men and guns.

The great War of the Spanish Succession was over by 1713, yet there was no rest for the British Navy. Charles XII of Sweden was engaged in a life-and-death grapple with Russia, Denmark, Poland, and other enemies; and a British fleet cruised in the Baltic in order to support the diplomacy of Lord Carteret, who succeeded in bringing about peace between the hostile states in 1720-21. Another fleet, commanded by Admiral George Byng, had to fight the battle of Cape Passaro (off Sicily) against a Spanish fleet; for the Spanish Government had set out to upset the settlement of Italy made by the Treaty of Utrecht. The battle (1718) prevented this design from being achieved; the victor, Byng, was the father of Admiral John Byng, the hero of the tragedy of Minorca in 1756.

Nine years after the battle of Cape Passaro another war occurred between Spain and Great Britain over Gibraltar, the Spaniards claiming that it should be restored to them. The Rock was successfully defended. A British fleet was sent to South America under Admiral Francis Hosier; but as the Prime Minister, Walpole, believed—correctly—that the war could be ended by diplomacy without further fighting, Admiral Hosier was not allowed to attack Porto Bello. His men wasted away without fighting a battle, and the Admiral himself died of fever.

In 1739 occurred the celebrated and wholly unnecessary War of Jenkins' Ear over commercial questions, which Walpole and La Quadra, Ministers of Great Britain and Spain, were settling in a perfectly fair manner by diplomacy; but an unreasoning Opposition in the House of Commons drove Walpole into war. A naval expedition was again sent to South America, and this time Porto Bello was really taken by Admiral Vernon. Another naval commander, Commodore Anson, sent to destroy Spanish commercial ships, circumnavigated the world. His chaplain wrote an admirable account of this voyage.

The War of Jenkins' Ear soon merged, as Walpole feared that it would, into a great European war, indeed, almost into a world war, for it was fought on the continent of Europe, on the sea, in North America, and in India (the ' War of the Austrian Succession '). The French Army, being engaged against the Austrians, naturally seized the Austrian Netherlands as a ' pledge.' For Great Britain nothing was more dangerous than that a powerful maritime enemy should hold Antwerp and the mouth of the Scheldt; therefore, a great part of the British Navy had to be kept in home waters, to watch Antwerp. An expedition of Royal Naval ships and New England volunteer soldiers operated in colonial waters, capturing Louisbourg, the fortress of Cape Breton Island, in the mouth of the Saint Lawrence (1745). The fate of the French colonies, however, was obviously bound up with the fortune of war in Europe. Here the struggle, as between France and Spain on the one hand and Austria and Great Britain on the other, was indecisive. The French were still in occupation of the Austrian Netherlands in 1748; and in India they had taken Madras from the British. So Louisbourg, the sole gain of the British Navy and the North American colonists, had to be restored to the French in order to make them evacuate the Austrian Netherlands and Madras.

The War of the Austrian Succession ended with the Treaty of Aix-la-Chapelle in 1748, but it gave place only to an uneasy peace. In 1756 a great European war broke out again, to be known in history as the Seven Years War. This time, as before, France and Great Britain were enemies, but Austria was the ally of France (against Prussia). Accordingly, France could not seize Antwerp, but would only be able to make use of this port by consent of Austria. As, however, Austria was not at war with Great Britain, France could not use the Austrian Netherlands as belligerent territory. This fact set free the British Navy from having to watch the mouth of the Scheldt, and enabled it to send large forces to colonial waters.

British naval historians consider that the Seven Years War shows almost perfect examples of combined strategy. France was on the whole defeated on the Continent by the Prussian and British Armies, but her defeats on land were not so decisive that she would have had to cede her colonies at the end of the war. These colonies, however, were nearly all in British hands when hostilities ceased in 1762, so that the British diplomatists were in a position to negotiate with great advantage. Without the British Navy, the French colonies would never have been ceded.

The most famous episode of these seven years is probably the capture of Quebec in 1759, an event which is for ever associated with the name of the young General James Wolfe. His naval colleague, Admiral Saunders, is less well remembered, although without the faultless co-operation of Saunders and his men Quebec could not have been taken.

Charles Saunders was born in 1713. He joined the Navy in 1727 and served at first under a relative, Captain Ambrose Saunders. In 1734 he was promoted lieutenant, after passing the usual examination. In 1740–43 he commanded a ship in Anson's squadron which sailed round the world. In 1756, after numerous voyages and terms of active service, and also after a period as Member of Parliament, Saunders was promoted Admiral. He served in the Mediterranean under Hawke, and in 1759 was sent to the Saint Lawrence. The first step towards the conquest of Canada was to open the Gulf of the Saint Lawrence by capturing Louisbourg on Cape Breton Island. This was accomplished by Admiral Boscawen and Generals Amherst and Wolfe in June 1758. Quebec, however, was still a long way off; the Gulf of Saint Lawrence had to be traversed, and Quebec is 300 miles further up the river.

It was a wonderful achievement to navigate a fleet and troop-transports up the uncharted Saint Lawrence. Saunders was helped in navigation by Captain Cook, who later discovered Australia. The fleet with majestical spreading sails moved slowly up the great river, the low banks of which were covered with forest, except where, every few miles, the clearing and house of a ' habitant ' showed the presence of French civilisation. At last there appeared the bluffs of Quebec and the spires and fortress of the picturesque town.

The long and apparently hopeless strain of siege ended with the scramble of troops up a bluff, about two hundred and fifty feet high, and the battle on the Heights of Abraham (September 13, 1759). The sailors assisted and made possible this operation by the precision with which they conveyed the troops in boats through inky darkness to the unknown shore and landed them at the spot, hidden by trees and bushes, where the ascent of the bluff could be made.

In European waters two victories almost destroyed the whole French Navy—Lagos, fought by Admiral Boscawen off the coast of Portugal against the Toulon fleet; and Quiberon Bay fought among rocks in a tempest by Admiral Hawke against the Brest fleet (both in 1759). These battles occurred after bad weather had rendered impossible the continuance of the blockades hitherto maintained by Boscawen and Hawke against the French naval bases. They confirmed the command of the sea which had enabled troops to be conveyed safely not merely to the Continent but to India, where General Clive's victory of Plassey (1757) won Bengal from Surajah Dowlah, and where General Coote was to destroy the last French expeditionary force, at Wandiwash (1760).

The next time that the Navy was severely tested was in the War of American Independence or the American Revolution, as it is frequently called. When the American Revolution broke out, the ships and other material of the Navy were not in good condition. The political intriguing which was a feature of British domestic history all through the century seems to have been worse than usual in the early years of the reign of George III; and this had a bad effect upon the Navy. The Earl of Sandwich was First Lord of the Admiralty from 1771 to 1782; the money voted for the Navy in this period is said to have been spent in ' administrative jobbery and corruption.' [1] The sinking of the *Royal George* in Portsmouth Harbour, with Admiral Kempenfelt and nearly 800 men in 1782, was found to have been due to rotten timbers,[2] and not, as the poet Cowper sang in his beautiful threnody, to a land-breeze which shook the shrouds.

In the War of American Independence the British Navy failed to keep throughout the struggle the command of the sea. The Americans, naturally, had not a regular navy yet,

---

[1] See W. M. James, *The British Navy in Adversity* (1926), p. 16.

[2] See Minutes of the Court Martial held on the loss of the *Royal George*, in *Select Naval Documents*, edited by Hodges and Hughes (1922), 149–155.

G

but their ' privateers ' commanded by Paul Jones, a sailor of skill, daring, and enterprise, if not of genius, gained some notable successes. John Paul Jones was the son of a gardener of Kirkbean, Kirkcudbrightshire, and was born in 1747. When twelve years old he went to sea in a White-haven ship sailing to America. He rose to be skipper in the West India trade; sometimes he varied legitimate business with slave-trading, and also with smuggling between the Solway Firth and the Isle of Man. His daring career and reckless nature probably suggested to Sir Walter Scott later the characters of Nanty Ewart and Dirk Hatterick in *Redgauntlet* and *Guy Mannering*.

In 1773 Paul Jones settled down (as much as he ever settled down) on some property left to him by a brother in Virginia; and when the war broke out between the Colonies and Great Britain in 1776 he took service as a lieutenant with the Continental maritime forces. In 1777 he was given command of the frigate *Ranger*, and next year he sailed to British home waters and raided Belfast Lough and White-haven harbour. He even landed on the shore and spiked some guns. Next, he sailed into Kirkcudbright Bay, and landed on St. Mary's Isle with the object of kidnapping the Earl of Selkirk. The Earl was absent, however; the sailors plundered the earl's house, but Jones afterwards bought the loot from his men and sent it back to the owner. The rest of the voyage had plenty of exciting incidents. One is mentioned in an anonymous American naval ballad—Jones's escape from an intercepting British squadron:

> ' Out booms ! Out booms ! ' our skipper cried,
>   ' Out booms and give her sheet,'
> And the swiftest keel that was ever launched
>   Shot ahead of the British fleet.
> And amidst a thundering shower of shot,
>   With stun'-sails hoisting away,
> Down the North Channel Paul Jones did steer,
>   Just at the break of day.

He made his way safely back to France, and afterwards

to the colonies. In 1779 Jones, with the rank of commodore commanding a squadron of five ships, sailed round the north of Scotland and entered the Firth of Forth. In foul weather he beat up the Firth almost to Leith, but a fierce squall drove him back. After a most exciting fight with a British squadron in the North Sea, in which he captured H.M.S. *Serapis*, Jones made his way back to France and America. When the American War was over, Jones received the commission of Admiral in the Russian Navy from Catherine II and served under Potemkin in the Black Sea. He died at Paris in 1792.

In 1778 (after the Americans had gained a great success on land at Saratoga) the French joined in the war against Great Britain; in 1779 the Spanish joined the French side; and in 1780 the Dutch also entered the war against the British. Besides all this active hostility, Great Britain had to face the passive resistance of the ' Armed Neutrality of the North,' a union of Russia, Sweden, Prussia, Denmark, the United Netherlands, Portugal, the Two Sicilies, and the Empire (Germany), formed to insist that neutrals should be allowed freely to trade with the belligerents in all articles except contraband of war.

The French Navy, since the disastrous times of the Seven Years War, had been enormously improved both in respect of *personnel* and *matériel*. In the battles which took place in the years 1778–82 the French seamanship and gunnery were as good as the British. The tactics which the French adopted were also effective. These tactics were not, it is true, the simple and (if successful) decisive plan of finding the enemy's fleet and sinking it (the tactics of the British Admiralty's ' *Fighting Instructions* '); for this, perhaps, the resources of the French were not quite sufficient. What they did attempt, however, to do (and with marked success) was, when they met the British Navy, to cripple it by shooting down its masts and sails. If they were able to do this, they would break off the battle and sail away with their battered hulls (at which their adversaries had been steadily firing) to see what damage they could do to the British cause elsewhere. There were six serious engagements fought by the French and British fleets according to these tactics, and in all but the last the French had the best of the struggle.

The first engagement took place off Ushant (a French island in the Atlantic, 14 miles from Finistère) between Admiral d'Orvilliers and Admiral Keppel, on July 27, 1778. The British engaged the French, ship for ship, aiming at sinking their enemies, and were surprised to find the action broken off, and the French sailing away, leaving the British ships crippled in masts and rigging, and for the time being helpless.

The next battle was fought in July 1779 off Grenada, in the West Indies, by Admiral Byron,[1] a good sailor who had been round the world with Anson in 1740–43. The French handled their ships with great skill and crippled Byron's fleet by shooting away his rigging. After the action was over, Grenada, with no British fleet to defend it, fell to the French.

Another, and perhaps the most momentous of the naval battles of this war, was fought on September 5, 1781, off the mouth of the Chesapeake river, by Admiral Graves against Admiral de Grasse. It is true that the French were in greater force than the British in this action, so it is perhaps not remarkable that Graves went out of the battle badly damaged, leaving the French for the time being in command of the sea. Lord Cornwallis, commanding 7600 British troops in lines at Yorktown, had thus no chance of being relieved by sea; closely besieged by the troops of Washington and Lafayette, he capitulated (October 19, 1781) after failing grandly in an attempt to cut his way through.

From the time that Spain had entered into the war, the Spaniards had been straining all their resources to capture Gibraltar, which was valiantly defended by General Eliott (Lord Heathfield). On January 16, 1780, Admiral Rod-

---

[1] The poet, Lord Byron, was his grandson.

ney by the battle of Cape St. Vincent against a French
and Spanish fleet gained sufficient command of the sea to
bring relief to the hard-pressed garrison of Gibraltar. He
could not keep at sea indefinitely, and soon afterwards
French and Spanish ships were again standing off the
Rock, giving what help they could to the besieging land-
forces.

In September 1782 Admiral Howe defeated, although
not heavily, a combined French and Spanish fleet off Cape
Spartel, on the coast of Morocco. In this battle the man-
œuvring of the British fleet was greatly facilitated by the
Signal Book (used for the first time) which had been composed by Admiral Kempenfelt according to a system of his
own invention. The victory of Cape Spartel resulted in
the relief of Gibraltar, which was still being hotly besieged
from the land-side by Spanish troops.

In January 1782 Rodney had been sent out to the West
Indies to regain the command of the sea which had been
lost in Graves' battle off the Chesapeake. He sighted the
fleet of Admiral de Grasse near the little islands called Les
Saintes (April 12, 1782). De Grasse, ready to accept
battle, came to meet his opponent. For a short time the
two fleets sailed parallel with each other, in different directions; but a slight change in the wind enabled Rodney, by
a quick decision, to alter his course and to cut through the
French line. ' Admiral Hood, bringing up the British rear,
acted in fine emulation of his commander-in-chief, and sliced
through at a second fissure just abaft the enemy's van. In
that moment the French ceased to be a line of battle, and
became three dislocated fractions.' [1] The fight off Les
Saintes ended in a complete victory for Rodney, and placed
Great Britain once more in a fairly favourable position
for negotiating peace with the French at the end of the
disastrous American War.

---

[1] Callender, *op. cit.*, p. 181. But some critics thought breaking
the line a useless manœuvre (Hodges and Hughes, p. 177).

FOR FURTHER STUDY

A. T. MAHAN, *The Influence of Sea Power on History* (1889).
SIR W. L. CLOWES, *A History of the Royal Navy* (1897).
SIR J. S. CORBETT, *England in the Seven Years War* (1907).
Anson's Voyages (Everyman edition).
A. C. BUELL, *Paul Jones, Founder of the American Navy* (1900).

Chapter IX

COMMERCE

COMMERCE, as distinct from 'industry,' furnished, along with agriculture, the strength of England in the eighteenth century. Agriculture was deservedly considered to be the mainstay of the country. The yield of the soil was increasing. Rents were rising; and with this came the great political influence of the Whig aristocracy, based upon 'broad acres.' There was, however, another aristocracy that was arising unobtrusively, which, though not recognised as an aristocracy, was powerful, purposeful, and rooted in the necessities of the country. This was the class of merchants, called arrogantly by Bolingbroke the 'moneyed interest,' as if their aims were less pure than those of political intriguers whose avidity for office and pensions had no bounds.

The foundation of Great Britain's mercantile wealth was shipping. The island has good harbours. The islanders took to the sea, and fetched and carried not only for themselves, but, so far as they were allowed, for all the world. A policy of exclusion or restriction of foreign shipping prevailed then among certain Continental states; and the British, with their Navigation Acts, were just as bad. Yet in spite of this crippling conflict of national commercial policies, which really benefited no nation, but only retarded the increase of the wealth of the world, the aptitude and the natural advantages of the British for seafaring brought them great profit. British ships fetched and carried all over the world; and the payments for these services passed through the counting-houses of the merchants of London, Bristol, and Liverpool. The eighteenth century in England was the age of the counting-house.

The Navigation Acts stipulated that goods could only be brought to England (and after the Union of 1707 to Scotland) in British (including British Colonial) ships, or ships of the country which produced the goods; except goods of Asia, Africa, and America, which could be brought to Britain in British (including Colonial) ships only. Adam Smith, although he was the apostle of Free Trade, inclined to the view that this policy, by giving a virtual monopoly of the British import-trade to the British carriers, increased the volume of British shipping. It is very doubtful, however, if this was so. British shipping, in free and open competition with the shipping of the rest of the world, ought to have been able to secure most of the carrying of goods bound for British ports. On the other hand, the Navigation Acts lost, or helped to lose, for Great Britain, the American Colonies in 1776; and they naturally confirmed other states like France, Spain, and the Dutch in their policy of excluding British shipping, when they could, from their colonies. These policies of mutual exclusion were one of the causes making for war all through the century, and in 1739 were the sole cause of a war between Great Britain and Spain.

Adam Smith, whose *Wealth of Nations* was published in 1776, held that, on the balance, Great Britain lost commercially by the Navigation Acts. He maintains that while the Navigation Acts tended to a great increase in Britain's Colonial trade, they led to a very serious diminution of Britain's trade with the continent of Europe; and that even the increase in Colonial trade was not altogether sound, because it resulted in greatly increased prices charged to the colonists for English goods and in greatly decreased prices given by the English merchants for Colonial goods, and in the profits of trade being confined to a relatively few number of merchants. High prices to the consumer, low prices to the primary producer, and the concentration of profits in the pockets of a few individuals are results which every monopoly tends to produce. Adam Smith's explanation is as follows:

' When by the Act of Navigation, England assumed to herself the monopoly of the colony trade, the foreign capitals which had before been employed in it were necessarily withdrawn from it. The English capital, which had before carried on but a part of it, was now to carry on the whole. The capital which had before supplied the colonies with but a part of the goods which they wanted from Europe was now all that was employed to supply them with the whole; and the goods with which it did supply them were necessarily sold very dear.

' The capital which before had bought but a part of the surplus produce of the Colonies was now all that was employed to supply them with the whole. But it could not buy the whole at anything near the old price; and therefore, whatever it did buy, it necessarily bought very cheap.'

The profit earned by British merchants in Colonial trade under the monopoly created by the Navigation Acts resulted in capital being withdrawn from other branches of commerce for investment in commerce with the Colonies.

' This monopoly has been continually drawing capital from other trades to be employed in that of the Colonies.

' Though the wealth of Great Britain has increased very much since the establishment of the Act of Navigation, it certainly has not increased in the same proportion as that of the Colonies. But the foreign trade of every country naturally increases in proportion to its wealth, its surplus produce in proportion to its whole produce; and Great Britain having engrossed to herself almost the whole of what may be called the foreign trade of the Colonies, and her capital not having increased in the same proportions as the extent of that trade, she could not carry it on without continually withdrawing from other branches of trade some part of the capital which had before been employed in them, as well as withholding from them a great deal more which would otherwise have gone to them. Since the establishment of the Act of Navigation, accordingly, the colony trade has been continually increasing, while many other branches of foreign trade, particularly that to other parts of Europe, have been continually decaying. Our manufactures for foreign sale, instead of being suited, as before the Act of Navigation, to the neighbouring market of Europe, or to the more distant one of the countries which lie round the Mediterranean Sea, have, the greater part of them, been accommodated to the still more distant one of the Colonies; to the market in which they have the monopoly, rather than to that in which they have many competitors. The causes of decay in other branches of foreign trade, which by Sir Matthew Decker and other writers have been sought for in the excess and improper mode of taxation, in the high price of labour, in the increase of luxury, etc., may all be found in the overgrowth of the colony trade. The mercantile capital of Great Britain, though very great, yet not being infinite, and, though greatly increased since the Act of Navigation, yet not being increased in the same proportion as the colony trade, that trade could not possibly be carried on without withdrawing some part of the capital from other branches of trade, nor consequently without some decay of those other branches.' [1]

Adam Smith even denies that the Navigation Acts were useful as a naval measure. The English Navy was superior to that of the Dutch in the war in which the Cromwellian Government engaged in 1652; and in the war of Charles II's reign it was ' at least equal, perhaps superior, to the united navies of France and Holland.' All this happened, not indeed before the Navigation Acts had come into law,

[1] Adam Smith, *Wealth of Nations*, chap. VII, Part III.

but before they can have had any particular effect on the number of ships on the sea.

In the time of the Dutch Wars there was no great trade with the Colonies. ' The island of Jamaica was an unwholesome desert, little inhabited and less cultivated. New York and New Jersey were in possession of the Dutch, the half of Saint Christopher's in that of the French. The island of Antigua, the two Carolinas, Pennsylvania, Georgia, and Nova Scotia, were not planted.' Adam Smith concludes this part of his argument thus:

' The trade of the colonies, of which England, even for some time after the act of navigation, enjoyed but a part (for the act of navigation was not very strictly executed till several years, after it was enacted), could not at that time be the cause of the great trade of England, nor of the great naval power which was supported by that trade. The trade which at that time supported that great naval power was the trade of Europe, and of the countries which lie round the Mediterranean Sea. But the share which Great Britain already [1] enjoys of that trade could not support any such great naval power. Had the growing trade of the Colonies been left free to all nations, whatever share of it might have fallen to Great Britain, and a very considerable share would probably have fallen to her, must have been an addition to this great trade of which she was before in possession. In consequence of the monopoly, the increase of the colony trade has not so much occasioned an addition to the trade which Great Britain had before, as a total change in its direction.' [2]

Colonial trade in itself—when not vitiated by monopolies and prohibitions—was natural and wholesome. It gave employment to large numbers of men in Great Britain and in the Colonies. It supported a great mercantile marine on distant voyages without in any way drawing

[1] ' Already '—i.e., now, in 1776, when Adam Smith was writing.
[2] Adam Smith, op. cit., loc. cit.

British shipping from other trade-routes. It provided, in the vast undeveloped areas of the New World, opportunities for reasonable profit to men of all nations, including the British, without giving rise to the political jealousies—and the wars—which great territorial monopolies tend to produce. It made for content among the colonists, who had then—as all men have—a natural desire to trade with any customer, regardless of political frontiers.

'The effect of the colony trade, in its natural and free state, is to open a great though distant market for such parts of the produce of British industry as may exceed the demand of the markets nearer home, of those of Europe, and of the countries which lie round the Mediterranean Sea. In its natural and free state, the colony trade, without drawing from these markets any part of the produce which had ever been sent to them, encourages Great Britain to increase the surplus continually, by continually presenting new equivalents to be exchanged for it. In its natural and free state, the colony trade tends to increase the quantity of productive labour in Great Britain, but without altering in any respect the direction of that which had been employed there before. In the natural and free state of the colony trade, the competition of all other nations would hinder the rate of profit from rising above the common level, either in the new market, or in the new employment. The new market, without drawing anything from the old one, would create, if one may say so, a new produce for its own supply; and that new produce would constitute a new capital for carrying on the new employment, which, in the same manner, would draw nothing from the old one.'[1]

Commerce cannot flourish without the means of banking. Merchants must purchase goods long before they can sell them; ships and crews have to be provided for voyages,

[1] Adam Smith, *op. cit.*, *loc. cit.*

and paid during months or even years until the ship and its profitable cargo come home. Banks accept the savings of those who have some spare wealth, but not the means of investing it in trade; and with these savings the banks give credit to such men as can put out wealth profitably in trade, but have not themselves sufficient wealth to do so. Besides obtaining credit from banks, merchants frequently invited individuals who had spare wealth to place it directly with the merchants for use in trade, and to receive in return a share in the profits. Thus were formed Joint Stock Companies. Banks and mercantile joint stock companies were active from the earliest years of the eighteenth century.

William Paterson, the founder of the Bank of England, was born at Skipmyre Farm in the parish of Tinwald, Dumfriesshire, in 1658. Very little is known of his early life. He is said to have ' carried a pack through England.' During this time he doubtless made and saved a little money, and thus was able to set up in some kind of mercantile business at Bristol. Later he went to the West Indies; it is not known whether he went as ' preacher or buccaneer.' Towards the end of the seventeenth century he is found in London, where he made a fortune and founded the Hampshire Water Company. He also used his financial ability to reorganise and place upon a sound footing an institution for orphans which was bankrupt. His next venture was to promote the ' Darien Scheme ' for the establishing of a Scottish colony in the isthmus of Darien, or Panama (1698). He went out in the colonising expedition, which was a failure, and which engulfed all his fortune. Years later, in 1715, the Government compensated Paterson with £18,000 on account of his losses. He died in 1719.

Paterson's other scheme, projected about the same time as the Darien Scheme, has proved to be a permanent and increasing success. There were four great banking companies before him—those of Venice, Genoa, Hamburg, and Amsterdam. Paterson believed that London could support a greater bank than any of these. His grand innovation was the note payable to bearer, on demand, in gold, without indorsement—the ' bank-note ' of the present day.

' The rejection of the indorsement was a fundamental revolution. The notes that would be discounted in bullion by the goldsmiths would sometimes have a string of names on their backs. Each indorser was under a subsidiary liability on the failure of the original issuer of the note. The more indorsements, therefore, the more valuable became the note. But the security thus imparted was of a very clumsy kind; on the failure to pay of the party primarily liable, there was recourse through actions at law against others. A currency thus encumbered would be very unwieldy; but then there was the security. To accomplish this Paterson proposed—probably an experience of foreign practice—that the unindorsed note should be payable in gold.' [1]

The Bank of England was founded according to Paterson's plan in 1694; he himself was one of the original twenty-four directors. It was incorporated, in pursuance of an Act of Parliament, by Royal Charter on July 27, 1694. It was an independent corporation, perfectly free so long as it did not infringe the terms of its charter and the law of the land. It advanced to the Government the sum of £1,200,000, and received in return an annuity of £100,000, made up of interest at 8 per cent., which equals £96,000, and reward for expenses of management, £4000. In 1708 the bank advanced a further £400,000 to the Government, without receiving any increase in its annuity; in effect this meant that the Government was now paying 6 per cent. instead of 8 per cent. on its total loan from the Bank of England. At various times the Bank advanced further sums to the Government; and in 1722, in order to ease the strain upon

[1] J. H. Burton, *History of Scotland*, vol. viii, pp. 16–17. This work and *Chambers's Encyclopædia* (*s.v.* Paterson) give all that is known (and it is very little) of this remarkable man's career.

the credit of the South Sea Company, it purchased £4,000,000 of the Company's stock. This was probably the first time in which the Bank of England came forward to support the credit of private commerce during a time of crisis. Thereafter, in order to stave off financial panic, it frequently came to the help of great mercantile firms not merely in England, but in Germany and Holland. In 1763 it is said to have advanced for this purpose in one week £1,600,000.

The Bank of England in the eighteenth century had the great privilege of being the only banking company in England which could have more than six members or proprietors. The number of its proprietors (members or stockholders) gave it a great command of capital. A large part of its capital, which in 1750 stood at about £10,780,000, was loaned to the Government at interest, so that, as Adam Smith wrote, ' the stability of the Bank is equal to that of the British Government.' Besides doing business with the Government and issuing notes payable to bearer on demand without indorsement, the Bank discounted the bills of commerce of private individuals. Its operations were prudently conducted, and its dividend in Adam Smith's time was about 5½ per cent. It had always met its liabilities in full, and had cashed all its notes on demand, although on several occasions, wrote Adam Smith, ' this great company has been reduced to the necessity of paying in sixpences.' [1] The use of a paper currency which circulated as if it were bullion saved the enormous expenditure of effort and capital involved in a currency of gold and silver.

' The gold and silver money which circulates in any country may very properly be compared to a highway which, while it circulates and carries to market all the grass and corn of the country, produces itself not a single pile of either. The judicious operations of banking,

[1] *Wealth of Nations* (1904 ed.), ii, 357.

by providing, if I may be allowed so violent a metaphor, a sort of waggon-way through the air, enables the country to convert, as it were, a great part of its highways into good pastures and corn fields, and thereby to increase, very considerably, the annual produce of its land and labour.' [1]

The Bank of England was performing this service throughout the eighteenth century.

In its early years the Bank had a great rival in the South Sea Company. This famous corporation was founded when Harley was Prime Minister, in 1711—a Tory foundation, just as the Bank of England had been a Whig foundation. The South Sea Company was not a bank; it was a trading corporation, and, as its name implies, its chief function was to engage in trade with the South American colonies of Spain. The War of the Spanish Succession was going on in 1711. Doubtless Harley hoped that the war would end so favourably for the Allies that the Government would obtain great trading-concessions for the South Sea Company from Spain. The Treaties of Utrecht, however, did not give to Great Britain anything like what had been expected; and the South Sea Company had to be content to take over the right conferred by the treaties to send one trading ship a year to the Spanish Main and to have the contract for importing negro slaves into the Spanish colonies. It engaged in whale-fishing. The Company was also enabled to transact general financial business. It was this last power which led the South Sea Company into the famous Bubble of 1720.

For some years, probably ever since the Restoration, speculation and stock-gambling had been a marked feature of English commercial life. The Government itself took advantage of this and encouraged it by issuing public debt with lottery prizes. There was an idea current among politicians that flourishing commercial corporations

---

[1] *Wealth of Nations*, ii, 357–358.

might be induced to take over portions of the National Debt; the holders of the Debt would become, instead, holders or proprietors of stock in a company; and the Government would only be liable for paying over the interest (or an agreed part of the interest) on the converted debt to the company on terms which would result in a saving of public charges; in addition the Government would be free of all liability for paying back the principal of its debt.

By the year 1717 the South Sea Company already held £10,000,000 of the National Debt. It now proposed to take over liability for all the rest, amounting to £51,300,000, on which it was to receive 5 per cent. interest from the Government. The people who held the debt, the Government's creditors, could exchange their share of debt for South Sea Stock, apparently at the price of the day, which was in 1717 about £110 for £100 of stock; if they did not make the exchange, they would receive their interest from the South Sea Company, which hoped, however, to establish a Sinking Fund out of its profits sufficient to pay off the whole National Debt in twenty-five years. For the privilege of taking over the Government liability the Company was to pay to the Government £7,567,000. The Bank of England had offered £5,000,000.

The public readily bought the stock of the South Sea Company. On January 1, 1720, this was worth 128½ for £100 of stock which paid a dividend of 10 per cent. By July it had risen to £1000 for £100 stock which only paid a dividend of 8 per cent., although the Directors promised 50 per cent.;[1] thus the return to a person who bought £100 of stock at £1000 was under 1 per cent. Meanwhile the mania for speculation was intensified. ' There are few in London,' wrote Edward Harley, ' that mind anything but the rising and falling of stocks.' Many of the joint stock companies which were formed during the period of speculation, the Bubble period, were honest enterprises,

---

[1] M. Postlethwayt, *The Universal Dictionary of Trade and Commerce* (1751), ii, 744, 747.

such as the Royal Exchange Insurance Corporation and the London Assurance Company. These two enterprises were incorporated, and authorised to carry on business, by Royal Charter for which, between them, they paid £600,000 into the Treasury. Others were mere ' wild-cat ' schemes, like one for ' a wheel for perpetual motion,' and some were impudent frauds, like one ' for carrying on an undertaking of great advantage, but nobody to know what it is. Every subscriber who deposits £2 per share to be entitled to £100 per annum.' The promoter of this company decamped with the £2000 which gullible members of the public had subscribed.[1]

After August 1720 the confidence of the public in the South Sea Company began to be weakened, and nervous or prescient stockholders took to selling their stock. When sellers are more eager than buyers (or, as economists used to say, when Supply exceeds Demand), prices fall. Every month now brought with it a fall in South Sea Stock. By the middle of November (1720) £100 of stock was worth £135. Stockholders who had bought it in July at £1000 were probably ruined. Many people lost practically all their savings. Doubtless many others had paid for stock at the high prices with borrowed money. The South Sea Company itself was solvent, but was not making any great profit.

Robert Walpole, who was in the Government with the position of Paymaster of the Forces, was now called upon to investigate the affairs of the South Sea Company. A Parliamentary Committee was formed to aid him. It was discovered that some of the Company's directors had been guilty of corruption and breach of trust. They were condemned, not by due process in a lawcourt, but by Act of Parliament, and their estates were confiscated for the relief of people who had suffered in the Bubble. The amount thus appropriated was £1,659,523. Great difficulty was

---

[1] I. S. Leadam, *The Political History of England*, vol. ix, 1702–60 (1909), p. 295.

ROBERT WALPOLE, EARL OF ORFORD
J. B. Van Loo
National Portrait Gallery

found in distinguishing between suffering stockholders who had been the victims of fraud and those who had bought stock for speculation with their eyes open.

The South Sea Company was not destroyed by the Bubble. The Government excused it from paying the £7,567,000 which the Company had agreed to pay for the privilege of taking over the National Debt; *per contra* of course the Government took back the National Debt (it had only made over a small part of it) into its own hands.

The Assiento contract for the import of slaves by the South Sea Company into Spanish America was not profitable. Neither was the other privilege lucrative which the Treaties of Utrecht permitted, that of sending one ship annually to the Spanish Main. Only ten voyages were made, and the Company appears to have lost by them all, except that of 1731 made by the *Royal Caroline*. In 1734 the Company gave up this privilege. The whaling business of the Company, which was not a monopoly, was not undertaken until 1724. ' Of the eight voyages which their ships made to Greenland, they were gainers by one, and losers by all the rest.' [1] The War of Jenkins' Ear which merged into the War of the Austrian Succession put a stop to the trading privileges of the Company with the Spanish Empire; the Treaties of Aix-la-Chapelle abolished them. The trading capital of the Company was then turned into annuity stock—that is, it was invested in the Funds (the National Debt) for the benefit of the stockholders. ' The Company ceased in any respect to be a trading company.' [2] It had an office and a small clerical staff to keep the register of the annuitants. Charles Lamb in 1790 was a clerk in South-Sea House for a short time, and later wrote an essay about it.

' Reader, in thy passage from the Bank—where thou

---

[1] Adam Smith, *Wealth of Nations* (1904 ed.), ii, 377.
[2] *Ibid.*, ii, 378.

hast been receiving thy half-yearly dividends (supposing thou art a lean annuitant like myself)—to the Flower Pot, to secure a place for Dalston, or Shacklewell, or some other thy suburban retreat northerly—didst thou never observe a melancholy-looking, handsome, brick and stone edifice, to the left, where Threadneedle Street abuts upon Bishopsgate? I dare say thou hast often admired its magnificent portals ever gaping wide, and disclosing to view a grave court, with cloisters and pillars, with few or no traces of goers-in or comers-out— a desolation something like Balclutha's.

' This was once a busy house of trade—a centre of busy interests. The throng of merchants was here— the quick pulse of gain—and here some forms of business are still kept up, though the soul be long since fled. Here are still to be seen stately porticos; imposing staircases; offices roomy as the state apartments in palaces— deserted or thinly peopled with a few straggling clerks; and still more sacred interiors of court and committee rooms, with venerable faces of beadles, door-keepers— directors seated in form on solemn days (to proclaim a dead dividend) at long worm-eaten tables, that have been mahogany, with tarnished gilt-leather coverings, supporting massy silver inkstands, long since dry;—the oaken wainscots hung with pictures of deceased governors and sub-governors, of Queen Anne, and the two first monarchs of the Brunswick dynasty;—huge charts, which subsequent discoveries have antiquated;—dusty maps of Mexico, dim as dreams, and soundings of the Bay of Panama; the long passages hung with buckets, appended in idle row, to walls whose substance might defy any, short of the last, conflagration:—with vast ranges of cellerage under all, where dollars and pieces of eight once lay, an " unsunned heap," for Mammon to have solaced his solitary heart withal—long since dissipated, or scattered into air at the blast of the breaking of that famous *Bubble*.'

The affairs of the South Sea Company were wound up, and it came to an end in 1853.

The East India Company was a more flourishing concern and had a longer history. It began in 1600 with the monopoly of trade between England and India secured to it by Royal Charter. As a matter of common law, however, it was doubtful whether the Crown by charter could grant such a monopoly unless confirmed by Act of Parliament. This question was never quite cleared up, and the Company suffered considerably from the competition of ' interlopers.' In 1698 a new Company was empowered by Act of Parliament to trade with the East Indies, but the old East India Company, in the name of its treasurer, subscribed for £315,000 of stock in the new Company, and thus gained the right to go on trading (as a member of the new Company) even if its charter was not renewed on its expiry in 1701. In 1702 the new and the old Companies were amalgamated into the United Companies of Merchants of England trading to the East Indies. ' The United Company thus formed is the famous corporation which acquired the sovereignty of India during the century extending from 1757 to 1858.' [1]

It is by no means certain that the amalgamation of the two Companies, and the legalising of the monopoly of trade under Act of Parliament was in the public interest. In 1730 a proposal was brought forward in Parliament for opening the trade, though only to a limited extent, to individual merchants. The East India Company strongly opposed the proposal; and the Directors stated that the competition which prevailed when there were two Companies in the trade in the years 1698–1701 had had miserable effects. ' The miserable effects,' wrote Adam Smith later, ' of which the Company complained, were the cheapness of consumption, and the encouragement given to production; precisely the two effects which it is the great business of political economy to promote.' [2] The East India Company, by reason of its

[1] Vincent Smith, *The Oxford History of India* (1919), p. 341.
[2] Adam Smith, *op. cit.*, ii, 381.

great resources and experience, ought to have been able
to make a good profit in unrestricted competition with
private individuals. If it had had to meet such competition, it would undoubtedly have managed its business with
greater efficiency, and would probably not have incurred
the scandals which are its reproach in the latter half of the
eighteenth century.

Down to 1740 the East India Company was a purely
trading corporation. It maintained factories—that is,
settlements containing offices and warehouses—at Bombay,
Madras and Calcutta. The officials of the Company were
like bank clerks or the officials of any merchant's counting-
house, except that they belonged to the more adventurous
kind of Englishmen who went abroad. Enterprising young
men, with no ' prospects ' of their own, like the boys of
Christ's Hospital, eagerly sought for places in the Company's
service, although the first grade, that of writer, carried with
it in the early part of the eighteenth century a salary of
only £10 per annum, with, however, board and lodging
at the Company's charges. The grade above writer was
factor with £20 a year; above factor, merchant with £40
a year. Out of the merchants the chiefs of factories were
chosen. These received £500 a year, and board and
lodging.

A factory was an area of ground, usually bought or
leased from a neighbouring rajah, and partly built over
with houses (quarters for the officials) and with offices and
warehouses. Open spaces were preserved as gardens or
pleasances, with small lakes or ' tanks ' which could be
used for swimming. The factory usually had a wall round
it; and the Company in some places maintained a few native
police or soldiers. It was really, however, just a place for
commerce. A traveller who visited the factory at Surat
shortly before the eighteenth century opened wrote:

' Here they (the English officials) live in shipping
time in a continual hurly-burly, the Banyans (native

agents) presenting themselves from the hour of ten till noon; and in the afternoon at four till night, as if it were an exchange in every row; below stairs the Packers and Warehouse-keepers, together with merchants bringing and receiving, make a meer Billingsgate; for if you make not a noise, they hardly think you intent on what you are doing.' [1]

The boys and young men who went out to these factories lived no very pleasant life amid the heat and noise of the warehouses and offices, with no society but their own, without comforts of home, with only irregular and infrequent letters. It is not surprising that Robert Clive in his early time as a writer tried to commit suicide. Yet these young men, like their successors who generation after generation go forth to make their career abroad, were the salt of the earth. They broke away from the circumscribed life inside England of the eighteenth century, and received the larger vision that comes to those who are prepared to take a risk and to draw their bow at a venture.

Although the trade between England and India was the monopoly of the East India Company, trade inside India was, of course, free, subject only to the regulations, if any, of the native sovereigns. Throughout a good part of the eighteenth century the officials of the Company were permitted to engage in private trade in India, and some made large fortunes. This did not occur, how-ever, until after 1750; the age of the 'Nabobs' was not yet.

At home considerable fortunes were made in commerce, but the first half of the eighteenth century was still very far away from the captains of industry of the Industrial Revolution. As a class, the merchants had considerable political influence, at any rate when the Whigs were in power; but few of them went into politics, and none of them

[1] Fryer's *Travels* (1696), quoted in Ramsay Muir, *The Making of British India* (1915), p. 23.

obtained high positions. On the other hand, merchants were sometimes employed in diplomatic business of the highest importance. Louis XIV negotiated the preliminary peace towards the end of the War of the Spanish Succession through Nicolas Mesnager, a merchant of Rouen.[1] The preliminary peace-treaty of November 30, 1782, at the end of the War of American Independence was negotiated and signed by Richard Oswald, a London merchant. Oswald was a Scotsman, born in 1705. He made some money in business in Glasgow, where a flourishing trade with America grew up after the Act of Union. In time he came to own considerable estates in the West Indies. In 1782 Lord Shelburne, Prime Minister, sent Oswald to Paris with confidential instructions to cede Canada and Nova Scotia, if necessary, to the Americans. Oswald, assisted by two other commissioners, made peace without these sacrifices. He was a friend of two of the American Commissioners, Franklin and Laurens. After the peace he retired to an estate which he had purchased in Scotland called Auchincruive, where he died in 1784.

London and Bristol were the chief ports; Liverpool and Glasgow were steadily increasing their volume of trade. London was then the greatest port in the world, as indeed it probably still is. In the late seventeenth century Samuel Pepys, the Diarist, who was Secretary of the Admiralty, used to enjoy going to the wharves and harbours in the Thames estuary and watching the concourse of shipping. James Thomson, a Scotsman who came to London in 1725, and wrote *The Seasons* (1730), says:

> Then COMMERCE brought into the public walk
> The busy merchant; the big warehouse built;
> Rais'd the strong crane; choak'd up the loaded street
> With foreign plenty; and thy stream, O THAMES,
> Large, gentle, deep, majestic, king of floods,
> Chose for his grand resort.

---

[1] See Mowat, *A History of European Diplomacy*, 1451–1789 (1928), p. 172

FOR FURTHER STUDY

W. CUNNINGHAM, *The Growth of English Industry and Commerce* (vol. ii, 1903).

J. R. McCULLOCH, *Select Collection of Early English Tracts on Commerce* (1856).

J. W. GILBART, *The History, Principles, and Practice of Banking* (new ed., 1882, revised by A. S. Michie).

MORLEY, *Life of Walpole* (1889).

W. R. SCOTT, *Joint Stock Companies* (1910).

C. R. WILSON, *The Early Annals of the English in Bengal* (1895–1911).

CHAPTER X

SCIENCE

THE eighteenth century, at any rate the middle period from 1714 to 1783, can show no such progress in natural science as the seventeenth century, during which Bacon, Galileo, Decartes, Boyle, Newton, and Huygens made their great advances. These grand geniuses established their conclusions upon most careful experiments. The eighteenth century was an ' Age of Reason.' It is recognised that philosophers like Rousseau, who made theories about the origin of human society and the State, depended upon intellectual speculation rather than upon historical investigation. In a similar manner, the scientists, although they did not neglect the method of experiment, tended to rely upon thought and speculation, to produce theories, and to be satisfied if the theories seemed to fit the facts.

Besides being an Age of Reason, the eighteenth century was also an age of materialism. There was a firm belief in the existence of substances which might be of no weight, but which, though imponderable, still were substances. Heat, for instance, which Bacon, early in the seventeenth century, had recognised as a form of motion, was in the eighteenth century held to be a caloric, a hot substance or stuff. Light, which the Dutchman Huygens in the late seventeenth century explained as waves in the air, was considered by most scientists in the eighteenth century to be material, corpuscles emitted by the luminous object.

The celebrated ' phlogiston ' theory is an instance both of the materialism of the eighteenth century, and of its failure to use the method of experiment as thoroughly as the previous century. The author of this theory, Georg Ernst Stahl (1660–1734), was a Bavarian professor in the University of Halle, which in his time was one of the most advanced institutions in Europe. Stahl argued that

' a burning body gave off a substance which he called phlogiston. Had he made more use of the balance, he would have noticed that metal when calcined or oxidised, may give off " phlogiston " but remains heavier than before.' [1]

Nevertheless, the phlogiston theory was held by scientists until disproved by Antoine-Laurent Lavoisier, who was guillotined in the French Revolution.

It was perhaps in researches upon electricity that the greatest advances were made in eighteenth-century science. The existence of electricity had been recognised for two thousand years, but it was not until the Renaissance that any substantial advance was made in the study of this phenomenon. It was left to the eighteenth century to produce something like a scientific theory of conductivity. This was the work of an Englishman, Stephen Gray (1696–1736), who, like Colonel Newcome, spent his last years as a pensioner in the Charterhouse. Gray discovered

' that the difference in electrical conductivity depends, not upon the colour of objects or some similar quality, but on the material of which bodies are composed. Thus, metal wire conducts; silk does not. . . . Gray observed that conductors can be insulated by placing them on cakes of resin.' [2]

Meanwhile in North America a native, self-taught genius was growing to his mature powers. The Royal Society of London was in the habit of publishing the results of the experiments of its members. Franklin, who lived at

---

[1] F. Cajori, *A History of Physics* (1929), p. 108.
[2] *Ibid.*, pp. 123–124.

Philadelphia, entered into correspondence with Peter Collinson, a member of the Royal Society, who was interested in electricity, and who had presented a glass tube, for use in electrical experiments, to the Philadelphia Subscription Library. In this correspondence Franklin explained a theory which he had formed about atmospheric electricity, and the way in which it could be conducted to earth and controlled. Hitherto the two-fluid theory of the Frenchman Charles-François du Fay (1698–1739) had been accepted as the explanation of the two properties of electricity, attraction and repulsion. Franklin argued for a one-fluid theory with plus and minus, or positive and negative, effects.

In 1752 Franklin sent up a kite equipped with a sharp pointed wire into a thundercloud, and received an electric spark on his hand from a key attached to the end of the string. Having found that electricity from the clouds could be conducted to the earth, Franklin conceived the idea of protecting buildings from lightning by placing a conducting wire from their highest parts down to the ground. With a view to testing this plan he endeavoured to collect sufficient money to enable him to build an experimental tower. While he was doing this, news came from France that Thomas-François D'Alibard, a friend of the naturalist Buffon, had successfully erected a lightning-rod at Marly-la-Ville. Franklin went on with his experiments. In 1760 his lightning-conductors were put into use to protect buildings in Philadelphia. John Winthrop, Professor of Physics at Harvard, obtained his electrical equipment from Franklin, and by means of his excellent lectures and demonstrations spread in the United States the knowledge of Franklin's work.

Franklin was made a Fellow of the Royal Society of London in 1756. The famous letters sent to Collinson were published by him in London, and were translated into several European languages. It is a proof of the solid culture of the eighteenth century that in order to make the letters available to the widest circle of scholars they were also translated into Latin.

In England another notable scholar, Henry Cavendish (1731–1810), made remarkable researches in chemistry and electro-physics, but was content to leave them buried in unpublished manuscript. After passing through Peterhouse, Cambridge, Cavendish, who was comparatively wealthy, confined himself to his house and library in London. It was not until late in the nineteenth century that much of his work was made known to the world by the Cambridge professor, James Clerk Maxwell.[1] By that time his results had been thought out independently by later scientists, like the Frenchman Coulomb and the Englishman Faraday.

In mathematics the British achievement of the eighteenth century was notable; the University of Cambridge, preeminent, was closely followed by those of Glasgow and Edinburgh. The British mathematicians developed a school of their own, basing their work upon that of Sir Isaac Newton, and almost entirely ignoring the work of the German Leibniz and the Swiss brothers, James and John Bernoulli.

' It was almost a matter of course that the English should at first have adopted the notation of Newton in the infinitesimal calculus in preference to that of Leibniz, and the English school would consequently in any case have developed on somewhat different lines to that on the continent, where a knowledge of the infinitesimal calculus was derived solely from Leibniz and the Bernoullis.' [2]

It is a remarkable fact that while, as a rule, science and learning recognise no national boundaries, in early eighteenth-century mathematics there was a regular national feud. John Bernoulli

[1] Cajori, *op. cit.*, p. 135.
[2] W. W. Rouse Ball, *A History of Mathematics* (1888), pp. 356, 357.

' regarded the controversy on the origin of the infinitesimal calculus as a convenient opportunity to vent his dislike of Newton and Newton's countrymen. It was only natural, though it was unfortunate, that the English should have resented this by declining to see any merit in the works of Leibniz and John Bernoulli; and so for forty or fifty years, to the mutual disadvantage of both sides the quarrel raged.' [1]

One of the most eminent English mathematicians after Newton was Brook Taylor (1685–1731), of St. John's College, Cambridge. Many of his theorems and proofs are of the highest interest and use to modern mathematicians. Roger Cotes (1682–1716), a Fellow of Trinity College, Cambridge, edited Newton's *Principia*, but died before he had reached the maturity of his powers. Robert Smith (1689–1768), Master of Trinity College, Cambridge, wrote the standard English eighteenth-century treatise on optics. The most promising Glaswegian was Colin Maclaurin, who, after finishing his college course at Glasgow, was made Professor of Mathematics in the University of Aberdeen at the age of nineteen. He was afterwards for twenty years professor at Edinburgh. He died in 1746 at the age of forty-eight in consequence of hardships incurred during service with the loyal troops and volunteers against Prince Charles and the Highlanders in the Jacobite rebellion of 1745.

Maclaurin's output of high-class mathematical work, in books and papers printed in *Philosophical Transactions*, was remarkable. The most able British mathematician of the eighteenth century, he is nevertheless considered to have had an unfortunate influence. ' By himself abandoning the use both of analysis and of the infinitesimal calculus, he induced Newton's countrymen to confine themselves to Newton's methods.' It was not until 1817, ' when the differential calculus was introduced into the Cambridge curriculum, that English mathematicians made any

[1] Ball, *op. cit.*, p. 356.

general use of the more powerful methods of modern analysis.' [1]

Physics and mathematics have obviously a close relation to the practical affairs of everyday life. The materialistic outlook of the men of the eighteenth century served to stimulate a desire to make practical applications of the theoretical results arrived at in these sciences. The eighteenth century was, therefore, rich in mechanical experiment; it was on this work that the marvellous successes of the nineteenth century in the sphere of mechanical invention were based.

One of the most marked advances in the eighteenth century was in the means of observing distant objects. Copernicus (1473–1543), the ecclesiastical astronomer of East Prussia, had to carry on his astronomical observations with the naked eye. The first telescope appears to have been made by a Dutchman, Hans Lippershey, in the year 1608. The great Huygens (1629–95) experimented with the making of telescopes, but the first really efficient one was made by the Englishman John Dollond in 1758. This was further improved by William Herschel.

Herschel (1738–1822) was a Hanoverian who, as a youth, had served in the band of a Hanoverian regiment in the Seven Years War. Migrating to England, he earned his living for some years by teaching music, and later secured the post of organist of the Octagon Chapel in Bath. Here he developed an interest in astronomy which moved him to undertake, with the assistance of his sister and brother, the construction of a large telescope. With the aid of this telescope he discovered two satellites of Saturn.

On one occasion Herschel and the recluse Henry Cavendish sat next to each other at dinner. ' Is it true, Dr. Herschel, that you see the stars round ? ' asked Cavendish seriously. ' Round as a button,' replied Herschel. Nothing more was said between the two until dinner was nearly over. Then Cavendish, who appeared to be turning the matter

[1] Ball, *op. cit.*, p. 363.

over in his mind, said doubtfully, ' Round as a button ? '
' Round as a button,' sharply rejoined Herschel. Cavendish
relapsed into complete silence.[1]

The value of the association of the scientific scholar and
the man of practical genius was never better demonstrated
than in the friendship of Joseph Black (1728–99) and James
Watt (1736–1819). Black, who, after spending some years
on the staff of Glasgow University, became Professor of
Chemistry at Edinburgh, is famous for his discoveries of
fixed air—*i.e.*, carbonic acid—and latent heat. Watt was
the mathematical instrument-maker at Glasgow University,
where he often discussed with Black the possibility of
improving the steam-engine, of which at that time New-
comen's was the most advanced type. Applying what he
learnt from Black, Watt set out to improve this wasteful
and clumsy engine. The success which Watt achieved
marks the close of an era in the world's history and the
beginning of an age of steam.

[1] See article by A. M. Clerke in the *Dictionary of National
Biography*, s.v. Herschel.

CHAPTER XI

THE AGRICULTURAL REVOLUTION

IT is impossible to think about the eighteenth century without frequently referring to revolutions—that of 1688, which determined the political development of Great Britain; the French Revolution towards the end of the century, which led to the great war; the Industrial Revolution, which created the vast cities and crowded masses of workers of to-day; and the Agricultural Revolution, by means of which alone could eighteenth-century England be plentifully fed.

The mediæval ' open-field ' system persisted into modern times, although giving way in many districts to ' enclosures.' In the seventeenth century there was a very large proportion, probably about three-fifths, of the country, still in open fields. Writing of the Restoration period, Macaulay states :

' Agriculture was in what would now be considered a very rude and imperfect state. The arable land and pasture were not supposed by the best political arithmeticians of the age to amount to more than half the area of the kingdom. The remainder was believed to consist of moor, forest and fen. These computations are strongly confirmed by the road books and maps of the seventeenth century. From these books and maps it is clear that many routes which now pass through an endless succession of orchards, hayfields and beanfields, then ran through nothing but heath, swamp and warren. In the drawings of English landscapes made in that age for the Grand Duke Cosmo, scarce a hedgerow is to be seen, and numerous tracts, now rich with cultivation, appear as bare as Salisbury Plain. . . .'[1]

At Enfield, hardly out of sight of the smoke of the capital, was a region of five and twenty miles in circumference, which contained only three houses and scarcely any enclosed fields. Even the enclosures, when used for growing grain, had to be cultivated according to the 'three-field' system —one year in wheat, another in barley, a third year lying fallow.

A result of the three-field system was not only that land was unproductive for one year in three, but also that meat was scarce. It was impossible to keep a large number of beasts throughout the winter, because there was nothing to feed them with. The best could be kept for breeding, and would be fed upon hay, but the rest of the animals were slaughtered and the meat was salted. The mediæval man, if he had meat at all in the winter months, had it salted; and anything, like a little pepper, which could give a relish to the tough, tasteless, and briny viand was highly prized, and fetched an enormous price. It was a great occasion in the mediæval Oxford colleges (which were by no means comfortable places) when a benefactor gave some money enabling the Fellows to have a small allowance of pepper.

The introduction of root-crops changed all this for England, as it did also, although not quite so rapidly, for all the Western European countries. Turnips and other root-crops could be grown, without exhausting the soil, on ground which otherwise would be fallow for a year. These root-crops such as turnips and mangel-wurzels, seem first to have been developed in the Low Countries, where also drainage and irrigation were skilfully practised. Dutch methods were already influencing England in the time of Charles I, just as was Dutch art (Vandyke). The Bedford Level which has rendered fertile and cultivable so large a part of the Fen Country was begun to be made in 1634, and

----

[1] *History of England*, chap. III.

was completed about 1660. The connection of England with the Low Countries was strengthened by the accession of William III of Orange. One Samuel Hartlib, a native of East Prussia, came to England about 1628, and published in 1652 a book, *Flanders' Husbandry*. Towards the end of the century the practice of raising turnips as a field-crop was introduced into England from Germany. Turnips were not unknown in England before the seventeenth century, but they were only cultivated as garden-vegetables.

The credit of seeing the possibilities arising out of the culture on a large scale of the turnip as a root-crop appears to belong to Charles Townshend, Viscount Townshend of Rainham, in Norfolk. He was a great Whig magnate and was one of the English commissioners who arranged the Union with Scotland in 1707. During the War of the Spanish Succession he conducted important diplomatic negotiations in the Netherlands. After the war was over he was Secretary of State in the Ministry of Stanhope. In Walpole's famous Ministry of 1721 Townshend was again Secretary of State. After about ten years of co-operation the two friends—they were also brothers-in-law—parted. Townshend henceforward devoted himself to his estates. ' It is to him,' writes Lord Mahon, ' that England, and more especially his native county of Norfolk, owes the introduction and cultivation of the turnip from Germany.' [1] Townshend died in 1738. Probably he had been experimenting at Rainham in the cultivation of the turnip for many years before he retired. It was not, however, introduced into Scotland until 1764.

The turnip was grown in the ' third year,' in which formerly the field had lain fallow. Moreover, it matures in the autumn and will keep all through the winter. By this means cattle could be fed, and fed well, in winter as in summer. Fresh meat was now to be had at any time.

The Agricultural Revolution of the eighteenth century took effect in two directions. One was a movement in the

[1] Mahon, *History of England*, chap. XII.

direction of better crops; the other was in the direction of better beasts. Both movements depended upon enclosures.

Enclosures had been taking place ever since the Black Death of 1349. They were made sometimes by a land-owner taking in waste or common-land and enclosing it for making cultivable fields; sometimes the enclosures took the form of putting together ' open fields,' various ' strips ' held by peasants on a manor, so as to convert the holding of each peasant into one solid piece of land, which might continue as his holding or which might by purchase or other legal arrangement be added to the lord's farm.

It is obvious that without enclosed fields no marked improvement in agriculture could come about. Good strains of cattle could not be bred on common-land; and proper ploughing, draining, and weeding were very difficult to achieve by small farmers who held only scattered strips of land in open fields. ' Enclosing,' which was usually carried out on each manor or village after the Restoration by a private Act of Parliament, made scientific farming on a large scale possible; and the growth of population, so prominent a feature in modern as compared with mediæval times, made this profitable.

While the Enclosure Movement of the eighteenth century increased the productivity of the soil, and made for better crops, it also helped towards effecting a revolution in the weight and quality of animals. It was a meat-revolution quite as much as, indeed more than, a crop-revolution. Bakewell, Tull, and Coke were especially famous for live stock, which they fostered and developed.

In addition to the open, but cultivated, fields, which could be enclosed, there were at the beginning of the eighteenth century, about 3,000,000 acres in forest, park, and common, 3,000,000 in woods and coppices, 10,000,000 in heath, moor, mountain, and barren land; altogether there were only 9,000,000 acres under the plough. All this refers to England and Wales taken together; the total area of the country (without Scotland) was estimated at 39,000,000 acres.

That England was a wealthy country, able to sustain the crushing expenses of prolonged wars on the Continent, is a remarkable fact; for, throughout at any rate the first forty or fifty years of the eighteenth century, it was ' mainly an agricultural country with its agriculture still rude and primitive, and large areas still in a wild state.' [1] The enormous economic drain of the wars was supported almost wholly by the commerce of England, by the mercantile houses of London, Bristol, and a few other ports. Almost all the wealth and most of the population were in the South. The North was poor, little populated, unprogressive. The energy, enterprise, and other businesslike qualities which are now rightly imputed to the North seem to be products of the Industrial Revolution, or at any rate, only to have been ' released ' by this new force, this black, but really beneficent, demon.

The owning and holding of land was a real business and livelihood for the gentry as well as for the farmers and yeomanry. Even the great families still depended on agricultural land for most of their income, although they sometimes invested their surplus in colonial undertakings. The smaller country gentry with incomes of £200 to £500 in the early eighteenth century lived closely attached to the land, and depended entirely for their living upon careful management of their small estates. Classes were not clearly marked off from each other; the small squires ' shaded off into the well-to-do yeomanry, as these again did into the poorer.' [2] There was no distinct labouring class, although hired labour was not uncommon. There were numerous small freeholders and copyholders, many of whom had not much more than a cottage and garden with rights upon a common; they increased their livelihood by hiring themselves out as labourers or by carrying on some domestic manufacture, like spinning. There were, however, also

[1] W. H. R. Curtler, *The Enclosure and Redistribution of our Land* (1921), p. 139.
[2] *Ibid.*, p. 140.

landless labourers, who received a wage agreed upon for a whole year, and who were boarded in the farmer's house. These must have been unmarried men. There was a future on the land, for starting with a few poles or an acre the thrifty and efficient labourer could add here and there to his holding and rise to be a cultivator of some size, with leasehold and freehold land. Farmers and labourers were not separate classes as they are now, although agricultural labourers still can, and not infrequently do, rise to be small farmers.

Features on the picturesque commons are still the patches enclosed by squatters, who cleared and drained and hedged small portions, and somehow remained long enough there to acquire a customary title. Rural England cannot have looked very different then from what it is now, in spite of the construction of railways and new roads, except in one respect—the hedges which are to-day so striking a feature in almost every English countryside and which mark off little field from little field did not exist in the early eighteenth century.

Everyone has a general familiarity with the story of the ' Enclosure Movement,' resulting in the increase of large estates and farms and the class of landless labourers. The Industrial Revolution undoubtedly fostered this process, by gradually destroying the domestic industry of the small landholders, and by offering them prospects of wages in towns. Enclosures, however, are much older than the Industrial Revolution; and those of the eighteenth century were caused more by the wars which Great Britain fought than by the Industrial Revolution which, as a matter of fact, had scarcely begun then. Popular opinion in the eighteenth century was strongly in favour of making the country self-supporting in food. England had been a grain-exporting country down to about the middle of the eighteenth century or a little later, but in the time of the War of American Independence it ceased for ever to export wheat. During peace-time the import of wheat had been practically prohibited by heavy duties, but in 1773 a Corn Law was passed, permitting import when the domestic price was over 48s. a quarter at the nominal duty of sixpence. There was always a serious danger in war that Great Britain would be absolutely cut off for some time from foreign sources of supply. Meanwhile the population was increasing rather more rapidly than formerly, and therefore the need for securing the domestic supply of food was all the greater. So successful was the Enclosure Movement and improved methods of farming that in the ten years 1770–80 wheat averaged only about 40s. a quarter (previously about 50s.) and remained low down to the French Revolutionary War, when it rose to about 75s. The production of meat went on favourably too; in 1773 the price of butcher's meat was fourpence a pound; by 1800 it had risen to one shilling. As the price of wheat and meat rose, the labourers, both in town and country, had less to spend on milk and butter; bread being their staple food, they even bought little meat. Down to the French Revolutionary War, however, everybody seems to have been able to use butter, milk, and meat, as well as bread.

In general two types of enclosure have been distinguished in English history—enclosure for wool, and enclosure for wheat and meat. The first, the woollen, are the characteristic Tudor enclosures; the second, the wheat and meat, are the eighteenth-century enclosures. The first kind were retrogressive, in the sense that they meant usually the sacrifice of a fairly highly organised, intensive kind of farming (tillage) for the simpler, easier, extensive sheep-farming. The second sort of enclosures, those of the eighteenth century, always meant better farming of the land; poor pasture became good grazing- or mowing-lands; miserable ' open fields ' were put under a well-capitalised system of tillage; capital also, wrote Arthur Young, ' converted barren heaths into smiling corn-fields.'

The eighteenth-century Enclosure Movement was slow in the first sixty years. From 1700 to 1760 there were 162

Acts, enclosing about 237,845 acres of open fields; in addition there were 56 Acts enclosing about 74,000 acres of common and waste land. In the next forty years, 1761–1800, there were 1479 Acts enclosing nearly two and a half million acres of open fields, and 521 Acts enclosing over 750,000 acres of common and waste. The rate of enclosure according-ing to reigns can be judged from the numbers of Acts passed: in Queen Anne's reign, 2 ; under George I, 16 ; under George II, 226 ; under George III, 3554. The part of the country most affected was the ' Great Central Plain ' which includes part of Somerset and Dorset, and extends across England through the Midlands to Yorkshire and East Anglia.

The enclosure movement could no more be stopped in England than could the rising or setting of the sun. It was absolutely inevitable that with the increase of population (which was bound to come with better hygiene and with the Industrial Revolution) the methods of agriculture would be improved; and no great improvement could take place without the abolition of the open fields. The enclosure of common might have been avoided, but this would very seriously have restricted the enclosable area. No more common can be enclosed now, and there is a great deal left (over 1,500,000 acres).

The chief criticism which can be levelled against en-closures is in regard to the expense. Throughout the whole of the eighteenth century, every award was made by means of a private Act which had to be promoted in Parliament with legal expenses. The cost of a private Act is estimated at about £1 for each acre enclosed. The parliamentary expenses were the smallest element in the cost of an en-closure award.

The following facts are the results of investigations of Mr. Curtler, who gives an unvarnished and judicious account.[1]

As a typical parish, applying for enclosure, may be taken

[1] *The Enclosure and Redistribution of our Land*, chap. xiv.

Inkpen, in Berkshire, in 1736. According to the private Act passed for it in that year, the Inkpen proprietors were thirty-four, consisting of the Lord of the Manor, the rector, four ' squires,' three ' gentlemen,' eleven yeomen, a cordwainer, a haberdasher of hats, a carpenter, blacksmith, labourer, potter, bricklayer, maltster, shopkeeper, two widows, a spinster, and the churchwardens.

The first stage in the process of enclosure was the convening of a public meeting in the parish after proper advertisement. At the meeting a draft petition to Parliament was prepared and approved, and signatures were attached representing a majority of the value of all the properties. The petition if approved in Parliament, after having been referred to a committee, issued as a Bill which defined the area to be enclosed and appointed commissioners to make the award or division.

The commissioners were often selected from the neighbouring farmers (not resident in the parish or farming in it), and they were usually paid about two guineas a day in addition to reimbursement of expenses. Their task, obviously one of great difficulty, was to divide all the open fields and any common or part of a common designated in the Act, and to award to each proprietor enclosed land of such fertility and situation as made his new holding equal in value to his former rights. A necessary result of the award was the fencing, hedging, ditching, draining of the whole area and the making of new public roads. All this was done at the expense of the whole enclosed area. The sum necessary to meet this expense was raised usually by assessment on all the properties, or sometimes by selling a certain amount of land, deducted *pro rata* from the amount allotted to each proprietor. £25 an acre may be taken as the average value of the land at the time of enclosure. The expenses were usually about £21 per acre. Therefore unless the result of enclosure was a very great increase in the productivity of the land the owner was much worse off after than before. As a matter of fact, enclosure did result in increased fertility, and from the first year; but the poor or unthrifty small proprietor may have sold his land to a wealthy neighbour rather than pay his share in the assessment. The immediate effect of enclosure upon housing was on the whole good. In many places new farm-houses and cottages had to be built to suit the new distribution of land. The conditions of housing for the poorer members of the population were bad. Nathaniel Kent, a diplomatist turned agriculturist, who managed estates for great gentry in the years 1775–1810, aspired to see the labourers and smallest cultivators in a cottage with ' a warm comfortable plain room for the poor inhabitants to eat their morsel in, an oven to bake their bread, a little receptacle for their small beer and provisions, and two wholesome lodging apartments, one for the man and his wife, and another for the children.' [1] Probably this ideal is more closely approached to-day in the countryside now than it was in the eighteenth century.

In considering the developments which took place in agriculture and in the English land-system of the eighteenth century, we must bear in mind that the wealthier among the landed gentry monopolised all political influence. Doubtless, they aimed at being just and fair in their treatment of the rest of the people who were on the land; but the rest of the people, although they were summoned to meetings to decide upon enclosures, were not likely to exert much influence.

The great landed gentry were not a frivolous, selfish class as the French nobility—with, naturally, notable exceptions —on the whole undoubtedly were. ' There [in England],' wrote Alexis de Tocqueville, in regard to the eighteenth century, ' the aristocracy has taken upon itself the heaviest public charges in order that it may be allowed to govern; here [in France] it has retained to the end its immunity from direct taxation in order to console itself for having lost the power of governing.' The English aristocracy was,

[1] Quoted in Curtler, *op. cit.*, p. 172.

indeed, proud but not haughty. Goldsmith wrote in *The Traveller* :

> Pride in their port, defiance in their eye,
> I see the lords of human kind pass by.

They were, however—and are—genial to their tenants and to their neighbours, even the humblest. ' Arthur Young, accustomed to the bearing of English landlords, was struck by the very distant condescension with which the French *seigneur* treated the farmer.' [1] The great English landed gentry lived in the country and knew their neighbourhood; they were all bred with a sense of fairness and public duty. Nor were the tenants entirely overcome by their landlords' rights and sense of rank. Goldsmith wrote that

> . . . even the peasant boasts these rights to scan
> And learns to venerate himself as man. [2]

Nevertheless it could not be satisfactory for the interests of the people as a whole that both central and local Government should be as unrepresentative as it was in England in the eighteenth century. Through their wealth, and especially through their ownership of land, the aristocracy and great gentry controlled parliamentary elections in most of the boroughs, and even in the counties, as the franchise was confined there to freeholders. They controlled and directed local government by another means. It was the duty of the Lord-Lieutenant of each county to nominate justices of the peace for the approval of the Lord Chancellor; these nominations were practically always accepted. As the Lord-Lieutenant was always one of the chief landholders of the county, and as he naturally believed that the ' landed interest ' was the best for England, he nominated landed gentry like himself. The justices of the peace, in Quarter Sessions, and in other ways, were the men charged with the duty of administering or adjudicating upon the enclosure

---

[1] J. L. and B. Hammond, *The Village Labourer* (1912), p. 3.
[2] *The Traveller*.

Acts. They were a great official body, unpaid and enjoying the full confidence of the central Government. The same men, through ownership or ' patronage ' of presentations to clerical benefices, nominated the parish clergy. The public schools and the two universities were practically given over to their sons. Cabinet, Parliament, Quarter Sessions—all were the country gentlemen's.

' Thus on every side this class is omnipotent. In Parliament with its ludicrous representation, in the towns with their decayed government, in the country, sleeping under the absolute rule of the Justice of the Peace, there is no rival power. The Crown is for all purposes its accomplice rather than its competitor. It controls the universities, the Church, the law, and all the springs of life and discussion. Its own influence is consolidated by the strong social discipline embodied in the family settlements. Its supremacy is supreme and unquestioned. Whereas in France the fermentation of ideas was an intellectual revolt against the governing system, and all literature spoke treason, in England the existing *régime* was accepted, we might say assured, by the world of letters and art, by the England that admired Reynolds and Gibbon, or listened to Johnson and Goldsmith, or laughed with Sheridan and Sterne. To the reason of France, the Government under which France lived was an expensive paradox; to the reason of England any other government than the government under which England lived was unthinkable. Hence de Tocqueville saw only a homogeneous society, a society revering its institutions in the spirit of Burke, in contrast with a society that mocked at its institutions in the spirit of Voltaire.' [1]

The writers of the above paragraph close with a passage from Burke's letter to the Duke of Richmond in 1772. ' You people of great families and hereditary trusts and fortunes are not like such as I am. . . . You, if you are

[1] Hammond, *op. cit.*, p. 24.

what you ought to be, are in my eye the great oaks that shade a country, and perpetuate your benefits from generation to generation.'[1]

The method of agriculture was bound to change during the eighteenth century, and the system of landholding had inevitably to be remodelled. This could have been done with more effectual safeguards for the 'landed labourer' than were employed during the Agricultural Revolution. On the other hand, it must be constantly borne in mind that the decline of the 'small man' on the land is not apparent before the great wars which began half-way through the French Revolution; and that these wars had probably far more to do with the creation of rural (and of urban) poverty than either the Agricultural or Industrial Revolutions or the bad Poor Law system of dole inaugurated by Berkshire Justices of the Peace in 1795.

[1] Burke, *Correspondence,* i, 370

FOR FURTHER STUDY

R. E. PROTHERO, *English Farming Past and Present* (1912).

W. CUNNINGHAM. See under chap. IX.

ARTHUR YOUNG, *The Farmer's Tour through the East of England* (4 vols., 1771).

—— *On the Husbandry of the Three Celebrated British Farmers* (1811).

NATHANIEL KENT, *A General View of the Agriculture of the County of Norfolk* (1794).

CHAPTER XII

SCOTLAND

UNTIL 1603 Scotland and England were independent of each other. From 1603 to 1707 they were joined in a personal union, having the same monarch, but separate legislatures. This form of union, tolerable while the Crown held absolute authority, was becoming intolerable after 1688, when limited monarchy and parliamentary government were being established in both countries. By the year 1707 the situation was quite intolerable, Queen Anne having had to consent to the Scottish Bill of Security (1704). This Bill ensured that when Anne died the Scots should choose a different sovereign from the successor to the English throne, unless in the meantime conditions had been obtained, securing ' the honour and sovereignty of this Crown and kingdom.' The Bill or Act of Security brought the Anglo-Scottish crisis to a head; and earnest negotiations among the wiser heads on both sides led to a treaty for complete union (1707). The treaty passed the English and Scottish legislatures. It was ' the end of an old song,' as the Scottish Chancellor said at the last meeting of the Estates in Parliament House at Edinburgh. Henceforth England and Scotland were to be one kingdom, with the same Cabinet and the same Parliament. There were a few local differences under the Act of Union. The Church, as established in Scotland, was Presbyterian, and the law that was in force in Scotland was still to be Scots law, supplemented by British statute law enacted after 1707. The Act of 1707 is a remarkable and indeed unique achievement of permanent union between two peoples who for years had been growing

nationally inflamed against each other, so that every year
the rent, as Queen Anne said at the time of the Act of
Security, had only become wider.[1]

The prosperity of Scotland is to be dated from the Act
of Union, which opened England and the English Empire
to Scottish trade and enterprise. Yet the Act of Union was
' burned at every market cross '; and during the Porteous
Riots in 1736 the old hatreds seemed to blaze up more
furiously than ever. It was their last effort. Scott's *Heart
of Midlothian* is the swan-song of the old animosities.
Jeanie Deans walks through England and is treated as a
friend. She finds the great Scottish nobleman, the Duke
of Argyle, apparently almost as much at home and almost as
influential in London as in Inverary. She is treated with
sympathy by the English Queen, and so can return to Edinburgh, her mission accomplished, her sister's life saved.

The irritation caused by the Act of Union, which was
fairly general and long sustained, must be distinguished
from Jacobitism, with which it had no part. Jacobitism
was the fantastic cult of a few Scottish gentry, chiefly in the
Highlands. The Stewarts, while they were reigning, had
never been really popular in Scotland, and least of all during
the hundred years before 1688. Yet when the Stewarts had
fled the country, a perverse, though not ungenerous, conception of loyalty kept a few families faithful to their cause.
There seem to have been never more than a handful of
these families, either in England or in Scotland, but they
were occasionally supported, for political reasons, by foreign
Governments—the Papacy, France, Sweden, or Spain.
The Jacobites had some money, and considerable social
influence. The Highland chiefs would call upon their
tenantry to follow them; but, even so, they were never able
to raise forces of more than a few thousands, and a following
of this size was secured only on two occasions.

James Francis Edward, the Chevalier de Saint George,
the ' Old Pretender,' was the son of the late king, James II.

[1] J. H. Burton, *History of Scotland*, vol. viii, p. 99.

His birth in 1688 had been the occasion of the English Revolution. ' My whole life from my cradle,' he remarked in 1715, ' has been a constant series of misfortunes.' Except for a few months spent in Scotland, he was in exile all his life. Brought up in France, he lived after the Peace of Utrecht (1713) at Bar-le-Duc, in Lorraine. At the time of the Rebellion he was still unmarried.

In 1715 James wrote to the Earl of Mar, proposing that an insurrection should be started in favour of the exiled dynasty. Mar, the Lord of Badenoch, in Inverness-shire, was a powerful Highland nobleman, but he was also a courtier and accomplished politician. On the accession of George I he had been dismissed, along with all the other Tory Ministers, from his office of Secretary of State for Scotland. His motives for becoming Jacobite seem to have been of the most sordid kind, ' greed of place, power and emolument, mortified ambition and revenge.' He, the polished courtier, the high politician of London who alone knew all the risks, the desperateness, of his ' bloody game,' [1] lured the rough-handed, ignorant Highland chiefs into rebellion. Mar invited the heads of the clans to come to a great hunting-party at Braemar, in Aberdeenshire, on August 26, 1715. So the rebellion began.

There were also some rather feeble efforts at rebellion in the South of Scotland and the North of England; Preston, under Thomas Forster, a Roman Catholic gentleman, was held for three days against the Government troops and then capitulated. While Preston was being held by the English Jacobites, Mar and his Highlanders, some 9000 men, were fighting the Duke of Argyle and a loyalist army of regular troops and volunteers, somewhat inferior in number, at Sheriffmuir, near Perth (November 13, 1715). The Jacobite right wing broke the opposing left; but the Hanoverian right wing, under the consummate commander Argyle, broke the Jacobite left. Mar retreated to Perth; King George's troops had possession of the field.

[1] J. H. Burton, *History of Scotland*, vol. viii, p. 255.

K

> Some say that we wan,
> Some say that they wan,
> Some say that nane wan at a',

ran a contemporary jingle. As a matter of fact, the rebellion was broken. When the melancholy Pretender, with his ' to me it is no new thing to be unfortunate,' landed at Peterhead from Dunkirk (January 2, 1716), failure was evident everywhere. ' Alas ! this too clear-sighted prince was not the leader who could rekindle a dying enthusiasm.' [1] He went to Perth and held chilly royal state in Scone. On January 30 the retreat northwards was begun along the coast. At Montrose James and the Earl of Mar slipped away on a ship, and sailed to France (February 3). The army, under a Colonel Gordon, continued its march, melting away like snow. The last few hundreds were overtaken at Aberdeen and made prisoners.

King George was merciful. ' In the infliction of penalties the Government, as compared with the Stewart sovereigns, acted with moderation and lenity.' [2] Though all who had engaged in the insurrection were liable to the penalty of death, none of the undistinguished rebels were executed. Six great lords, leaders of their people, were impeached in Parliament and sentenced to death. Three were reprieved. Two, the Earl of Derwentwater (an Englishman) and Viscount Kenmure (a Scotsman), were beheaded at London on Tower Hill on February 24, 1716. A third, the Earl of Nithsdale, who was held for execution, escaped from the Tower in his wife's clothes. ' Though her act was treason, the Government was generous enough to let her go free.' [3]

There was another attempt at rebellion in 1719, financed by Alberoni, the ambitious Minister of Spain. A small Spanish force was landed on the Ross-shire coast. It was joined by about 1000 Highlanders, brought by Lords Sea-

---

[1] R. L. Mackie, *A Short History of Scotland* (1931), p. 348.
[2] I. S. Leadam, *The Political History of England*, vol. ix, 1702–1760, p. 265.   [3] *Ibid.*, p. 267.

forth and Tullibardine. They were speedily attacked by General Wightman, who came with 1100 regular troops from Inverness. The Highlanders were driven away in rout; the Spaniards, 274 in number, were made prisoners of war. In consequence of these two insurrections, the 'Fifteen and the 'Nineteen, a systematic scheme of road-making was undertaken by General Wade in 1724 and following years. The wild and roadless Highlands now became accessible to soldiers, travellers, and traders. The roads, skilfully engineered, with handsome, though simple, bridges, can still be seen—some are still used—threading the glens, following the river-banks, and winding in the passes of the sterile savage mountains.

> If you had seen these roads before they were made,
> You would have held up your hands and blessed General
> Wade.

After the Old Pretender escaped to France in 1716, the British Government insisted that the French Government should refuse him permission to reside in France. The Regent Orleans was complaisant, so the prince had to depart for Italy. Here he married (1719) Clementina Sobieski, and lived mainly at Rome, or in a villa at Albano, given to him by Pope Clement XI, until he died, in 1766.

Though communication went on between the Jacobites in Great Britain and France—largely by means of French privateers [1]—Scotland showed no inclination to restore the Stewarts and was far better without them, and went on steadily increasing in prosperity. The English and Scots peoples were settling down together happily enough, although the Porteous Riots, in 1736, for a short time revived the old prejudices and antipathies. John Porteous, captain of the Edinburgh city guard, fired upon a disorderly mob when a smuggler was being publicly executed. Porteous was tried, sentenced to death, then respited. He was

---

[1] See *French Privateers and Jacobites*, by W. B. Johnson, in *The Quarterly Review*, April 1931.

lying in the Tolbooth Jail in Edinburgh, when the mob broke in and killed him (September 7, 1736). There were serious disputes in the Government, in which some of the Ministers were for taking away the charter of Edinburgh. In the end Walpole had a Bill put through Parliament imposing upon the corporation of Edinburgh a fine of £2000 for the benefit of Captain Porteous's widow. The story of the Porteous Riots and of the strong feelings which were then aroused are familiar to readers of Scott's vivid and moving romance *The Heart of Midlothian*. The political effects of the incident were not important, apparently it had no bearing at all upon the Jacobite rebellion which broke out in 1745. This rebellion was the affair of a moment, the result of a chance seized by the Jacobites, while England was entangled in a Continental war, to make a last wild venture.

There were, indeed, favouring circumstances in 1745. Great Britain being engaged in the Continental war, there were few troops at home. The king, George II, was himself away at Hanover. The Highlanders were restive, for with Wade's roads there had come Government interference and regulation, and also new ways and fashions of life; the untutored men of the mountains, moors, and glens were feeling ' the pressure of Saxon order and industrial civilisation.' At this time they were ready to be stirred up against all this, but in a few years' time they would be used to it. For the Jacobites it was now or never.

Prince Charles Edward Louis Philip Casimir Stewart was the elder son of the Old Pretender, and was twenty-four years of age when his great adventure began. He received practically no support from the French Government. He borrowed 180,000 livres (about £75,000), and obtained the use of two small ships, the *Elizabeth*, a French privateer belonging to an Irishman, Anthony Walsh of Nantes, and the *Du Teillay* (or *Doutelle*), a small warship lent by the French Government. He embarked at Saint-Nizaire, at the mouth of the Loire, on July 13, 1745. On August 2 he landed on the island of Eriskay, between Barra and South Uist, with seven men, Lord Tullibardine, Æneas Macdonald, Sir Thomas Sheridan, Sir John Macdonald, the Reverend Mr. Kelly, Francis Strickland, and O'Sullivan.

The landing on the mainland was made in Moidart, on the west coast of Inverness-shire. A few chiefs, young Clanranald, Cameron of Lochiel, Macdonald of Kinloch-Moidart, came unwillingly and against their better judgment, and joined their forces to him. There was no spontaneous rising when the Stewart standard was raised at Glenfinnan, but the appeals of the eloquent, confident young Prince, who bore himself like a king and called upon ancient, hereditary loyalties, could not be withstood by the generous clansmen.

The amazing Highland raid into the Lowlands of Scotland and England was an initial and temporary success, because the British Army was on the Continent, the public were tranquil and unenterprising (' apathetic ' was the epithet often employed), and because this was not yet the age of railways and telegraphs. Distance and lack of information put the Government at an initial disadvantage in meeting the insurrection of the swift-moving clansmen.

When the Prince's troops of about 5000 ill-armed men, led by their chiefs, approached Edinburgh, the ' Whigs ' organised themselves in volunteer companies for the defence. Young Alexander Carlyle, a graduate of Edinburgh University, whose father was parish minister of Prestonpans, says that two-thirds of the citizens were for King George, and two-thirds of the ladies for the Prince. Colin Maclaurin, the brilliant young Professor of Mathematics, joined one of the volunteer companies, and employed his mathematical ability in locating the most suitable places for artillery.[1] The rout of two regiments of dragoons by the Highlanders at Coltbridge, two miles west of Edinburgh, on Monday,

[1] *The Autobiography of Alexander Carlyle of Inveresk* (1910 ed.), p. 123.

September 18, discouraged the authorities in the city. In the late afternoon of the same day the Jacobite forces entered the city. The castle was, however, held for King George. James VIII was proclaimed at the Market Cross, and took possession of the Palace of Holyrood, a dignified but rather gloomy *château* in the French style, situated in the shadow of the magnificent steep hill known as Arthur's Seat. Here Charles held receptions in the long gallery; and for a short time a touch of royal brilliance rested upon the desolate rooms. On September 21 the Prince and his little army marched out, and at Prestonpans met General Cope's troops, which had come from Aberdeen by ship to Dunbar. Prestonpans is about seven miles east of Edinburgh. The battle there was short and sharp, ending in complete victory for the Highlanders. Alexander Carlyle, who was in his father's manse at the time, was wakened in the early morning by the noise of cannon. Dressing hastily, he went out into the garden and stood upon a bank or mound whence he could see the battlefield. Although it was only ten or fifteen minutes after the firing of the first cannon, ' the whole prospect was filled with runaways, and Highlanders pursuing them.' The common clansmen were wild and excited, with the blood-lust upon them; their officers were in much the same state. Lord Elcho, leader of a Highland company, passed by Alexander Carlyle, ' and had an air of savage ferocity that disgusted and alarmed.' [1]

After the battle of Prestonpans the Prince returned with his forces to Edinburgh and delayed there for nearly six weeks, until October 31 ' while regular troops poured into English harbours from the Continent.' [2] The Dutch Government, according to its obligation under the Barrier Treaty of 1713, sent 6000 troops to defend the Hanoverian Succession, as it had done in 1715. The battle of Fontenoy (May 11, 1745) was long past; Cumberland and his veterans were ready for a campaign in Great Britain. In the late autumn

---

[1] *The Autobiography of Alexander Carlyle*, p. 152.
[2] Mackie, *op. cit.*, p. 358.

Charles started off on the march into England, and crossed
the Border on November 10. On the 18th the Highlanders
entered Carlisle, and on the 29th Manchester. They had
left Edinburgh after six weeks' sojourn there, rested, re-
freshed, well-fed, well-armed, in the best of spirits; yet
even excellent spirits could not hold up against the sustained
apathy of the settled population. In spite of the easy capture of Carlisle and Manchester, only 300 recruits joined
the Prince's forces in England. Alexander Carlyle,[1] who
had planned to go to the University of Leyden in the
autumn of 1745, saw no reason to postpone his going; he
sailed from South Shields in October, apparently in no
anxiety about the insurrection which he left behind him.

On December 4 the Jacobite army, about 4500 strong,
entered Derby in good trim. The invasion of England,
however, was already a failure. The population was wholly
indifferent. The Jacobite army was less numerous than the
army with which William the Norman had conquered a
feeble and divided England. The England of 1745 was
neither feeble nor divided. There were three armies of
trained troops, each led by an efficient veteran general, and
each twice as large as Prince Charles's army, ready to engage
him in battle. Marshal Wade was marching south from
Newcastle, with 10,000 troops; the Duke of Cumberland,
recently arrived from Flanders, was in the Midlands with
another 10,000; a third army of 10,000 was waiting on
Finchley Common, commanded by George II himself, who
had come over from Hanover and had no thought of yielding.
On December 5 Prince Charles reluctantly accepted the
advice of Lord George Murray, his chief of staff, and began
the retreat. Lord George Murray took the arduous, responsible, and thankless task of commanding the rear-guard.
The retreat was conducted with swiftness and skill. On
December 21 the Highlanders recrossed the Esk into Scotland, and reached Glasgow on Christmas Eve. After a
week's rest they marched northwards to Stirling, actually

[1] *The Autobiography of Alexander Carlyle*, p. 167.

growing in strength through the accession of fresh forces
from the Highlands. With 9000 men the Prince defeated
a similar number of King's troops under General Hawley
at Falkirk on January 17, 1746. Prince Charles continued
his northward march, crossed the Tay, traversed Perthshire,
and entered Inverness-shire. The Duke of Cumberland
with the regular army, moving slowly but steadily with
artillery and supply-wagons, followed by the coast route.
There was no chance of the war being long maintained by
the Prince in the Highlands. Desertions were daily occur-
ring as men went off to their homes. If there was not a
battle soon, the Prince would have no army at all. He
would have done better to have dismissed them to their
homes or hiding-places. The fatal battle occurred in the
early morning of April 16 on the waste land called Drum-
mossie Muir or Culloden. The Highland army, no longer
in good condition, but half starved, ill-equipped, led by
dispirited, quarrelling commanders, stood up to Cumberland's army of 10,000, fed, trained, heavily armed, and led by
the cool and daring officers of Dettingen and Fontenoy.
The Highland army was broken in irretrievable ruin, and
Prince Charles escaped. It would have been better for him
if he had died on the field of battle. Life held no more
for him; the man who had borne hardship gaily, marching
at the head of his men into England, escaped to France
and thence to Italy, to a life of idleness, sensuality, and
drink. He seems to have visited England again in 1750,
and to have joined the communion of the Church of
England.[1] He died in Rome in 1788.

The Highlands were pacified after savage retribution.
In 1746 a Bill was passed through Parliament abolishing
heritable jurisdiction. Thus the chiefs lost their powers as
judges, the powers on which their autocracy over the clans
had been based.

Scotland now entered upon a period of marked prosperity,

[1] Sir C. Petrie, Bart., ' The Elibank Plot,' in *Transactions of the
Royal Historical Society*, 1931.

material and intellectual. It never became a rich country, but it was more than self-supporting. The careful and strong-minded Scot, who is imaginative as well as prudent, directed his attention to enterprises both at home and abroad. Inside Scotland there were important commercial corporations, some of which originated before the Act of Union, such as the Bank of Scotland and the British Linen Bank. Without anything of the ' Bubble ' element about them, they made steady progress, although nobody acquired a spectacular fortune. Overseas the staffs of the East India Company and the Hudson Bay Company were to a great extent recruited from Scotland. The Scot was always ready to go abroad; the Act of Union opened the English Empire, which became the British Empire, to him. There were still Scots regiments in the Dutch service; young men of good landed family still accepted commissions as Dutch officers.

The epic of eighteenth-century Scotland is Scott's novels. In these living pages there survive the society of the Highlands and Lowlands, the general characteristics and the individual man and woman, their conversation and their actions, their way of life, and their thought. It is a complete social picture, the ever-thrilling life-story of a whole people. It is too the life-story of a people in its infinite variety, told with the simplicity that comes of the author's complete sympathy and understanding. *Rob Roy* reproduces the wild society of the Western Highlands in 1716. *The Pirate* describes the Shetlanders in the last years of the reign of George I; *The Heart of Midlothian* the social life of peasant and squire around Edinburgh in the reign of George II, particularly in 1736; *Waverley* and *The Legend of Montrose* Scotland in the Rebellion of the 'Forty-five; *Guy Mannering* South-west Scotland, the Ayrshire and Dumfriesshire regions, in the early years of George III; *Redgauntlet* Galloway in the earlier eighteenth century. *The Antiquary* tells the story of society in the small towns of Fifeshire. Scott was himself essentially a man of the eighteenth century, a member of ' the Club ' which Dr.

Johnson founded. Every novel which he wrote, except the purely mediæval romances like *Ivanhoe* and *The Talisman*, are instinct with the food, clothing, habits, the mind, speech, religion, humour, learning, and prejudices of eighteenth-century Scotland.

It was a people both rude and cultured. The leading man in the parish of Prestonpans was Lord Grange, a brother of the Earl of Mar of ' Sheriffmuir.' Lord Grange had been Lord Justice Clerk of Scotland in Queen Anne's reign, and was afterwards a Judge of the Court of Session and a Member of Parliament. His wife was a daughter of a Scottish squire, Chiesly of Dalry, ' the person who shot President Lockhart in the dark, when standing within the head of a close in the Lawnmarket, because he had voted against him in a cause depending before the court.' [1] Lady Grange seems to have had something of the violent temper of her father, justified, or at least explained, in her case, by the irregular habits and profligacy of her husband. Lord Grange, in order to put an end to her upbraiding, had her seized in his own house in Edinburgh in 1732. She was carried off to the desolate Western Isles, to St. Kilda, an island from which the inhabitants have now (1931) been all removed, as being a place not fit for human beings. She remained a prisoner, ' in the society of none but savages, often with scanty provision of the coarsest fare,' until her death, in 1745. The accomplices of Lord Grange in this atrocious act of abduction were believed to be two other gentry, Lord Lovat and the Laird of M'Leod. [2]

Yet at the same time as this wild incident was taking place, Scottish society in the university towns of Edinburgh, Glasgow, St. Andrews, and Aberdeen, was living, in the hours of leisure from hard work, a life of literature, philosophy, and conversation. The coffee-house habit had

---

[1] *The Autobiography of Alexander Carlyle*, pp. 8–9. Lockhart was President of the Scottish Court of Session.

[2] *Ibid.*, pp. 12–13.

spread from the London of Charles II and of Queen Anne, to the Scottish cities, although it was claret rather than coffee that the Scots gentleman usually drank in his tavern. Every coffee-house or good city tavern was the resort of a congenial group of men, who called themselves a club. They met, like the members of Johnson's Club in London, once a week or once a fortnight in their favourite tavern. For that evening they had a room to themselves; each member ordered what he pleased and paid his own reckoning. There were no entrance-fees, no annual subscriptions, and neither servants nor rooms to maintain. The club endured just so long as its members chose to come together for smoking, eating, and conversing. Every profession had its club and tavern: the medicals in one, the merchants in another, the lawyers in theirs. Some groups or clubs might have men of all professions; clergymen, university professors, lawyers, a soldier or two, and a few cultured merchants might be found together. Alexander Carlyle describes many such clubs. The members would be two or three lairds, a judge, a colonel in the Dutch service, another officer who had served with Braddock in Virginia, a historian (Robertson), a philosopher (David Hume or Adam Smith).

It was in society like this that the young Walter Scott grew up in Edinburgh, and this life, to some extent, he reproduces in the early chapters of *Redgauntlet*. These were the days before railroads and telegraphs, and therefore everything did not tend to be centred in the metropolis, London. Dublin and Edinburgh in the last half of the eighteenth century were independent centres of highly civilised life, colleagues with London in the world of European culture. The eminence of Edinburgh, the ' Modern Athens,' endured well into the nineteenth century, down to the time of the first Reform Bill. After that the movement of talent towards London became almost irresistible.

FOR FURTHER STUDY

PETER HUME BROWN, *History of Scotland* (1911 ed.).

J. ALLARDYCE (editor), *Historical Papers relating to the Jacobite Period* (Aberdeen, 1895–96).

W. L. MATHIESON, *Scotland and the Union : a History of Scotland from 1695 to 1747* (1905).

—— *Awakening of Scotland : a History from 1747 to 1797* (1910).

R. L. STEVENSON, *Kidnapped* (a story of 1752).

D. N. MACKAY, *Trial of James Stewart* (Glasgow, 1907).

CHAPTER XIII

TOWARDS AN UNDERSTANDING
OF IRELAND

THE way in which England has managed her colonies and dependencies has, on the whole, won the approval of most historians and observers who have directed their attention to the subject. There have been, indeed, grave and quite preventable miscarriages, for instance, in the handling of the American question between 1765 and 1775. In Colonial affairs, however, the British authorities, and the British public as far as it thought about the matter, did not persist for many years in the same error, but took lessons from experience and altered their ways. In regard to Ireland, on the other hand, England, throughout the greater part of the eighteenth century, seemed to forget nothing and learn nothing. The Irish problem was handled entirely without sympathy or understanding.

The story of the first three-quarters of the eighteenth century as told by Lecky in his great chapter is simply frightful.[1] It shows the British Government as being oppressive, ignorant, and arbitrary. It shows a policy which steadily and systematically, although not of set purpose, worked towards the demoralisation of a whole people. It shows the English acting with an intense national selfishness, and absolutely oblivious of the awful sufferings inflicted by a stupid and cruel policy. Nevertheless in the latter half of the eighteenth century things began to improve; and Burke, in the House of Commons in 1775,

[1] *History of England in the Eighteenth Century* (1879), vol. ii, chap. VII.

was able to speak of Ireland as a great and flourishing kingdom. Referring to the restoration by the Revolution of 1688 of the Irish Parliament (which Charles II and James II had practically suspended), Burke said :

> 'This has made Ireland the great and flourishing kingdom that it is; and from a disgrace and burden intolerable to this nation, has rendered her a principal part of our strength and ornament.'

And in another part of the same speech the great Irishman declared :

> 'England is the head, but she is not the head and members too. Ireland has ever had from the beginning, a separate, but not an independent, legislature; which, far from distracting, promoted the unity of the whole. Everything was sweetly and harmoniously dispersed through both islands for the conservation of the English dominion, and the communication of English liberties.'

Clearly, even if Burke exaggerated in his speech the peacefulness and prosperity of Ireland in 1775, he cannot have been wholly wide of the mark; unless Ireland was enjoying a reasonable degree of happiness and good government, the argument which he was developing (and in which the description of Ireland was an elaborate part) would have been torn to bits at once.[1] There is, then, a good side, as well as a bad side, to the story of England's relations with Ireland in the eighteenth century; and as people will not forget, it is right that they should bear in mind the good as well as the bad. Thus a just reading of the past will help towards the reconciliation of two peoples which, like the English and Welsh, the English and the Scots, must live together, for 'Nature has said it.'

Ireland in the early Middle Ages had a brilliant culture. The founder of Western monasticism, Saint Bernard, said:

---

[1] Speech on Conciliation with America, March 22, 1775, in *Works of Burke* (1906), ii, 208, 227.

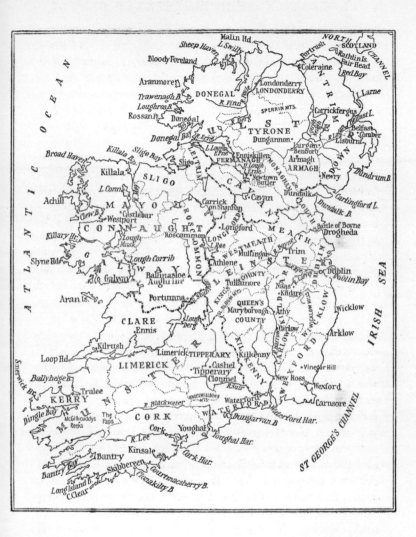

' From Ireland, as from an ever-flowing stream, crowds of holy men descended upon foreign countries.'[1] There are St. Columban, St. Kilian, St. Gall, Scotus Erigena, and a host of others who preached and taught in Scotland, Gaul, Germany, and Italy, and who fared across the sea to Iceland, becoming the first inhabitants of that island, and giving it Christianity and the possibility of a wonderful mediæval literature.

No people, however, can satisfactorily nourish its spirit with only memories of a great past. It is a confession of failure if a people cannot direct its mind's eye with legitimate pride on the present and near past as well as on its far-away, half-forgotten ages of grandeur. Now the first period, since the eighth or ninth centuries, upon which Irishmen can look with the solid satisfaction of being peers with the brightest societies of the rest of Europe, is the later eighteenth century.

The intervening centuries were dark and bloodstained. Like Anglo-Saxon England, Ireland went through a period of inter-tribal wars. Next, it had a Norman conquest, which failed to impress itself on the people as deeply as in England. In the fourteenth and fifteenth centuries there was a ' Celtic Revival ' which ended with the Reformation and the long-drawn-out Tudor wars in Ireland. After the Reformation Ireland was conquered three times: once in a war which lasted through most of the reign of Elizabeth and the early years of James I; once by Oliver Cromwell and the Commonwealth soldiers; and lastly by William III. All wars are cruel, and the Irish Wars, growing out of social, racial, and religious differences, were perhaps as bad as any; at any rate the Tudor and Commonwealth wars were ruthlessly waged. The third conquest, that of William III, though it left bitterness behind, was the least sanguinary, and was succeeded by a system of settled government which had the means, at any rate, of leading Ireland to stable peace and prosperity.

[1] Quoted by Lecky, *op. cit.*, ii, 258.

Unfortunately this means (a ' British Constitution ' in Ireland, as Burke called it) was not allowed to work un-impeded. The Penal Laws stood in the way—the deliberate effort of England to expel the Roman Catholic religion by imposing on it oppressive disabilities.

The confiscations and ' plantations ' carried out under Elizabeth and Cromwell had made the landlords of Ireland predominantly Protestant. There was still, however, at the close of the seventeenth century, a fairly large number of Catholic gentry. The peasants were Catholic almost to a man. In Ulster there were Protestant farmers, but few outside that province.

The Irish as a whole had taken the side of James II at the Revolution, and had fought bravely for him. The last place of any size to be taken was Limerick, which surrendered to Ginkel, the general of William III, on October 3, 1691. By the military articles of the treaty all Irish soldiers were free to go to the Continent with their portable goods, and the English Government was to provide shipping for them.[1] These articles were faithfully executed; and 12,000 Irishmen went abroad to take service in the armies of France, Spain, Austria, and other countries. By the religious articles Roman Catholics in Ireland were to enjoy such religious rights as they possessed in the reign of Charles II. The treaty required ratification by the Irish Parliament which after long delay refused its assent in 1697. The Irish Catholics considered themselves to be betrayed. The English Government should have and could have honoured the treaty by an Act of the English Parliament. It repeatedly legislated for Ireland, over the head of the Irish Parliament. It was an Act of the English Parliament which in 1691 debarred Catholics from sitting in the Irish Parliament, and so created the purely Protestant legislature which in 1697 refused to ratify the religious articles of the Treaty of Limerick.

The celebrated and disastrous Penal Laws were enacted

[1] Macaulay, *History of England* (1914 ed.), iv, 2069.

L

by the Irish Parliament in the years following the Revolution
of 1688. They amounted to a systematic plan for crushing
Roman Catholicism in Ireland and making the condition of
the Catholics there so wretched that they would either give
up their religion or become abject slaves. Burke, who paid
so warm a tribute to the prosperity of Ireland in the
eighteen-seventies, called the Penal Acts the most ingenious
and elaborate machine ever devised by man for oppressing,
impoverishing, and degrading a people.

The Penal Laws prohibited an Irish Catholic from sending his sons abroad to a seminary for priests (there were no
seminaries in the British Isles, at least not legally). No
Catholic could be a schoolmaster—thus, legally, there were
no Catholic schools in Ireland (nor, for that matter, in
England either)—nor hold any office under the Crown.
Catholics could not sit in Parliament; after 1727 by a law
enacted in the Irish legislature they could not vote for the
election of a member of the Irish House of Commons; and
by the imposition of a religious oath they were debarred
from municipal corporations. Eldest sons were encouraged
to become Protestant by a law entitling them to inherit the
whole of their father's estate; if all the children of a Catholic
landowner remained Catholic, the estate had to be divided
equally between them (so as to make the Catholic landholders small and unimportant). A Catholic could not
practise any of the learned professions except that of
physician. He could not invest his money in land-mort-
gages (this was to prevent him from acquiring any territorial
influence); and, if the profits of a Catholic tenant-farmer
exceeded one-third of the value of his land, any Protestant
who proved this could displace him and become the farmer
himself. A Catholic was not allowed to carry a sword, nor
to possess a horse worth more than £5; these two stipulations
were obviously meant to degrade him from the condition
of gentleman.

These laws were enforced as far as the Government could
do so, at any rate down to the viceroyalty of Lord Chester-

field (1745-46). Priests, unless they consented to be registered and to stay in their parish, were liable to penalties. There are numerous records of priests sentenced to transportation. Spies and informers abounded everywhere. The hideous system of cruel repression seems to have had very little effect in reducing the number of Catholics among the gentry. The poor inhabitants—who were the mass of the Irish people—not only became more poor, but also more numerous. Their families multiplied as happens always where people are poor, ignorant, and careless of the future, and especially in a Catholic religious system which encourages early marriages and large families. The terrors and rigours of the law did not diminish the number of priests, of whom in the eighteenth century there were in Ireland thousands, perhaps 30,000, for a Catholic population of between two million and three million. The memories of country people are long. The tradition of the inveterate hatred and oppression of the peasants' religion remained firmly implanted in Ireland and became the basis of the political thought which their leaders put before the Irish people. A consideration of this fact should induce the inhabitants of the rest of the British Isles to regard with sympathy the Irish attitude towards England, for sympathy, not prejudice or argument, is the only way to assuage rankling historical memories.

Every nation is (like all individuals, too, except the rarest spirits) egocentric. England has tended to become less egoistic, less egocentric, through having to live in a community of vigorous and assertive young nations—her colleagues in the British Empire. In the eighteenth century, however, the English people were just as selfish as any people of whom they may now feel inclined to complain. For the English did not merely ' protect ' their own manufactures, as other nations do to-day, by prohibiting the importation of foreign products; but where they had the opportunity they deliberately suppressed manufactures in dependent countries. The Colonial Manufactures

Prohibition Act of 1750 is an arresting instance of such policy. English economic legislation with regard to Ireland is another.

Ireland, in the age of steam and coal, was not and could not be a great industrial country; but in that same age (the nineteenth century) it gradually became a land of prosperous agriculture. In the eighteenth century, before the age of steam and coal, Ireland could have been rich in agriculture, and rich, too, in the kind of manufactures which depended on hand-industry, water-power, and a plentiful supply of the raw materials which can be grown in a temperate zone. This was forbidden to Ireland, not by Nature, but by the arbitrary will of a foreign and dominant people—that is, the English.

The readiest source of Irish wealth in the eighteenth century would have been stock-farming. The country has some of the richest pastures in the world. In the eighteenth century the English were becoming large consumers of fresh beef and mutton; and the English Agricultural Revolution was as much a vast development in stock-raising as it was in the growing of wheat. Before the eighteenth century opened, however, the import into England of beef, pork, and mutton, as well as butter and cheese, had been forbidden —not taxed, but simply prohibited (1680). This was done in order to ' safeguard ' English graziers in their profits and English landlords in their rent. Its effect on Ireland was to annihilate a great source of Irish prosperity; on England its unnoticed effects could only be to raise the price of meat for the consumer, and to cut off a profitable trade in the goods which England exported to Ireland in exchange for meat. Yet the exclusion of Irish produce was not necessary for the maintenance of high rents and of high graziers' or butchers' profits in England, as Irish cattle (owing to the long journey) really did not seriously compete with the home-grown article in England, but were probably eaten by people who could not afford English meat. The cattle had to be brought alive to the English market—there was no

' freezing ' system then. England did what she could to ruin an Irish industry by diminishing her own trade and raising prices to her own people.

Irish shipping was never likely to be a serious competitor with English shipping, which in modern times has maintained itself in unexampled efficiency against (to some extent because of) the most intense competition of the subsidised marine of wealthy countries. The Navigation Act of 1660, according to the accepted Protectionist theories of the day, practically excluded foreign shipping from British colonial ports, and, to a large extent, from English ports, but had included within the privileges of the Act not merely the shipping of England and Wales, but also of Ireland and the lands and plantations of His Majesty beyond the seas. This fact has been widely noticed in historical works. In 1663, however, an Act of Parliament quietly took Ireland out of the Navigation Act and put it in the category of foreign, prohibited shipping in respect of trade with the colonies. This was the barbarous, blighting Act of Navigation, to which (as Swift wrote on behalf of the Irish) ' we had never consented,' and which was ' pinned down upon us and rigorously executed,' so that ' the convenience of ports and havens, which Nature hath bestowed so liberally on this kingdom, is of no more use to us than a beautiful prospect to a man shut up in a dungeon.' [1]

This economic policy which was destructive for Ireland was not even in the interests of England. Unlike the Penal Laws, however, it was impartial; it pressed as hard upon Protestants as upon Catholics. Lecky points out that in the years between the Restoration and the Revolution a remarkable industrial spirit was being developed and displayed in Ireland, especially, although not exclusively, among the Protestant elements of the population. Wool of excellent quality was being raised; it could be exported legally, but only to England. It was, however, being

[1] *A Short View of the State of Ireland*, 1727 (1745 ed.), pp. 153, 154.

manufactured into cloth, which found a ready market in the export trade. Where capital was wanting, Englishmen and Scotsmen supplied it, and their skill and energy too, for many came over to Ireland to take part in the industry. In 1699 a British Act of Parliament absolutely prohibited the export of woollen manufactures from Ireland. ' So ended the fairest prospect Ireland had ever known of becoming a prosperous and happy country.' [1] As a set-off to the ruin of the cloth trade, some little encouragement was given by the Irish and British Parliaments to the linen trade in qualities which did not compete noticeably with English and Scottish goods.

Robbed of their natural right to trade in the most profitable channels and to develop the industrial resources of their country, the Irish might have had hopes from its agricultural fertility. The Penal Laws, however, prevented Catholic landowners or tenants from putting capital into agriculture or from reaping a reward proportionate to their exertions. Large numbers of the Protestant landlords, owing to their recent origin, their home ties in England, and other intelligible causes, were absentees. The small tenants were given over to bailiffs and middlemen, who swarmed in Ireland. The readiest way in which money could be made from the land was by grazing, so owners tended to evict the small cultivators and to lease the land in great blocks to graziers, and in this way even Catholics made profits; but the miserable peasantry sank in hopeless degradation, oppressed not only by rents which competition of the starving population sent up to unmanageable heights, but also ' tithed,' even in their potato crop, to support the established Protestant Church.

The religious system of Ireland was obviously unsatisfactory when the Established Church represented only about one-seventh of the people, and the Roman Catholic religion of the great majority was despised and persecuted by the Government. The Established Church was not

---

[1] Lecky, *op. cit.*, ii, 211

altogether an abuse: there were bishops and rectors who did their duty, working hard to relieve, educate, and uplift the people in their charge. The three successive primates, Archbishops of Armagh who, as Lecky points out, were practically at the head of affairs, civil as well as religious, from 1724 to 1764, were men of energy and ability. These were Archbishops Boulter, Hoadley, and Stone.

Hugh Boulter (1672–1742) was a man of high capacity, a Fellow of Magdalen College, Oxford, and afterwards Bishop of Bristol and Dean of Christ Church. In 1724 he was translated from Bristol to Armagh. As Primate of Ireland he was active and public-spirited, but his policy was too much directed to furthering the English and Protestant interest in Ireland. John Hoadley (1678–1746) was a graduate of St. Catharine's Hall, Cambridge. He was chaplain to Bishop Burnet of Salisbury. In 1727 he was made Bishop of Leighlin and Ferns in Ireland. He was translated to the Archbishopric of Dublin in 1730, and in 1742, on the death of Boulter, to Armagh. His policy in Ireland was to be tolerant towards the Roman Catholics, whom he allowed to practise their worship without hindrance. He also gave both time and money to promoting Irish agriculture. Shortly before his death, in 1746, he was able to say: ' I never asked anything for any relation of mine own, and but one small thing for a dependent.' George Stone (1708–64) was a graduate of Christ Church, Oxford. In 1733 he was made Dean of Ferns, and in 1740 Bishop of Leighlin and Ferns. After several other translations he became Archbishop of Armagh in 1747. Stone became so powerful in the civil as well as in the religious system of the country that he was called the ' Wolsey ' of Ireland. He was luxurious and extravagant, but active and also tolerant in religion. His personal character was not of the same degree of earnestness and integrity as was that of Boulter and Hoadley. At the same time, it could not be said that he neglected the affairs of his dioceses or of Ireland.

There were, however, some prelates of another kind who stayed away from their dioceses as much as they could; and there were rectors who left their benefices in the hands of curates—as, indeed, happened often in eighteenth-century England too. The majority of the Irish Protestant benefices were exceedingly poorly paid, and several of them had usually to be combined to provide a living for one parson.

The Protestant Established Church was an anomaly among a predominantly Catholic people, but it did, as a whole, try to do its duty. The real scandal outside the commercial system and the penal code was the pension system. Lecky gives a list of influential English men and women throughout the eighteenth century who were drawing pensions of £2000 to £9000 a year each from the Irish revenue, without ever doing anything in return. There was something particularly heartless in the English governing class enriching itself with enormous sinecures at the expense of what was in fact a chronically starving country.

It is impossible for a historian not to conclude from the evidence that most of the Irish in the rural districts outside Ulster were in a continuous condition of hunger all through the eighteenth century. There was no census taken at that time, and there are only the estimates of travellers to work upon. There appear to have been always some 30,000 regular beggars in Ireland in this century, some of them permanent beggars, others small cultivators who ' took to the road ' at the end of winter when the household stock of potatoes was used up. Mortality, both in grown people and children, was undoubtedly high in ordinary times; in famine years like 1739, 1740, and 1741 it is believed to have increased by hundreds of thousands in a population of some three millions.

Concisely, the result of the whole hideous process of mismanagement may be summarised as (1) chronic poverty and misery among the vast majority of the Irish people;

(2) the steady draining of all the best individuals—the most self-respecting, the most enterprising, the best educated—who went abroad, to England if they were Protestant, to the continent of Europe if they were Roman Catholic; and (3) the continuous if unspoken disbelief in the law of the land on the part of the mass of the population. All this must be allowed for in estimating the difficulties of Irish problems since that time.

Dean Swift is not an absolutely unbiased witness, but his account, published in his *Short View* in 1727, and in other essays, has never been contradicted. The Viceroys, he wrote, passed only four-fifths of their time in Ireland. One-third of the rents of Ireland was spent by absentees in England. Strangers did not resort to the country, because they did not wish to see continuing misery and desolation. Swift might have added that along with the body of Ireland, the English *régime* was doing almost everything that could be done to ruin the soul—to force the best elements to leave the country and to imbue the rest with a hatred of the law of the land, indeed of all civil law as such. The well-to-do and well-educated among the Irish gentry had not this lawless outlook; their faults—also largely due to the English *régime*—were of another kind: the Protestant party developed something like a slave-owner's attitude of mind; the Catholic party, because of their legal and economic disabilities, developed recklessness and extravagance. In a word all Ireland was being demoralised.

Yet if the English must remember their greatest failure in the government of a dependency—more striking, more disastrous, than the American failure—Irishmen on their side have to admit that the picture is not all dark. While there is almost nothing to relieve the tale of misery in the first thirty or forty years of the eighteenth century, there was a marked amelioration which began before the year 1750.

In the first place, although the Penal Laws remained on the Statute-book, the execution of them was relaxed, and as the years went on some of the laws were almost suspended. The public disabilities of the Roman Catholics remained, such as the bar against them in respect of any commissions in the Navy or Army, or of elections for Parliament; but ' priest-hunting ' was given up, and there was no organised interference with liberty of worship. The spirit of tolerance may be said to have come in with Lord Chesterfield, who during his period of Viceroyalty acted just as he did in England, with good-humour, liberality, and splendid hospitality.

In Dublin intellectual life flourished in the last half of the century. In number of inhabitants Dublin was the second city in the British Isles, having over 100,000 people. There Handel brought out the *Messiah*, its first appearance, on April 13, 1742. There was a flourishing stage. Garrick played in Dublin. Many of the most famous actors and actresses of the late eighteenth century came from Ireland, such as Wilkes, Macklin, Barry, Mrs. Wolfington, Mrs. Bellamy.[1] Richard Brinsley Sheridan, the dramatist, was born at Dublin, the son of an actor. Trinity College, Dublin, was already the imposing group of ' stately squares ' that it now is. It had about 700 students and a body of Fellows probably more eminent than those of any single college of Oxford or Cambridge.

The fact that Dublin was the place of residence of the Viceroy (even if he resided for only four or five months in the year) and the seat of the Irish Parliament gave it the distinction of a capital, and brought leisured and cultured people to it. Booksellers (who in these days were also publishers) were numerous in the city. The Library of Trinity College was being steadily built up until it has become one of the important libraries of the world. Irish architects beautified the city with public buildings of which the Parliament House (still standing), built in 1739, was one of the most graceful.

At last the British Government, learning by its experi-

[1] See the list in Lecky, *History of the Eighteenth Century*, ii, 325

ences in the American Revolution, gave Ireland almost complete freedom.

It could be argued by different schools of opinion that what might justly be called ' the freeing of Ireland ' was due to fear or to a tardy generosity. True it is that Ireland was only freed after the revolt of the American colonies had won its way to success and had inspired the Irish Protestants themselves with the American spirit. On the other hand, it must be remembered that the British Government had at any rate made a beginning with lightening the burden on Ireland before the American trouble began. Probably the wisest way to criticise the British attitude and the concessions which it made would be to say that the British Government gave way to facts, not to fear, and that, even in the eighteenth century, beneath a good deal of obscurantism and selfishness, it nevertheless had some generous inclinations. Grattan always realised this and bore witness to it.

One of the first acts of George III or his advisers was to decide (1761) that the Viceroy must reside continuously in Ireland. There was difficulty in finding a nobleman who would accept office on this condition, but at last Lord Townshend, the great Anglesey landowner, agreed. Described as ' good-natured and convivial,' Townshend was popular for a good part of his Viceroyalty, although owing to his lack of scruple in bribing and bestowing places he ended in 1772 amidst not hatred but contempt. The next Viceroy, Earl Harcourt, the head of one of the most ancient territorial houses of England, maintained the splendid hospitality which the Irish, and indeed all peoples, love; but he was faced with a steady decline in the Irish finances and with the unrest aroused in Ireland by the news of the American rebellion (1775); for there were numerous Irishmen, settlers in America, who fought in the Colonial forces. The British Government reduced the garrison of Ireland from 12,000 to 8000 men; and the Irish leaders, Protestant and Catholic, organised a volunteer defence force. About this time Paul Jones' squadron was cruising the waters around the British Isles, but the Irish, in forming their remarkable defence force, were, without doubt, as much actuated by the idea of peacefully yet forcefully impressing their views on the British Government as of defending themselves from the dashing American ' Commodore.'

The Irish House of Commons, in spite of pocket boroughs and other electoral anomalies, in spite of its being a House of the Protestant minority, was now fired with a spirit of independence and criticism. Its most stirring orator, Grattan, led it to approve a series of resolutions in favour of commercial and legislative freedom. The British Government gave way. In 1780 free trade was granted, in the sense that Ireland was put upon the same footing as England in regard to Navigation Acts and the right to manufacture goods and to exchange them for foreign products. On April 16, 1782, Grattan brought forward in the Irish House of Commons a Declaration of Rights. ' I am now,' he said, ' to address a free people.' The House was breathless with attention. Outside on College Green even the beggars knew that something was happening. The Declaration was approved by an overwhelming majority. Meanwhile Lord North's Government had conceded Irish commercial freedom, but had lost America and perhaps would be obstinate enough to lose Ireland. Lord North, however, had resigned in 1782, and the Marquis of Rockingham, sensible, tolerant, judicious, was now Prime Minister, with the two most open-minded men of England, Fox and Shelburne, as Secretaries of State. On May 27, 1782, the Duke of Portland, Lord-Lieutenant of Ireland, announced that the assent of the King had been obtained to the repeal of the Declaratory Act, 6 George I (1719), which had confirmed the legislative power of the British over the Irish Parliament. Ireland could now legislate through her own Parliament.

Lecky in his *History* testifies ' to the necessity of these concessions and to the grace and dignity with which that necessity was accepted.' In the same year, 1782, the Duke of Portland, Lord-Lieutenant, proposed to Grattan that the new relations which were to rule between Great Britain and Ireland should be defined and registered in a treaty. Grattan, however, refused this offer, as he held that the concessions which Ireland was demanding were a matter of right to which she had a claim without negotiation or treaty-making. Nevertheless a treaty would have been in the interest of both countries, because the grant of legislative freedom made by the British Parliament left the position of the Irish executive undefined. The British Government continued to appoint not only the Lord-Lieutenant (Viceroy), but the Chief Secretary and other important officials. The Irish Executive, in order to maintain harmony with the Irish Parliament, maintained— so far as it could—the old system of bribery and corruption. Yet matters had been enormously improved by the transactions of 1782, and Ireland entered upon what is claimed to be its finest period in modern times.

The position of Roman Catholics was greatly benefited. The laws against the existence of Roman Catholic bishops and priests were repealed in the Irish Parliament, as were also the laws restricting the purchase and the bequest of land by Catholics. The famous law making it illegal for them to possess a horse worth more than £5 was revoked. Catholics were to be able to become schoolmasters provided they took the oath of allegiance to the Crown. They still remained ineligible to sit in Parliament, but in 1793 an Act of the Irish Parliament gave them the right to vote at elections (on the same terms as Protestants)—a right not allowed to Roman Catholics in Great Britain. Endowed with ' the dignity of independence,' Ireland, in the period between the end of the American War and the outbreak of the French Revolutionary Wars, enjoyed a period of lustre, particularly in respect of parliamentary oratory, which is unequalled yet in the other periods of her history.

FOR FURTHER STUDY

W. E. H. LECKY, *Leaders of Public Opinion in Ireland* (2 vols., 1912).

HENRY GRATTAN (the Younger), *Memoirs of the Life and Times of Henry Grattan* (5 vols., 1839–46).

W. J. AMHERST, *The History of Catholic Emancipation* (2 vols., 1886).

R. MANT, *History of the Church of Ireland* (vol. ii, 1840).

CHAPTER XIV

THE EMPIRE OF INDIA

THE history of mankind is full of romance. Although the record contains much that is petty, sordid, or agonising, it still shows that on the whole the life of most nations, like the life of most individuals, has in it more of pleasure than of pain, more of success than of failure, more of romance than of dullness.

Romance may be internal or external. In the life of a man it may consist in the dreams which he forms and cherishes in his mind and soul; or it may be found in some outward action, some external relation, with other people; but the commonest way is for the inner romance to express itself externally in action, whether by the writing of a poem, or by a launching out on the deep to look for fortune. So too with a nation; its romance may lie in internal politics, but sooner or later, if there be any opportunity, the romantic spirit will seek to express itself in some external activity. The young United States had the Western movement; the European nations had their colonising, their 'imperial' activities; Japan had its great adventure, the adopting of Western civilisation and the winning of the position of a Great Power.

Surely India provides some of the most stirring romance of the eighteenth century. The great peninsula, a veritable sub-continent of Asia, is one of the cradles of mankind and of human culture. Its ancient states had a civilisation of their own when Alexander invaded India in 328 B.C. One martial race after another has descended into the plains of India, contributing to the immense and rich variety of the

peoples of this wonderful land. Trade, commerce, painting, architecture, poetry, all flourished for centuries before
India was known to the Europeans. When the Portuguese
touched the fringes of the country in the sixteenth century,
they found a rich civilisation, which later (1632) raised one
of the rarest of fine buildings—the glorious Taj Mahal of
Agra.

The problem of ruling India as an Empire was solved
for a time by the Moguls, from Babur, who established himself by the battle of Panipat in 1526, to Aurungzebe, who
died in 1707. Then administrative feudalism asserted
itself, as it did in Europe after the death of Charlemagne.
India became a mass of practically independent States,
and with independence came political competition, the
clash of ambitions, and war. The decay of the central
power of the Moguls gave the opportunity for the establishing of an Empire under the vigorous adventurers from the
West.

The word Imperialism has acquired an unfortunate
meaning, like the word ' Chauvinism ' in foreign policy.
' Imperialism ' is associated with the effort of an exaggerated
nationalism to open up and to monopolise new markets, to
seize territory, and to think of ' expansion ' as the chief
end of a State. The impartial study of history, however,
ought to make the Imperialist humble as well as proud,
ready to give praise to other nations as well as to attribute
it to his own. Thus, for instance, a true reading of the
history of India, while it displays the wonderful achievement of the British there, does not show them as the
great originators : it was the French who first conceived
the idea of an Indian Empire directed by a Western
people, and who pointed to the means for achieving this
result. Colonel Malleson, the English historian of the
French in India, writes:

' That the conception was the conception of Dupleix
cannot be denied. It was with him a well-thought-out

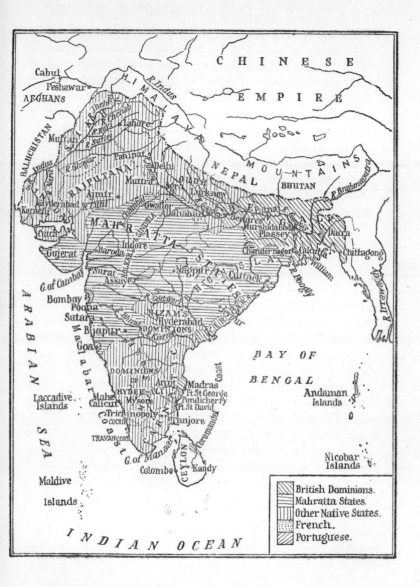

British Dominions.
Mahratta States.
Other Native States.
French.
Portuguese.

calculation, an organised scheme, an end to be obtained by patient striving. It was long before the English regarded it in that aspect. Contented with having defeated the plans of Dupleix, they were ready to fall back on their *rôle* of merchants. The quasi-imperial idea came to Clive only when he recognised that unless the English should crush Suraju-d-doulah, Suraju-d-doulah would crush the English. But how far, even after his victory, even after the annexation of Bengal and Behar, Clive was from having adopted the entire programme of Dupleix, was shown by the earnest injunctions he laid upon his successor not to advance the frontier beyond the point at which he had left it.' [1]

Perhaps the most remarkable fact concerning the British dominion in India is that it was never conceived as a plan by anybody, but was, as it were, the result of pressure and counter-pressure; that is to say, the French and neighbouring Indian princes naturally strove to limit the activities of the British merchants, and the British ' reacted ' against this pressure, took measures to safeguard themselves, and, when successful, pressed forward almost inevitably into the opponent's territory. This fact almost justifies Seeley's remark that ' We seem, as it were, to have conquered and peopled half the world in a fit of absence of mind.' [2] War was horribly expensive, and the Directors of the East India Company were for this reason, if for no other, anxious to avoid it. Every political group, however, inevitably makes for itself a frontier. The British factories, having to defend themselves in a strange country, were, in a sense, a political group. Each factory or settlement therefore made a frontier. But, a frontier which one side at any rate does not recognise is not likely to be stable. The Indian princes,

---

[1] *Dupleix*, by Colonel G. B. Malleson (1890), p. 184. H. Dodwell, *Dupleix and Clive* (1920), whilst disputing much of Malleson's work, agrees in general with the passage quoted.
[2] *Expansion of England* (1895), p. 10 (Lecture I).

so long as the French were behind them, would not recognise the East India Company's frontiers; therefore collisions occurred, with the result that the more masterful power did not simply stay where it was, but advanced beyond the original frontier. It was not until this process had been going on for generations, probably not until the time of the Marquess of Wellesley, that the conception of a European Empire in India, in the sense in which Dupleix had conceived it, occurred to any Englishman's mind. And no sooner had the idea occurred to the Englishman's mind than it was changed into something new and strange; for the European Empire in India never came into being. Instead, a second Indian Empire was evolved by Great Britain out of the ruins of the Mogul dominion; and this second Empire, although administered for the most part by Englishmen, always had a certain Indian point of view, always had a history and a policy of its own.

If a study of the history of the British in India leads the student to appreciate the pioneer work of the French, so also it must result in a fairer appreciation of the actions of another Power, Spain. It is a commonplace of historical students that Spain brought upon herself the odium of other states by her blindly egotistical policy in regard to her colonies. Spain prohibited other nations from trading with Spanish colonies, closely preserving to herself the commercial monopoly. This was one of the causes of the revolt of the Spanish South American colonies in the early years of the nineteenth century, and was also one of the reasons why the British Government was deeply interested in the establishing of these colonies as free republics. Great Britain herself, however, was no more liberal, in regard to foreign traders, than was Spain. The Navigation Acts practically prohibited trade between foreign nations and British colonies; and the Charter of the East India Company gave to this corporation the complete monopoly of all trade between Great Britain and any part of India, or indeed any place east of the Cape of Good Hope. Further, the East India Company, owing to its possession of the Presidencies of Bombay, Madras, and Calcutta, brought all the best harbours of India under the conditions of the Navigation Acts, so that foreign ships could not carry any goods from those parts to Europe. Thus, except in the Portuguese settlement of Goa, and the small French settlements at Pondicherry and Chandernagore, the whole of Indian foreign trade was, throughout the eighteenth century (with an exception made in favour of the United States in 1794),[1] closed to the trade of all the world except the British.

The War of the Austrian Succession raged in Europe from 1740. Although France and Great Britain took part in the war from the first as ' auxiliaries,' it was not until March 1744 that war was declared between them as ' principals.' When this occurred they had to take into consideration the attitude which they should adopt towards each other in their Indian spheres. The Directors of the French East India Company wrote to the Governor of Pondicherry, Dupleix, instructing him to propose neutrality for the French and British possessions; if this proposal had been agreed upon it would have meant, in effect, that the whole Indian Ocean would be neutral in the war, as there would be no reason for keeping French and British squadrons there. Governor Morse of Madras refused Dupleix's offer of neutrality.

The action of Governor Morse may be defended on the ground that Great Britain was fundamentally a sea power and France a land power; and that consequently to neutralise overseas possessions of the two nations would be for Great Britain to sacrifice the advantages of command of the sea. On the other hand, it might be agreed with perhaps more

---

[1] The Jay Treaty, November 19, 1794, Article 13, permitted United States vessels to enter the ports of the British East Indies and to carry away, to the United States only, any articles, the importation or exportation of which were not prohibited in the East Indies. See Mowat, *The Diplomatic Relations of Great Britain and the United States* (1925), p. 25.

force that the war between Great Britain and France would be settled by its fortunes in Europe, by the success or failure of the British armies on the Continent, and of the British blockading fleets on the French coast. The French knew that this was so, and events proved them to be correct, for at the end of the Austrian Succession War (1748), which neither France nor Great Britain had won, conquests made overseas by either Power were given back to the other. A neutralisation agreement for the French and British possessions in India for the duration of the War would have been a great humanitarian work, and would not have influenced the general course of the war at all.[1] The effect of this argument is not to depreciate the work of the soldiers and statesmen of British India. It is only right to notice, however, firstly, that the great successes (except the victory of Wandiwash) of these soldiers and statesmen were achieved not against the French, but against powerful Indian princes who were in collision with the British. The fact that the French were encouraging these Indian princes to attack the British is not of much significance; similar collisions occurred after the removal of French influence. Secondly, it must be observed that the wars in India have not resulted in the expulsion of the French from India, therefore the original proposal to neutralise the French Settlements might as well have been accepted.

The English administration in Madras, having decided to reject the French offer of neutrality, had now to make the best of a bad condition of affairs. Its position was perilous enough, for within the bounds of the English settlement were about 250,000 Indians and only 300 English— one hundred of these being civilians and two hundred soldiers.

---

[1] A similar proposal made by the German Government at the opening of the War of 1914 to neutralise the areas of West and East Africa contained within the ' Berlin line ' of 1885 was rejected by the British and French Governments. If the proposal had been accepted, Germany would still have been compelled to surrender her colonies after her collapse in Europe in 1918.

Robert Clive, aged 17, landed at Madras on June 1, 1744, after a voyage which (including nine months for repairs to the ship at Pernambuco, in Brazil) lasted for nearly fifteen months. He had no friends, and was too shy to introduce himself to any of the resident families. He had very little money, and was charged ruinously high prices for the clothes and other things which he had to buy after his long journey. He lived with the other writers in the quarters provided by the Company. He had no taste for drink and cards, but employed his leisure reading in the library of the Governor, who placed the books at his disposal. Clive was able to read the Latin classics, perhaps also the Greek; Horace at any rate was among the books which he read at Madras. He eagerly waited for letters from home, and pathetically wrote to his father for some books; ' a little news would also be agreeable to me.' Stirring times, however, were soon to come; for over the shining waters of the Indian Ocean and the surf on the Coromandel Coast it was not a British ship with cargo and letters which soon was seen but a French squadron.

The French found Madras unprepared for defence, and they captured it without losing a man. After the Peace of Aix-la-Chapelle in 1748 they had to restore it again to the British, just as the British had to restore Louisbourg, on Cape Breton Island, in North America. The War of the Austrian Succession was therefore wholly indecisive in India as in North America; but it left a legacy of hostility behind it between the French and British in India, who, in spite of the Peace of Aix-la-Chapelle and the restoration of Madras, did not stop fighting each other. From the military point of view the importance of the War of the Austrian Succession so far as it was fought in India was that it gave a taste for military affairs to Clive, who had escaped from Madras when it was captured by the French and had taken service with the Company's troops. In 1751 he held the rank of captain.

The French were never a serious danger to the British

in India; that is to say, their fate there absolutely depended upon their success or failure in any war in Europe in which they might be engaged with Great Britain. It is doubtful whether the European factories were worth conquering even for the purpose of being held as ' pawns or counters ' for bargaining in the final negotiations at the end of the war. The case of Canada was quite different from that of the Indian factories. The French colony was a huge affair with a settled population; if Canada had not been conquered by Wolfe and Amherst, the French would, as things turned out, have been in a sufficiently good position, both in Europe and America, to refuse to give it up at the end of the Seven Years War.

The British in India were contending not so much with the French as with warlike Indian princes. In the existing condition of dissolution of the Mogul empire, ambitious chieftains, as in the bad early days of European feudalism, had opportunities for establishing themselves as princes over extensive territories. One such territory, large and wealthy, although not one of the greatest, was the Carnatic, the long coastal strip in which Madras and Pondicherry were situated. On the death of Anwaru-d-din, Nawab of the Carnatic, whom Macaulay in his famous essay on Clive calls Anaverdy Khan, in 1749, a disputed succession arose. The French and British in India, in the course of their struggle with each other, had learned to find allies among the Indian princes. In the dispute for the Carnatic the British gave their support to the worthless Mohammed Ali, whose ' debts ' later caused so much thought and trouble to Edmund Burke.[1] The French supported Chanda Sahib, who, according to the contemporary English historian, Orme, was best man for the place of Nawab—' a brave, benevolent, humane and generous man, as princes go in Indostan.' In the course of the struggle Chanda Sahib was murdered (1752), and Mohammed Ali held the throne

[1] Burke, Speech on the Nabob of Arcot's Debts, 1785, in *Works of Burke* (1884), ii, 1 ff.

of the Carnatic until his death in 1795. The internecine war had been brightened by the magnificent defence of Arcot, the capital of the Carnatic, by Clive. The young captain—twenty-six years old—had made a ' sporting offer ' to his commander, Stringer Lawrence, to seize Arcot, which was Chanda Sahib's capital (this was when Chanda was winning and for the time being held the throne of the Carnatic). With 200 European soldiers and 300 Indian soldiers (sepoys) Clive seized and held Arcot, sustaining against Chanda Sahib a siege for fifty-three days (September 23–November 14, 1751), until the assailants gave up the attempt. Clive's ascendancy over his soldiers was complete. He could speak the language of the sepoys and thoroughly understood their ways. The news of the brilliant defence of Arcot went through the bazaars of India, travelling swiftly and silently in that mysterious way which has so often aroused wonder among Europeans. It was understood that there was now a new Power in India. The star of the French paled.

It was a crying scandal that the British and French authorities and their military men in India should intrigue against each other and engage in hostilities on one side or the other of contending Indian princes. The Directors at home took strong measures to put an end to this intolerable state of affairs. That Dupleix began the policy of taking sides with Indian princes and interfering in their internal affairs is not improbable, for in 1753 the French Directors recalled him to France, where he lived in retirement until his death in 1763. Before this the French position, which was firm only in the Carnatic, had been broken at the battle of Wandiwash (inland, and about half-way between Pondicherry and Madras), fought by Generals Eyre Coote, and Lally de Tollendal on January 22, 1760. The battle was fought by European forces which on each side consisted of about 2000 men. The British Navy, since the victories of Lagos and Quiberon Bay, in the Atlantic, commanded the sea, and the French in India were practically isolated. The shadow of a French empire never again appeared in India. During the American Revolutionary War and the Napoleonic War French agents, for military reasons, stirred up Indian princes against the British, but there was no effort made to revive French power there, nor was there any opportunity.

The ' making of British India,' so far as it was made by force of arms, was the result, not of the French episode, but of events in Calcutta in which the French were scarcely involved at all.

In the great Mogul province of Bengal the Nawab, Allahvardi Khan, had made himself completely independent of the Emperor of Delhi. He was a good ruler, and was in excellent relations with the British merchants at Calcutta. He died at the age of eighty in 1756, the year of the outbreak of the Seven Years War in Europe. The struggle, which soon took place in Bengal, had, however, nothing to do with the European struggle, and would have happened just the same if there had been no Seven Years War.

Allahvardi Khan's successor was his grandson, Surajah Dowlah (Suraju-d-doulah), who was probably twenty-four or twenty-five years old. He had been softly brought up and was self-indulgent and careless. Attracted by the reputed riches of the British settlement at Calcutta, he marched from his capital, Murshidabad, with an army of 50,000. The settlement was captured. A few of the British escaped by ship down the river. The remainder, or most of them, about 140, were herded by the Nawab's officers into a detention-cell of the Fort (Fort William) eighteen feet long and fourteen wide (June 20, 1756). Only twenty-three survived the night in the ' Black Hole.' The Nawab neither ordered the detention nor, so far as is known, censured his officers for inflicting it. He seems to have been a debased young man, entirely insensible to the tragedy, for, according to Orme's account, when one of the survivors of the Black Hole was brought before him, Surajah ' was so far from showing any compassion for his condition, or remorse for the death of the other prisoners, that he only talked of the treasures which the English had buried.'[1]

The historical importance of the episode is that it aroused the British to action and led to their becoming the chief power in Bengal.

The horror of the Black Hole still vibrates in the passage of Macaulay's great essay on Clive. ' Nothing in history or fiction, not even the story which Ugolino told in the sea of everlasting ice, after he had wiped his bloody lips on the scalp of his murderer, approaches the horrors which were recounted by the few survivors of that night '; and ' then was committed that great crime, memorable for its singular atrocity, memorable for the tremendous retribution by which it was followed.' The British authorities at Madras had no alternative but to send the strongest expedition which they could equip. It was not, however, until October 16 (1756) that the ships and the men were ready and the Commander-in-Chief, Colonel Clive, appointed. Some difficult operations were carried out successfully in the estuary of the Ganges, and Calcutta was recaptured on January 2, 1757. More fighting and a good deal of intriguing ensued until June 23 (1757), when Clive's forces met Surajah Dowlah's at Plassey, ninety-six miles north of Calcutta.

The number of men engaged were for Clive 613 European infantry, 50 sailors, and 2100 sepoys ; he had ten field-pieces manned by 171 white artillerymen and by the sailors. Surajah had 35,000 infantry, 15,000 cavalry, and 53 guns; there were also fifty Frenchmen. The fight was opened at 8 A.M. and lasted until 5 P.M. It was conducted mainly as an artillery duel. Clive's forces, small in number and skilfully placed in cover, suffered little. The Nawab's forces had considerable casualties and became partly demoralised. At the moment when great confusion became evident in

---

[1] R. Orme, *A History of the Military Transactions of the British Nation in Indostan* (1803), ii, 77.

the enemy's ranks, Clive ordered Eyre Coote to attack the redoubt held by the French as well as by Indians. The redoubt was carried, and with it the battle was won. Part of the Nawab's forces had been immobilised all through the battle because their Commander, Mier Jaffier (who was afterwards made Nawab of Bengal), was passively on the British side. The numbers killed were four European soldiers and fourteen sepoys on Clive's side; on the Nawab's, 500. The Nawab himself was captured by Mier Jaffier's men, and was done to death at the order of Meeran, son of Mier Jaffier, on July 2 (1757).[1]

Plassey was no more of a pitched battle than was Valmy forty-five years later, but it marks a turning-point in the history of the world. Both events demonstrated that something new had come on to the scene of history—in the case of Valmy, the national French republic; in the case of Plassey, the British dominion in India.

The point of this chapter will have been entirely missed if the interest of the history of British India is considered to be in wars and battles. It is not; the significance of the British effort in India is in administration, and it has been so ever since the time of Plassey. The actual amount of fighting has not been great; such fighting as has been done was, in the eighteenth century, conducted by armies of some thousands, sometimes only hundreds. In the nineteenth century the forces were larger, from 3000 to 20,000. Since 1849 there has been no war in India, except the Mutiny of 1857; the Afghan wars, various frontier hostilities, and the Burmese wars were outside India.

The work achieved by the British in India is definite and well recognised. It has given political unity (and therefore peace) to the mass of peoples of the sub-continent who in the middle of the eighteenth century either did not know each other or were enemies to each other. Secondly, British rule has given impartial administration. Looked at, so to speak, from the outside, the achievement is remarkable:

[1] G. W. Forrest, *The Life of Lord Clive* (1918), ii, 13-14

a huge, thickly populated sub-continent of the Orient, a vast collection of warring groups, rendered peaceful and at last prosperous by a handful of administrators coming from a land 3000 miles away. It must be remembered that this was only done by using the services of the Indians themselves, in large numbers, in the public offices, in the police, in the Army. It is a work comparable to that accomplished by Imperial Rome in the Mediterranean world during the early Christian era.

Macaulay, whose two great Indian essays contain some inaccuracies of fact, has made true generalisations when he says that from Clive's first visit to India ' dates the renown of the English armies in the East. . . . From Clive's second visit to India dates the political ascendancy of the English in that country. . . . From Clive's third visit to India dates the purity of the administration of our Indian Empire.' [1]

The crowning work of the great soldier was therefore his administration. He was absent from India from February 1760 to May 1765. These years are the worst, indeed, the only bad years in the history of British adminis- tration, and the evils seem to have been limited to Bengal. The officials of the Company had not the responsibility of authority, although practically they wielded enormous power. In theory they were the servants of a trading company which in Bengal had obtained from Mier Jaffier, the Nawab, a grant of some 882 square miles of land, mainly to the south of Calcutta. The curious system of a trading company maintaining armed forces for its defence still went on. In 1764 Mier Jaffier's son, who had become Nawab, made war, along with the Mogul Emperor and the Nawab of Oudh, upon the British. They were met at Buxar by Major Hector Munro, who commanded some 6200 sepoys and about 850 European troops. The Nawab's forces were about 50,000, but neither trained nor armed so well as

[1] Essay on *Clive*.   Clive's periods in India were (1) 1744–53 ; (2) 1755–60 ; (3) 1765–67.

LORD CLIVE
N. Dance
National Portrait Gallery

Munro's troops. The battle of Buxar was fought on October 23, 1764, and completed the work of Plassey. This happened about six months before Clive landed in India on his last mission.

Clive found the officials of the Company enriching themselves by private trade and misusing their power for their own advantage. The way to stop this was to convert the officials into responsible governors and to bind them by precise regulations. The Nawab of Bengal was just a shadow. He received a large pension and became simply a rich, titled nobleman. The Mogul Emperor granted to the Company the right of collecting the taxes in Bengal (the Dewani). A large pension was assigned to him from these revenues, and so ended the political influence of the Moguls. All this happened in 1765. Clive had two years in India facing insubordination and even mutiny; he quelled disorder and suppressed abuses, and then left India in February 1767. On this, his last, mission, he made no money for himself: in fact, he was £6000 poorer than when he came out two years previously.

Clive when in England (he lived until 1774) was regarded as a representative of the type of ' Nabob '—the official who returned from India, rich, prodigal of money, not too scrupulous in his means of employing it. There is no doubt that Clive was rich, as his income from investments and rents derived from Bengal was £40,000 a year. But he was not the reckless ' Nabob ' of the play or novel; he was serious-minded and deeply interested in India; and he remained in touch with Indian affairs after he retired to England. Alexander Carlyle, the author of the *Autobiography*, saw him in the Granby Hotel at Harrogate in 1763, in the interval between the second and third visit to India. The great nobleman had come to the fashionable Northern spa for a few days' relaxation, but dispatches followed him like a Cabinet Minister.[1]

Between the departure of Clive and the appointment of

[1] See above, pp. 75–76

Warren Hastings to be Governor of Bengal one event stands forth, an arresting landmark in Indian history. It was not the first of such occurrences by any means, but it was the first seriously to attract the attention of the British. This was the famine of 1770, when it is computed that one-third of the population of Bengal died, and a British official reported that corpses were eaten for food. After this time the British officials accepted responsibility for doing their best to cope with famine. Such calamities had occurred under the Moguls, and, indeed, were almost inevitable in a country so large, so densely populated, and of such varying climates. Nothing but improved communications and careful organisation of surplus supplies could deal in any satisfactory way with famines. British administration has gradually reduced and at last wholly prevented these dearths and their consequent appalling misery.

Clive, although he purified and disciplined the administration, left Bengal still with a very imperfect organisation. The grant of the Dewani, made by the Mogul to the Company in 1765, was not fully taken up until 1772, when the Board of Revenue of Bengal was moved from Murshidabad to Calcutta, which henceforth became the capital of Bengal and until 1911 of all British India. The transfer of the Board of Revenue was one of the first acts of Warren Hastings when he became Governor of Bengal in 1772.

Hastings, who had been a hardworking servant of the Company for twenty-three years before he became Governor, was a great administrator. His letters and dispatches show him working with untiring zeal in his office throughout the hot Indian days and into the night, with scarcely a holiday, yet finding time to read widely in literature (every ship bringing out a large packet of books) and helping Sir William Jones (a judge in the Supreme Court of Bengal) to found the Asiatic Society.

The administration of the revenue was simplified, and the system of making regular periodical settlements or revised assessments of the land was begun. The opium and salt administrations, the monopoly of which was taken over from the Mogul by the Company with the Dewani in 1765, were organised into smoothly working offices. A judicial system was established for all British subjects in Bengal (under the Regulating Act, 1773), with Elijah Impey, a learned English lawyer, as Chief Justice. The Supreme Court which was thus set up was entitled to deal with all cases between or against British subjects—in effect, all the population of Bengal. Impey proved to be an excellent judge who by his verdicts, by his organising ability, and by his compiling of a legal code could claim when his work was drawing to an end to have 'settled the internal quiet of a great Empire.' He has been described, quite wrongly, as being, in Macaulay's famous phrase, 'rich, quiet and infamous.' The Directors in London recalled him; and Impey sadly wrote (with, it appears, complete truth) that he had given peace and justice, restored confidence to suitors and regularity to courts, 'without any reward, and for my recompense shall have lost my office, reputation and peace of mind for ever.' After leaving India in 1789 Impey entered Parliament and sat until 1796. He resided for the last years at Newick Park, Sussex, farming. When on a visit to France at the time of the Peace of Amiens, he was caught on the reopening of war and was imprisoned by Bonaparte for a time. He died in 1809.

Hastings was highly successful not only in giving regularity to the internal administration of Bengal, but in adjusting its external relations. He made the Treaty of Benares in 1773, entering into an engagement of alliance and protection with the Nawab-Vizier or King of Oudh. The Oudh alliance proved to be the corner-stone of Bengal's external policy for many years, and greatly conduced to the peace of the British dominions and of Oudh itself, particularly during the Maratha Wars. It was in consequence of this alliance that Hastings sent a brigade to assist the Nawab-Vizier in his war with Rohilkand. This was an area of north-west territory situated between the Ganges and the hills, and was inhabited by an Afghan tribe ruled over by their own chiefs. British intervention in the Rohilla War, which can scarcely have endangered the independence of Oudh, was not necessary under the terms of the Treaty of Benares. Hastings would have done better to be neutral; the conduct of the war, however, seems on the balance of the evidence not to justify the invective of Macaulay against it. The occupation of Rohilkand by the Nawab-Vizier strengthened him against the Marathas, who had invaded Rohilkand several times before and who henceforth ceased to trouble it.

Hastings may be called the founder of the system of subsidiary alliances, by which all the Indian Ruling Princes have been one by one associated with the British Crown in a kind of feudal system. This process has been one of the big steps taken in the creation of a solid framework of peace over the whole sub-continent. Actually the beginning of the alliance system was made by the Madras authorities, in the settlement into which they entered with the Nawab of Arcot. Hastings took up this policy and put it into the Treaty of Benares of 1773. In a dispatch of 1775 he advocated the creation of an honourable tie of feudal allegiance between the Indian Princes and the British Crown. ' Their confidence,' he wrote, ' would be strengthened by such a relation, which would free them from the dread of annual changes and the influence of individuals; [1] and their submission, which is now the painful effort of a necessary policy, would be yielded with pride by men who glory in the external show of veneration to majesty and even feel the respect which they profess where they entertain an idea of the power [2] to command it.' Thus as early as 1775 Hastings was looking forward to the political unity of all India under the British Crown.

Political unity, however, was a long way off. Hastings' work of peaceful organisation was interrupted by two

[1] *I.e.*, of British officials.   [2] *I.e.*, of the Crown.

serious wars. The first was the Maratha War, which lasted intermittently over the years 1778–84.

The Maratha country is in the west centre of India, south of Bombay and north of Goa. It contains the mountains called the Western Ghats—mountains or hills with flat tops and smooth, almost perpendicular sides. Some of these, in themselves natural fortresses, had been converted by Indian princes and their possessors into places of remarkable strength. They are the more suitable for fortresses inasmuch as most of the hill-tops have springs of plentiful water.[1] The Marathas were the most formidable antagonists whom the British met in India in the eighteenth century. They are described as ' small, sturdy men, well-made though not handsome, . . . laborious, hardy and persevering.' There were several Maratha states, with no very fixed frontiers. The chief state had its centre at Poona, and was governed by a ruler called the Peshwa, who was nominally only Prime Minister of the Raja of Satara. Satara itself, the parent state of the Maratha power, had been founded by the warrior Sivaji, who died in 1680; it was unimportant in Hastings' time. Gwalior, with its perpendicular rock-fortress, 340 feet high, was a Maratha state of considerable strength, ruled by a dynasty called Sindia. The Marathas are adherents of the Hindu religion.

In 1772 the Government of the Bombay Presidency took sides with a pretender to the throne of the Peshwa. This led to some desultory fighting. The real struggle, however, did not come until 1778. A British force under Colonel Carnac surrendered to Marathas at Wargaon in January 1779. Hastings had not approved of the adventure of the Bombay Government; but when he heard of the Convention of Wargaon, which he said made him almost sink with shame, he decided upon energetic action. His daring, resolute mind conceived the plan of a march of British troops right across India, from Bengal to Bombay. Colonel Goddard's expedition, consisting of about 6000 troops,

[1] See Vincent Smith, *Oxford History of India* (1919), p. 430.

N

CHAPTER XV

LIFE IN THE AMERICAN COLONIES

THE War of American Independence is one of the decisive events in world history. It is futile to consider how it could have been averted. History can only deal with what has happened, why it happened, and what have been the results. No serious observer can deny that the United States is a wholesome influence in world affairs. It is not aggressive; the principles which actuate its foreign policies are those of justice and fair-dealing. Its influence upon world affairs is, however, a new thing; for the first hundred years of its existence the United States was absorbed in the task of its own internal development. Nevertheless the revolution, carried into effect in the years 1775–83, definitely altered the course of world history, which, until that date, had pointed in another direction. Until 1775 the New World was given over to the colonies of European states, directed from Europe. The American Revolution resulted, sooner or later, in European political control being entirely excluded from the New World; and, instead, free, powerful communities grew up, able, not indeed to control Europe (nor did they wish to do so), but to influence and impress Europe.

It was not, however, the American Revolution which made the American nation. Existence within the British Empire never prevented the development of a people along its own lines, even in Ireland, where the English Government at certain times tried to prevent such development. In the American colonies it made no such attempt. The Americans had developed a culture of their own before the time of the Revolution. 'Whence came all these people?' wrote Hector St. John Crèvecœur in 1781. 'They are a mixture of English, Scotch, Irish, French, Dutch, Germans, and Swedes. From this promiscuous breed that race now called Americans have arisen.'[1] Burke, in his famous speech on Conciliation and Taxation in America, delivered in 1775, obviously regarded the Americans as a nation when he said: 'I should hold myself obliged to conform to the temper I found universally prevalent in my own day, and to govern two millions of men, impatient of servitude, on the principles of freedom.'

It had not taken long for this nation of two million of men to grow up on the continent of North America. At the opening of the century there was not much more than a tenth of that number. The country was still uncleared even near the coast.

'In 1690 along the entire length of the colonial shore, everywhere sweeping backward from the sea, creeping up the slopes of the mountain barriers and over their untrodden crests, lay the shadow of the virgin forest, illimitable, silent, starless. So thick was this covering in parts that an Indian trader two generations later reported that at times for miles he could find no place the size of his hand where the sunshine penetrated on the clearest day. The innumerable tree-trunks, dusky beneath the green covering of summer or bare and gaunt above the winter's snow, formed a trackless maze save for the labyrinth of Indian trails.'[2]

The men who came over the seas to settle in this new land took a chance and ran a terrible risk. Their lot must have been very miserable in the old country if they thought it worth while to incur the dangers and miseries of the voyage and of the early days of settlement. Large numbers died on the way over from disease or shipwreck; large

[1] Quoted in J. T. Adams, *Provincial Society* (1928), p. v.
[2] *Ibid.*, p. 1.

numbers died from the hardships of life after they had
arrived. Of the ordinary class of poor emigrants, about
one-third, probably, died on the way out or immediately
after arrival.[1] The survivors were bound to be a hard-
bitten race, uncompromising, almost reckless, determined
not to give up the prize of a free existence which they
had won with so much toil and suffering.

The conditions of life were still so severe in 1700 that there
was little opportunity for culture on the part of the average
man, although Harvard College existed at Cambridge, near
Boston, and William and Mary College at Williamsburg,
Virginia. An American culture was beginning, made up
from the intellectual heritage of the New England Puritans,
the Southern planters, and the recent arrivals of Quakers at
Philadelphia, Lutheran Germans at Germantown,in Pennsylvania, and French Huguenots in the Colonies both of the
North and the South. Yet the culture was still very slight,
the life of the people closely circumscribed. The whole continent behind the narrow coastal strips was still the red man's.

The next seventy years was a time of steady growth.
The Autobiography of Benjamin Franklin shows the American
colonies growing to something of more than merely local
importance. Franklin was indeed a genius, but his development was not independent of his environment. He grew
up in rude but not uncultured surroundings. His ancestors
belonged to an obscure family, all strongly Protestant, of the
village of Ecton in Northamptonshire. Although members
of the Church of England, they objected, or some of them
objected, to the legislation of the reign of Charles II against
' Conventicles.' Accordingly, Josiah Franklin managed to
gather together sufficient money to migrate with his wife
and three children to New England in 1682.

Benjamin, born January 17, 1706, was the fifteenth child
of Josiah Franklin, who had seventeen children altogether.
Benjamin in the *Autobiography* says that he could remember

[1] See Lecky, *History of England in the Eighteenth Century*
(1879), ii, 261.

THE AMERICAN COLONIES IN 1734.

thirteen children at one time sitting at the family table. Conditions of life were healthier in the New England than in the old, where in almost every large family a great proportion of the children died young. The Franklin family lived at Boston, where the father worked as a soap-boiler, a trade which brought him a very poor living. Boston had about 3000 or 4000 inhabitants. It was just a simple country town, with a large green or ' common ' which still exists, and with winding lanes trodden by the cows; already it had the Latin School, which is a famous institution to-day. Benjamin spent a year there, and was then withdrawn because his father grudged the fees and also thought that the colony already had too many learned men who could not earn a decent living. In Boston's noble natural harbour, among its interesting islands, Benjamin often went sailing with other boys, and always, when difficulties were encountered, he took command.

Although working as a soap-boiler and tallow-chandler with his father from the age of ten to twelve, Benjamin was able to find time for reading (of which he was always fond). He saved enough money to buy books and thus collected all Bunyan's works in separate volumes. These he a little later sold in order to buy R. Burton's *Historical Collections*, which he picked up from travelling chapmen in cheap volumes to the number of forty or fifty. A people among whom such books were offered from door to door by chapmen was not uncultured.[1] Benjamin's father had some books, including Plutarch's *Lives* and Defoe's *Essay on Projects*, which the boy read.

In 1717 one of the brothers, James, having gone to England, returned with a printing-press and set up in

---

[1] I may be allowed to mention that in 1926 in a small Canadian inn in the Rocky Mountains I found a complete edition of Balzac in translation and an edition of Pailleron's comedy, *Le Monde où l'on s'amuse*, doubtless sold by some itinerant chapman or *colporteur*.

business in Boston. Benjamin was bound as an apprentice to his brother, to serve until he was twenty-one years old. There were a number of booksellers in Boston, and Benjamin was allowed to borrow their books if he returned them ' good and clean,' after sitting up at nights to read them through. A Mr. Matthew Adams, who had ' a pretty collection of books,' also lent him many. He used to argue about the subjects of his reading with another ' bookish boy,' called John Collins. Before he was sixteen Benjamin had found a copy of Addison and Steele's *Spectator*, the third volume, in Boston. He read it and modelled his style upon it.

At the age of seventeen Benjamin was released by his brother from the apprentice's indentures. He went off to New York in a sloop, knowing nobody there and with very little money in his pocket. Finding his chances at New York not promising, he went on by ship to Amboy. From there he walked fifty miles to Burlington. There he found a party of people going by row-boat up the river. Benjamin went with them, earning his passage by rowing till midnight. They passed Philadelphia in the dark without knowing it, and had to go back to find the city. On landing, Benjamin had in his pocket one Dutch dollar and a shilling in copper. Taking a lodging at the Three Mariners Inn, he went in search of work, and was taken in at Keimer's Printing-house. In Philadelphia he gradually made friends with other young men. They used to meet frequently to read their essays and poems to each other. These meetings were in effect a sort of ' Mutual Improvement Society ' of the kind that was so common among the young men of the smaller *bourgeoisie* of Great Britain in the Georgian and Victorian ages. The Governor of Massachusetts, Sir William Keith, took notice of Franklin and frequently had the young man at his house.

In 1724 Benjamin sailed to London. This visit lasted for eighteen months. He earned his living as a printer, extended his knowledge by reading in the London bookshops, and discussed British politics in Batson's Coffee House.

After eighteen months spent in England, Franklin sailed from Gravesend on July 21, 1726, and landed at Philadelphia on October 11. He travelled with an English merchant who was going to open a store in Philadelphia and who took Franklin into his employ. On the death of his employer two years later, Franklin took service again with the old printer, Keimer. Among the journeymen of Keimer was one George Webb, an Oxford scholar, working for small wages under a bond and indenture. After saving enough money at Keimer's, Franklin started in the printing business in a small way on his own account with a fellow-printer, Meredith. The business was soon fairly prosperous, and they were able to embark on the printing and publishing of a small newspaper. This newspaper had a better type and was better printed than his competitors', and gradually increased its circulation. In 1730 he was able to marry and to set up house. In his club, the Junto, the members kept their books or some of them in the Club meeting-room for the use of one another. This suggested to Franklin the idea of starting a subscription library. He induced fifty people to subscribe £2 each as capital and 10s. annually. Books were purchased, the Assembly of Massachusetts gave a charter. 'This was the mother of all the North American subscription libraries, now so numerous,' wrote Franklin in later life (1771). After the library, Franklin, in 1744, founded the Philadelphia Philosophical Society.

In 1739 Boston was stirred in its soul by the preaching of Whitefield, who arrived from Ireland. After several of his open-air meetings had been held, ' one could not walk thro' the town in an evening without hearing psalms sung in different families of every street.' Franklin, always scientific, studied Whitefield's fine voice and articulation, and calculated that in a properly filled area the preacher could be heard by 30,000 people.

BENJAMIN FRANKLIN
J. Wright
National Portrait Gallery

In 1742 Franklin had invented a new kind of stove for heating houses by means of warm fresh air—a great boon in the severe winter climate of Philadelphia. He gave the model to a friend who had a blast furnace. A London ironmonger imitated the stove, took out a patent, and made a small fortune. Blast furnaces were fairly numerous in the North American colonies until 1750, when the stupid Colonial Manufactures Prohibition Act passed in the Prime Ministership of Henry Pelham prohibited the manufacture of bar or pig-iron in the colonies. Thus the British Parliament caused all the blast furnaces to be dismantled.

Franklin was now a considerable person, although only of local fame. In 1749 he induced some of his fellow-citizens of Philadelphia to subscribe for forming a college; scholars came to it; and so the University of Pennsylvania was founded. He was elected to the Pennsylvanian Assembly and held his seat for ten years, without ever asking any of the electors for their vote. To his many duties he added that of Postmaster-General for all the American colonies in 1753.

In 1754, when war between Great Britain and France seemed likely to occur (as it soon did), the Home Government (Board of Trade) ordered a congress of commissioners from all the colonies to be held at Albany, in New York State. The Governor of Pennsylvania nominated Franklin as one of the commissioners. He went with the others to Albany and brought forward a scheme for the union of the colonies in defensive measures and for their taxing themselves in common for defence. This scheme, if it had been adopted, would, he says with reason, have prevented the secession of the colonies from England which took place twenty-two years later. The plan was discussed in the Congress of Albany, but failed to be approved either among the colonists or by the English authorities. Franklin was disappointed and endeavoured, but without success, to revive the plan next year.

When General Braddock came over from England with

regular troops in 1755, Franklin met him at Fredericktown, in Maryland, and rendered great service in procuring wagons for the expedition. He even advanced £1000 of his own money for the collecting of wagons and other supplies. After the general had gone off on his fatal march, Franklin sent him the account for the money advanced. Braddock immediately sent back an order for repayment; a few days afterwards he suffered defeat and death at the hands of the French and Indians (July 1755). This defeat, and more particularly the panic shown by Braddock's reserve troops who had been left behind in camp, ' gave us Americans,' writes Franklin, ' the first suspicion that our exalted ideas of the prowess of British regulars had not been well founded.' The troops, unfortunately, had behaved badly towards the inhabitants, looting and insulting and even ' totally ruining some poor families.' Braddock was greatly at fault in allowing this. Franklin testifies, however, to the general's courage and readiness to learn by experience. Braddock's *aide-de-camp* told him that after being carried off fatally wounded from the field, the general lay silent for a whole day; at night he said, ' *Who would have thought it ?* ' Next day he remained silent again, saying only at last, ' *We shall better know how to deal with them another time*,' and died a few minutes after.

In 1757 Franklin visited England for the second time. Although he had been living for years in America, among the backwoods as people commonly thought, he had been carrying on a learned correspondence with English scientists, had written pamphlets, which were published in London, on his experiments in electricity, and had been elected a member of the Royal Society. He was known in two hemispheres as a philosopher, scientist, and statesman; he was the great citizen of Pennsylvania; but he was recognised also as a citizen of the world. This visit to England, begun in 1757, was to last for five years, during which period he lived in the society of London politics and literature. His third visit was to last from 1764 to 1775, when he represented the views of the Colonies against direct taxation of America by the British Parliament. The American Colonies at the mid-century were places of great activity, commercial, literary, scientific. If, when Franklin started his press in Philadelphia, there was not one bookshop south of New York, this state of affairs had been amply remedied by the year 1750. Newspapers were reasonably numerous, and the books which they advertised in their sales lists—religious works, the Latin classics, the works of Shakespeare, Milton, Molière, Dryden, Smollett, Gay— show the degree and breadth of the prevailing taste.

' By 1753 New York and some of the other larger centres, both South and North, were having frequent concerts of the best music of the day, performed by orchestras large enough to render overtures, *concerti grossi* and symphonies. In 1759 the Orpheus Club was formed in Philadelphia and three years later was founded the celebrated Saint Cecilia Society at Charlestown.' [1]

John Singleton Copley was painting in Boston in 1753, and Benjamin West, who became—the only American to do so—President of the Royal Academy, was starting his career as an artist in Philadelphia. There was a small American school of sculpture, chiefly for memorials in churches. In 1759 Colonel George Washington of Mount Vernon, Virginia, ordered busts from London—busts of Alexander the Great, Cæsar, Charles XII, Marlborough. If there was yet no great literature in America, there was science and philosophy. Besides Benjamin Franklin, Jonathan Edwards (1703–58) was recognised as an original thinker; he ranks now among the world's classical theologians and metaphysicians. The men who conducted the American Revolution were educated and, many of them, travelled gentlemen. The diplomatists of the Revolutionary days, and the subsequent ten or twenty years—Franklin, Jay, Gouverneur Morris, Monroe—were able to deal with the

[1] Adams, *Provincial Society*, p. 358.

most experienced of the trained European diplomatists. The many-sidedness of the great Americans is the best proof both of their intellectual vigour and of their open and comprehensive attitude towards world-influences. Franklin was not the only man who attained European fame in many directions. Jefferson, one of the makers of the American constitution and the second president, attained distinction as a statesman, philosopher, political scientist, and educationist. Had he never drafted and signed the Declaration of Independence he would still be remembered for his treatises on law and politics.

FOR FURTHER STUDY

W. B. WEEDEN, *Economic and Social History of New England* (1896).

The Diaries of George Washington, 1748–99 (edited by John C. Fitzpatrick, 1925).

H. W. PIERSON, *Jefferson at Monticello: The Private Life of Thomas Jefferson* (New York, 1862).

A. M. SCHLESINGER and D. R. FOX, *A History of American Life* (vols. i–iv, New York, 1927).

CHAPTER XVI

THE ORIGIN OF THE AMERICAN
UNION

NO British historian is ever likely to underrate the significance of the American Revolution. Its effect upon the development of the British Empire has been marked and permanent; its effect upon world history grows more impressive every year.

The causes of the Revolution or Secession are not obscure. It had been prophesied years in advance; the secession, however, of other Dominions from the British Empire has been prophesied, yet has not occurred. There was about the American Revolution nothing inevitable, so far as can be ' historically ' inferred; it just happened through mismanagement and lack of the spirit of compromise and tolerance—faults which without doubt lay chiefly at the door of the British authorities. Although not inevitable, the Revolution was likely to occur or to be attempted, if the Home Government tried to govern the Colonies from London. The observant British Commissioner of Customs at Boston, among his letters written between 1767 and 1776, writes : [1]

' In Connecticut the houses are pretty well built, and the people dressed a good deal in homespun. Nobody in these parts has the idea of a Superior or of a Gentleman, other than themselves. They seem to be a good substantial kind of farmers, but there is no break in their Society; their Government, Religion and Manners all

[1] *Letters of Ann Hulton* from Boston, 1767–76. (The above letter is from Henry Hulton, brother of Ann, and Commissioner of Customs at Boston.)

tend to support an equality. Whoever brings in your Victuals sits down and chat (*sic*) to you. . . . They are all politicians and all Scripture learnt.'

The description of the men of Connecticut cannot be applied to the peoples of all the American Colonies. The nature of their society differed widely, for instance, between North and South; but they were all firm-minded and independent in outlook, habituated to governing themselves, impatient of outside interference. They had what Burke called ' a fierce spirit of liberty.'

The Northern colonies, although each had its own individuality, had as a whole a different character from the Southern colonies, although these too were not a distinct group, but differed markedly one from another. The physical division between North and South has been conventionally understood to be the line drawn by two English surveyors, Charles Mason and Jeremiah Dixon. These men in 1764–67 were employed to draw a line in accordance with an agreement between the heirs of William Penn, the original proprietor of Pennsylvania, and of Cecil Calvert, Lord Baltimore, the original proprietor of Maryland. ' Mason and Dixon's Line ' runs from the Atlantic coast northwards and then westwards, separating firstly Maryland from Delaware, and secondly Maryland from Pennsylvania. The total population of the American colonies was in 1775 nearly 2,500,000, of whom between 400,000 and 500,000 were negro slaves. Most of the slaves were to the south of Mason and Dixon's Line. The white population north of the line was much larger than that to the south.

The Revolution had its origin in the North. The first distinct cause of serious friction appears to have been the determination of the British Government in 1761 to enforce rigorously the Acts of Trade or Navigation Acts which had hitherto been commonly evaded. Trading between New England merchants and the French colonies had been quite brisk, even during the Seven Years War. The manufactured goods which the colonists had to buy from England were more expensive than the raw materials which they shipped to England. Consequently there was a balance of trade against the colonists which they could only meet by paying over money. Trade with the French West Indies was one way of obtaining a supply of money. The rigid enforcement of the Navigation Acts after 1760 stopped this. Governor Shirley of Massachusetts applied to the Courts for general search-warrants or ' Writs of Assistance.' The King's Advocate, James Otis, resigned his office in order to make a speech against general warrants. This speech ' is conveniently regarded as the first act in the American Revolution.' [1]

Otis's speech maintained the principle that ' an act of Parliament against the constitution is void.' Accordingly, the writs of assistance, even if declared legal by Parliament, would not be legal. In 1764 Otis explained his argument at greater length in an *Essay on the Rights of the Colonies*. ' The Parliament cannot make two and two, five; Omnipotency cannot do it. The supreme power in a state is *jus dicere* only.' [2] Thus from the inception of the trouble between Great Britain and the Colonies we see clearly the Americans taking their stand on the idea of a fixed constitution, a fundamental law—the essence of the Constitution which later they made and adopted in 1787. This principle, however, did not and does not hold good in Great Britain. Parliament has gradually, since the close of the Middle Ages, assumed the more than Omnipotency which Otis denied to it; whatever it enacts is law for the citizens of Great Britain, whether it be reasonable or unreasonable, good or bad. Such is the British Constitution, and it is unlikely to be altered. Obviously, therefore, the stability of British Government and society depends upon Parliament

[1] E. Channing, *The History of the United States*, 1765–1865 (1896), p. 43.
[2] Text in S. E. Morison, *Sources and Documents illustrating the American Revolution*, p. 7.

o

using this ' more than omnipotence ' tactfully—never using its ' omnicompetence ' to declare laws which will only provoke resistance. When in 1767 Parliament declared the Writs of Assistance legal, it was asserting its right, but it was provoking armed opposition; and, after all, its right in this particular case was not worth asserting. In England itself the Law Courts, in the case of John Wilkes (1763), had declared General Warrants illegal; and Parliament had forborne to reverse this decision (as it could have done) and to declare the warrants legal.

In 1763 there occurred another constitutional case, this time in the South. Patrick Henry, an able and industrious young lawyer, argued before a Virginian court that the King had not power to veto an Act of the Virginian Legislature passed for the good of the people of Virginia. This is, indeed, the convention of the Constitution determining the relations of the Crown towards the Dominions at the present day; it was not the law of the land in 1763. The Patrick Henry argument (and the verdict which a jury gave after hearing his argument) ' attracted little attention in the colonies at the time, and, what was extraordinary, the English Government gave way in the Virginian case.' If the British Government had gone on, judiciously and on occasion, giving way like this (as it does now), there would have been no American Revolution. For ' there seems every reason to believe that at the beginning of 1764 no more loyal and faithful subjects could be found than the American colonists.' [1]

A result of the Seven Years War was that Canada passed from French to British hands. The removal of the French danger might have been considered by the British Government to be a reason for totally removing British troops from the American Colonies. The Home Government, on the contrary, thought that the possibility of French revenge, the presence of a probably hostile French population on the northern frontier, and the likelihood of Indian wars (one, called

[1] The quotations on this page are from Channing, *op. cit.*, p 47.

the Conspiracy of Pontiac, actually occurred in 1763–64), rendered the presence of increased garrisons necessary. The American colonists thought that they could undertake their own protection, just as all the British dominions do now. The military advisers of the Home Government, however, believed that a force of 12,000 regular troops was required in the American Colonies. Until 1763 there had been no permanent garrisons of regular soldiers, no standing army, in the British American Colonies. The Home Government was prepared to find £200,000 of the sum of money required annually for this; to produce the remaining £100,000 that was needed the British Parliament passed the Stamp Act.

The circumstances in which the Stamp Act was passed should be carefully noted; for, however unwisely the Government acted, it did not proceed rashly or without considering the susceptibilities of the Americans. On March 9, 1764, George Grenville, Prime Minister, brought forward in the House of Commons a resolution that it might ' be necessary to charge certain stamp duties in America.' This motion, which the House of Commons easily passed, was not sprung upon the Colonies. The Agents, whom every colony maintained in London, had been officially informed of the coming resolution and had been asked to consult with their principals ' with a view to having the colonists themselves propose some more agreeable method of raising the necessary revenue.'[1] The colonists were given plenty of time in which to frame proposals, but they did not do so. The Stamp Act passed through Parliament in March 1765 and received the Royal Assent by commission, George III being ill at the time.

The news of the passage of the Stamp Act aroused practically no excitement in the Colonies. It was not to come into force at once, and nobody can say how the coming into force would have been taken by the colonists. ' It chanced, however, that the matter did not rest until the day

[1] Channing *op. cit.*, p. 49.

came for buying stamps.'[1] Patrick Henry, who had just been elected to the Virginia House of Burgesses, made on May 29, 1765, a fiery speech against the Stamp Act and carried resolutions against it. Henry cried: ' Cæsar had his Brutus, Charles his Cromwell, and (pausing) George the Third (here a cry of " Treason! Treason! " was heard, supposed to issue from the chair, but with admirable presence of mind he proceeded) may profit by their examples. Sir, if this be treason,' continued he, ' make the most of it.'[2] The chief resolution was as follows :

> ' *Resolved*. That the taxation of the people by them-
> selves or by persons chosen by themselves to represent
> them, who can only know what taxes the people are able
> to bear, or the easiest method of raising them, and must
> themselves be affected by every tax laid on the people,
> is the only security against a burthensome taxation, and
> the distinguishing characteristic of British freedom.'

When the Virginia resolutions were reported in the North and printed in the newspapers there, they became a banner of opposition. By the time the stamps and stamped paper arrived in America, the opposition was universal, and the officials almost at once gave up trying to enforce the Act. Except for a few instances in Georgia, no stamps at all were used in any of the Colonies. The judges, after at first waiting for the agitation to subside, were obliged by congestion of business to open their courts and to administer the law as if the Stamp Act had never been passed. Moreover, on the motion of James Otis of the Massachusetts House of Representatives, a proposal had gone out to all the Colonial legislatures, inviting them to appoint delegates to a Stamp Act Congress. The invitations were accepted. The Congress met at New York in October 1765, and framed a declaration on the model of the Virginia Resolutions. The

---

[1] Channing, *op. cit.*, p 50.

[2] From John Burke's *History of Virginia*, 1855, quoted by Morison, *Sources and Documents*, p. 17.

importance of the Congress is in the fact that it was a Congress, and that all the Colonies sent representatives to it. What the British Government had been trying for years to do, namely, to make the Colonies act jointly in regard to defence and taxation, had now been accomplished in the most disastrous manner. The Stamp Act Congress is the beginning of the American Union.

CHAPTER XVII

THE OUTBREAK OF THE WAR OF
AMERICAN INDEPENDENCE

IN 1765 King George dismissed Grenville. A Whig of
another kind, the Marquis of Rockingham, a *grand
seigneur*, and a man of moderate, tolerant views, became
Prime Minister. His Government, ' a landmark in the
reign of George III,' [1] was short-lived, but it repealed
the Stamp Act ; at the same time, it passed another Act
declaring the legislative supremacy of the British Parliament
which Otis and Patrick Henry impugned. Rockingham's
Ministry, however, only lasted twelve months. The next
was the Grafton-Chatham Ministry, in which Charles
Townshend was Chancellor of the Exchequer. This
Government, with a view to raising revenue, imposed taxes
upon imports into America. Such a tax was not unpre-
cedented, for the British Parliament had always regulated
commerce, and had imposed tariffs, although not for
revenue. The new taxes produced nearly as great a storm
as the Stamp Act, so the British Government lost all the
advantage which its tactful withdrawal of that Act had
gained for it. The Massachusetts House of Representatives
sent a circular letter to the other Colonial legislatures (1768)
suggesting that measures should be concerted against the
new taxes. This letter explicitly stated that independence
was not aimed at. The mention of the word and the
prospect which it opened up were ominous.

The Virginia House of Representatives, on account of
certain obnoxious ' Resolves ' which it passed in 1768, was

[1] D. A. Winstanley, *Personal and Party Government* (1910),
p. 240.

dissolved by the Governor, but, like the French Estates-General in a similar case at a later day, it met in another house. The members solemnly bound themselves not to import or use any goods taxed by Parliament until the new duties (the Townshend duties) should be repealed (1769). The well-known Virginian landholder and soldier, George Washington, took a leading part in this proceeding. Within the same year all the other Colonial Legislatures adopted similar non-importation agreements. If this state of affairs went on, the Colonies would soon stand in no constitutional relation at all to the Mother Country—that is, Great Britain must either face a revolution aiming at secession, or repeal the Townshend Acts. Either alternative would be, in the circumstances, not unreasonable. Great Britain could face the secession issue and do her best to conquer the Colonies, or she could give way, and thus maintain the Empire (it is true, in a much looser form than before) by concession—which has been the policy adopted now for a hundred years. In 1769, however, the Government really adopted neither alternative; it did not boldly challenge the Revolution; it did not repeal the Townshend taxes, for it left one, the smallest, on tea, in force (April 1770). It was a tax worth about £300 annually. Yet ' if it was important from the point of view of the English Government to retain the tax on tea as a species of continuing declaratory act, it was equally important for the colonists to pay no tax which could be drawn into precedent.' [1]

In March 1770, there was a collision in Boston and some fighting; and yet the Revolution actually did not break out for another five years. It is difficult to realise now how very slowly it came.

The collision of 1770, sometimes called the Boston Massacre, occurred between some soldiers and a mob in Boston. Anybody who has seen Boston and knows anything about its old families, can easily understand that the presence of a standing force—like a standing army in

[1] Channing, *op. cit.*, p. 60.

seventeenth-century England—would be highly unpopular. On March 5, 1770, a false alarm of fire had brought a crowd into the streets. Some boys and men used the opportunity to insult a sentinel who was on guard in front of a public building. A captain, corporal, and six soldiers came up to rescue or support the sentinel. The crowd surrounded the soldiers and began to use missiles. The soldiers, apparently, did not act without grave provocation. At last they fired, and five men of Boston were killed. The soldiers were charged at Boston with murder, and were defended by two of the strongest of the Boston opponents of the British attitude. These were two lawyers, John Adams and Josiah Quincy. The jury acquitted the soldiers of the charge of murder, but found two guilty of manslaughter. These two were ' slightly branded.' The whole episode shows that the responsible citizens of Boston acted, in the circumstances, with remarkable moderation. Governor Hutchinson bowed before the storm and sent the troops away from Boston. Thus the citizens triumphed, for they objected to the presence of a standing army, unless invited, as much as they objected to paying taxes which they had not voted.

On June 9, 1772, a British ship of war, the *Gaspee*, on revenue service, when chasing a suspected smuggler, ran aground in the mouth of the river Providence in Narraganset Bay, near Providence, the capital of the state of Rhode Island. On the same night a large party of men came from Providence in boats, boarded the *Gaspee*, overcame the crew, and set fire to the ship. No lives were lost; the crew were landed on shore and allowed to go free. Although the perpetrators of this outrage were perfectly well known to the rest of the inhabitants of Providence, a judicial commission sent to Rhode Island to enquire could obtain no evidence.

The destruction of the *Gaspee* was a sporadic outrage against the ship of an unpopular revenue officer. The next incident involved a calculated defiance of British taxing authority. In order to ease the financial difficulties of the East India Company this Corporation was permitted to ship tea to the American Colonies without paying the excise or export duty of twelve pence per pound when the tea was taken out of bond in England. The only duty which would have to be paid on the tea would be the Townshend duty of threepence per pound when it was landed in America. Doubtless the British Government believed that by letting the colonists have tea cheaply it would not merely increase the sales of the East India Company, but would induce the Americans, almost without noticing it, to pay a British tax. All the colonists refused to accept the tea, and it seems to have failed to find landing anywhere except at Charleston, South Carolina, where it was stored in a damp cellar until spoilt. In Boston harbour the tea-ship was boarded by a crowd on December 16, 1773, and the tea was thrown into the water. The ' Boston Tea-party ' was the first deliberately overt or violent act of rebellion.

The challenge was at once met by stern measures on the part of the British Government. An Act of Parliament closed the harbour of Boston to trade and removed the customs-house to the little port of Salem; the prosperity of Boston, which was nothing but a maritime town, would, while this Act was in operation, be completely destroyed. Another Act of Parliament revoked certain parts of the Charter of Massachusetts; while leaving the General Assembly (or House of Representatives) untouched, it caused the members of the Council—that is, the Upper Chamber, and all judges and magistrates—to be nominated by the Crown (May 20, 1774).

All the other American Colonies at once made the cause of Massachusetts their own, and offers of armed assistance were made. At the same time feeling was further influenced in the Colonies by passage through Parliament of the Quebec Act (June 22, 1774) which established the free exercise of the Roman Catholic religion (hitherto illegal throughout all British territories) in the province of Quebec. This Act also extended the limits of Quebec from the frontier of 1763 (which was even more restricted than the present

218 ENGLAND IN THE EIGHTEENTH CENTURY

frontier of Quebec) so as to include the country west of the Alleghanies and southwards to the Ohio river. Thus the rights or claims of Massachusetts, New York, Connecticut, Pennsylvania, and Virginia seemed to be overridden, although there were ' saving clauses ' reserving the rights of holders of grants from the Crown. These saving clauses, however, were not generally understood or even generally known in the Colonies. The difference between the frontier of Canada as it now is and as it was defined by the Quebec Act is represented by the territory of the present states of Ohio, Indiana, Illinois, Michigan, and Wisconsin.

The long process towards secession was now nearly complete. In 1774 Thomas Jefferson, a rich Virginian landowner, scholar, and man of affairs, published a *Summary View*, arguing now that the Parliament of Great Britain had no authority at all over the Colonies, and that the Colonies had complete legislative freedom. This view seems to have found at once general acceptance throughout the Colonies, where excitement was intense, and where the opposition to the British Government had thrown off all restraint or disguise. Unless, therefore, the British Government was prepared to grant what would now be called full ' Dominion status '—and this was actually, though vaguely, in the minds of, at any rate, Burke and Chatham, and was definitely in the mind of Adam Smith[1]—there was no alternative but secession, with the sure prospect of a deadly civil war. Great Britain chose the alternative.

In Salem, to which the Massachusetts legislature had removed itself, there took place in June 1774 a scene strongly reminiscent of the Parliament of the reign of Charles I—a similarity of which the stern Puritans of New England were keenly conscious. Samuel Adams moved and carried a resolution providing that a Continental Congress should be held at Philadelphia on September 1—a step the easier to be taken because of the precedent of the Stamp Act Congress of 1765. An invitation was sent to the other

[1] *Wealth of Nations*, Book IV, chap. VII, part III.

colonial legislatures. The Continental Congress which accordingly assembled on September 1, had representatives from all the Colonies except Georgia. On October 14 (1774) the Congress passed certain resolutions—not defiant, not incompatible with the sovereignty of the British Crown—which in effect were a Declaration of Rights. The chief rights claimed for the inhabitants of the Colonies were:

' That they are entitled to life, liberty and property, and they have never ceded to any sovereign power whatever, a right to dispose of either without their consent.

' That the foundation of English liberty, and of all free government, is a right in the people to participate in their legislative council; and as the English colonists are not represented in the British Parliament, they are entitled to a free and exclusive power of legislation in their several provincial legislatures, where their right of representation can alone be preserved, in all cases of taxation and internal polity, subject only to the negative of their Sovereign, in such manner as has been heretofore used and accustomed.

' That the keeping a standing army in these colonies, in times of peace, without the consent of the legislature of that colony in which such army is kept, is against law.'

Congress thereupon adjourned, after resolving to assemble again in the following May. It is said that there were still ' probably not a dozen men in all the colonies at that time (October 1774) who wished for independence.' [1] This may be true, and yet the colonists, at any rate in Massachusetts, were arming. The British garrison was now back in Boston, boycotted, as was also the Governor, Gage, by the inhabitants. On the night of April 18, 1775, Gage sent out from Boston a strong party of 800 soldiers to capture or destroy warlike stores which were being accumulated by the inhabitants at the village or small town of Concord, twenty miles away. When the soldiers reached the village of Lexington, they found, about 5 o'clock in the morning of

[1] Channing, *op. cit.*, p. 69.

the 19th, a band of armed men opposing them. Shots were exchanged on Lexington Common; some sixteen of the Americans were killed or wounded. The soldiers marched on to Concord, spiked a couple of guns and threw some powder-barrels into the river; but when they came to the bridge—a rough wooden structure just outside the village—they found it held by a large number of militia men, or 'minute-men,' as they were called. The British were hotly attacked and had to retreat. All the way back to Boston they were shot at and indeed were only saved from complete destruction by a relieving force of 900 men which, under Lord Percy, came out and met them at Lexington. They lost 65 killed, 180 wounded, and 28 men made prisoners. The losses of the Americans are believed to have been 90. The colonists pressed on and, their numbers steadily growing, laid siege to Boston. Thus the War of American Independence began.

Seven and a half years later the preliminary treaty, recognising the independence of the American Colonies, was signed by the British and American peace-commissioners at Paris (November 30, 1782). The Final Treaty between Great Britain and the United States was signed on January 20, 1783. The war was now over; and the characteristic English way was to regard it as an unpleasant episode which had better be forgotten. Facts are facts, and must be recognised. The United States was now an independent nation; but this was no reason why good-will and co-operation should not be resumed between the mother and the daughter even if the daughter should outgrow the parent. 'Upon this argument I always make my stand,' wrote one of the British peace-commissioners from Paris to the Foreign Office, ' that we may proceed to open an intercourse between our two countries, as nearly as possible, to the point of *as we were.*' [1]

[1] Dispatch to David Hartley, June 2, 1783, *Foreign Office Archives* (F.O. 4).

CHAPTER XVIII

REFLECTIONS ON THE AMERICAN REVOLUTION

IT has been stated by a modern scholar, referring to the present British Empire :

'The various Dominions composing the British Commonwealth had at times protested against what was known as Downing Street control, but now they were completely independent nations controlling their foreign and domestic affairs, and they formed a self-respecting group of nations who were working together. It was perfectly obvious that such a solution was impossible in 1776, for the one thing that made the problem difficult was that of finding unity between the thirteen states themselves.' [1]

The last sentence of this quotation has an inconsistency in so far as it says that the ' Dominion status ' solution was *impossible* in 1776, because it was *difficult* to find unity among the thirteen states—that is, among the New England colonies, New York, New Jersey, Pennsylvania, Delaware, and the colonies to the South of Mason and Dixon's line. True, it was difficult—but unity had at last been found in the Stamp Act Congress of 1765 and the Philadelphia Congress of 1774; and this occurred before the colonists had determined on secession. Down to the actual outbreak of hostilities, it is almost universally acknowledged, a substantial majority of the colonists were for remaining under the British Crown.

---

[1] Lecture on *Anglo-American Relations* by Philip Kerr, reported in *The Times*, December 4, 1928.

The views of George III were quite clear. He certainly had no conception of 'Dominion status.' His letters to Lord North show this. His views as expressed therein were that the claims of the Americans were inconsistent with the constitution of the Empire which he had inherited; would, in a sense, destroy the old Empire; and that his conscience would not allow him to acquiesce in this.

One bold writer advocated separation. Colonies which would do nothing for their own defence, which were in a condition of smothered rebellion, and which were continually waiting for the difficulties of the mother-country in order to assert their power, were a source of political weakness and not of political strength.' This was the argument of Dr. Tucker, Dean of Gloucester. The American trade-connection, Tucker held, was certainly not worth a war. The war of 1739 over the Spanish right of search had cost sixty million pounds; the Seven Years War had cost England ninety millions; 'and its most important result had been, by securing the Americans from French aggression, to render possible their present rebellion.' Besides, trade would always flow in the most lucrative channels; therefore so long as British capital was greater than that of any other country, a profitable trade would necessarily take place between Great Britain and America. 'Let England free herself from the cost, the responsibility, and the danger of defending them, retaining, like other nations, the right of connecting herself with them by treaties of commerce or alliance.'[1]

Adam Smith, in his *Wealth of Nations*, which was published, very *à propos*, in 1776, declared that peaceful separation of the American Colonies from the Mother Country would be the best for all parties, although, at the same time, he recognised that such a solution was practically impossible;

---

[1] The above quotations are from Lecky, *History of England in the Eighteenth Century* (1882), p. 389, paraphrasing Tucker, *Political Tracts* of 1763 and following years.

for, owing to what appears to be a curious and unreasonable, yet permanent and universal instinct, 'no nation ever voluntarily gave up the dominion of any province, how troublesome soever it might be to govern it, and how small soever the revenue which it afforded might be in proportion to the expense which it occasioned.'[1]

Whether the Americans had good reasons for wishing to be separate from Great Britain is a question which Adam Smith does not consider. He does indeed deal with the trade-grievances, which, however, were not the cause of the separation (taxation and taxation alone was, as a matter of fact, the point at issue throughout all the controversy which preceded the Declaration of Independence). On the whole, amid the illiberal fiscal conditions of the eighteenth century, the British Government was comparatively liberal in its treatment of the Colonies. If masts and other naval stores were placed on the list of 'enumerated' commodities and were not allowed to be exported to any country except Great Britain, on the other hand a bounty was given on the exportation of naval stores from the Colonies; 'and as both regulations were enacted at the same time, their joint effect was rather to encourage than to discourage the clearing of land in America.'[2] The most perfect freedom of trade was permitted between the British Colonies in America and in the West Indies; 'these Colonies are now become so populous and thriving, that each of them finds in some of the others a great and extensive market for every part of its produce.'[3] It is true that the Acts of Trade had a substantial list of 'enumerated' articles, such as tobacco, which were not allowed to be exported direct to any foreign country, but had to be landed in Great Britain. On the other hand, the Colonies had a legal monopoly in supplying such articles to Great Britain; foreign countries were prevented by tariffs or prohibitions from competing; and tobacco was not permitted to be grown in Great Britain.

[1] *Wealth of Nations* (1904 ed.), ii, 224.   [2] *Ibid.*, ii, 180.
[3] *Ibid.*, ii, 181.

The liberality of England, however, towards the trade of her colonies was confined to raw produce of the Colonies or to articles in the first stage of manufacture. 'The more advanced or refined manufactures, even of the colony produce, the merchants and manufacturers of Great Britain choose to reserve to themselves, and have prevailed upon the legislature to prevent their establishment in the colonies, sometimes by the high duties and sometimes by absolute prohibitions.'[1] For instance, Great Britain (since 1750) had imposed an absolute prohibition upon the erection of iron furnaces and slit mills in any of the American Colonies. 'To prohibit a great people from making all that they can of every part of their produce, or from employing their stock and industry in the way that they judge most advantageous to themselves, is a manifest violation of the most sacred rights of mankind.'[2]

On the other hand, 'in everything except their foreign trade, the liberty of the English colonists to manage their own affairs their own way is complete'[3]—or rather was complete until the enactment of the Stamp Act, the Townshend duties, and until the establishing of a garrison of regular soldiers. Indeed, there was more equality among the English colonists than among the inhabitants of the Mother Country, not merely socially, but also politically; for in some of the Colonies, in Connecticut and Rhode Island, the people elected the governor as well as the assembly-men. Without being autocratic, like Spain and Portugal, the British Government ensured safety. 'The government of the English colonies is, perhaps, the only one which, since the world began, could give perfect security to the inhabitants of so very distant a province.'[4]

The British people did not lightly undertake war with their own people overseas. Adam Smith writes: 'The expectation of a rupture with the colonies has struck the

---

[1] *Wealth of Nations,* ii, 181.   [2] *Ibid.,* ii, 183.
[3] *Ibid.,* ii, 186.   [4] *Ibid.,* ii, 187.

people of Great Britain with more terror than they ever felt for a Spanish Armada or a French invasion.' Great Britain was eminently suited to the task of producing manufactured goods, the Colonies to that of producing agricultural goods and raw materials. The reciprocal advantages of exchanging their surplus produce had triumphed over the actual disadvantages which, Adam Smith held, the monopolistic British mercantilist policy created. The monopoly of colony trade diminished colonial wealth without increasing the wealth of the Mother Country; by raising the ordinary rate of profit, it might benefit particular traders, although the London merchants had not become ' such magnificent lords as those of Cadiz and Lisbon ' in monopolistic and poverty-stricken Spain and Portugal.

Now, ' the maintenance of this monopoly has hitherto been the principal, or more properly, perhaps, the sole end and purpose of the dominion which Great Britain assumes over her colonies.' The expense of maintaining the monopoly was enormous; the returns inconsiderable. ' The expense of the ordinary peace establishment of the colonies amounted, before the commencement of present disturbances, to the pay of twenty regiments of foot; and to the expense of a very considerable naval force, which was constantly kept up in order to guard from smuggling-vessels of other nations, the immense coasts of North America, and that of our West Indian Islands.'[1] Adam Smith computes the bill at enormous figures. ' The late (Seven Years) war was altogether a colony quarrel; and the whole expense of it, in whatever part of the world it might have been laid out, whether in Germany or the East Indies, ought justly to be stated to the account of the colonies. It amounted to more than ninety millions sterling.' The Spanish War, which began in 1739 with the object of the preventing of the search of ships in the colonial trade, was a colony quarrel. ' The whole expense is, in reality, a bounty which has been given in order to support a

[1] *Wealth of Nations*, ii, 223.

monopoly.' Thus, from every point of view, ' under the present system of management Great Britain derives nothing but loss from the dominion which she assumes over her colonies.' [1]

Adam Smith's conclusion from all this argument was that Great Britain should voluntarily give up all authority over her Colonies, and leave them to elect their own magistrates, and enact their own laws, and to make peace and war, as they might think proper. This could have been done without the Colonies ceasing to acknowledge the British Crown, an acknowledgment which they were perfectly ready to give.

' By thus parting good friends, the natural affection of the colonies to the Mother Country would quickly revive. It might dispose them not only to respect, for whole centuries together, that treaty of commerce which they had concluded with us at parting, but to favour us in war as well as in trade, and instead of turbulent and factious subjects, to become our most faithful, affectionate and generous allies, and the same sort of parental affection on the one side, and filial respect on the other, might revive between Great Britain and her colonies, which used to subsist between those of ancient Greece and the mother city from which they descended.'

This is precisely the political system within the British Commonwealth of Nations of the twentieth century after the Great War. But in Adam Smith's time no nation, as he says, had ever voluntarily given up dominion over even the most troublesome and unprofitable province, and to advocate this ' would be to propose such a measure as never was, and never will be, adopted by any nation in the world.'

In place of the proposal, incapable of acceptance at that time, to give the Colonies independence either with or without allegiance to the British Crown, Adam Smith

[1] *Wealth of Nations*, ii, 224.

turned to another idea which has been put into practice, although not in the British Empire, in recent years, namely, representation in the central or supreme legislature. ' Great Britain insists upon taxing the colonies; and they refuse to be taxed by a Parliament in which they are not represented.' The answer to this problem is obviously—give the Colonies representation in the British Parliament, ' such a number of representatives as suited the proportion of what each (colony) contributed to the public revenue of the empire.' If some such method were not adopted, it was certain that the American leaders would never voluntarily submit; ' and we must remember that the blood which must be shed in forcing them to do so, is, every drop of it, the blood either of those who are, or of those whom we wish to have for our fellow-citizens.' As for these same fellow-citizens or their leaders—' from shopkeepers, tradesmen, and attorneys, they are become statesmen and legislators, and are employed in contriving a new form of government for an extensive empire, which, they flatter themselves, will become, and which, indeed, *seems very likely to become*, one of the greatest and most formidable that ever was in the world.' [1]

To say that the people of Great Britain in 1776 were not aware of the momentous issues involved in the American Revolution, or of the methods by which Great Britain's later imperial difficulties have been met, is obviously untrue.

Adam Smith undoubtedly had the right view, the only view that could have solved the problem between the American Colonies and Great Britain. George III was quite wrong when he wrote to Lord North—sincerely, of course, but entirely erroneously—' we must either master them (the Colonies) or totally leave them to themselves, and treat them as aliens.' There *was* a third, a middle course possible, the course which Great Britain follows now, and which Adam Smith saw clearly then and Burke, to some extent, also saw. The British Government's treatment of

[1] *Wealth of Nations*, ii, 223. (The italics are mine.)

the American problem—with the approval, it must be admitted, of a majority, although neither large nor enthusiastic, of Parliament and people—was stupid, perverse, blind, and is responsible for whatever ill-feeling has been shown on both sides of the Atlantic since.

Burke brushed aside the damnable doctrine of absolute and irresponsible sovereignty—a theory which, ever since it came into existence at the end of the Middle Ages, has poisoned and still poisons international relations. ' I do not enter into those metaphysical distinctions,' exclaimed Burke in passionate argument. ' I hate the very sound of them. Leave the Americans as they anciently stood; and those distinctions, born of our unhappy contest, will die along with it. They and we, and their and our ancestors, have been happy under that system. . . . Do not burthen them with taxes ; you were not used to do so from the beginning. Let this be your reason for not taxing. These are the arguments of states and kingdoms. Leave the rest to the schools ; for there only they may be discussed with safety. If intemperately, unwisely, fatally, you sophisticate and poison the very source of government by urging subtle deductions and consequences odious to those you govern, from the unlimited and illimitable nature of supreme sovereignty, you will teach them by these means to call that sovereignty itself in question.'

If Great Britain gave way in the crisis it would not destroy the Empire, she would simply transform it into a union which would be nearer to perfect freedom—a new kind of union like that advocated by Adam Smith. Why could not the Tory statesmen, who must in their heart of hearts have known what they perversely refused to see, agree with these men? It was not because of any suddenness in the crisis. ' For nine long years,' Burke reminded the House, ' Session after Session, we have been lashed round and round this miserable circle of occasional arguments and temporary expedients. . . . Invention is exhausted; reason is fatigued; experience has given judgment;

EDMUND BURKE
Sir Joshua Reynolds
National Portrait Gallery

228

but obstinacy is not yet conquered.'[1]   The truth is that the Tory statesmen never looked forward to the consequences of their attitude towards America: ' Never have the servants of the State looked at the whole of your complicated interests in one connected view.'[2]   And the futility of the Government's attitude—in order to raise a threepence in the pound tax on tea in America it had thrown away the shilling English export tax which the East India Company had always paid and which nobody, at home or overseas, objected to.   Yet— ' your dignity,' explained Burke to the House, ' is tied to it. I know not how it happens, but this dignity of yours is a terrible encumbrance to you; for it has of late been ever at war with your interest, your equity, and every idea of your policy. . . .   But what dignity is derived from the perseverance in absurdity, is more than I ever could discern.'

Burke did not dash recklessly forward to propose a remedy.   He sympathised with the difficulties of the executive Ministers.   It is always easy for those to make suggestions who have not the responsibility for carrying the suggestions into action.   ' I have in general,' he said, ' no very exalted opinion of the virtue of paper government; nor of any politics in which the plan is to be wholly separated from the execution.   But when I saw . . . that things were hastening toward an incurable alienation of our colonies, I confess my caution gave way.   Public calamity is a mighty leveller; and there are occasions when any, even the slightest, chance of doing good must be laid hold on, even by the most inconsiderable person.'   Well, Burke was not inconsiderable.   ' Great men are guide posts and landmarks in the State '; this remark he made elsewhere in the same speech, and applied, rather too generously, to the deceased Charles Townshend and George Grenville, the architects of the colonial trouble.

' To restore order and repose to an empire so great and

---

[1] Speech on American Taxation, 1774 (*Works of Burke* (1906), ii, 92).

[2] *Ibid.*, ii, 99.

there a power steps in, that limits the arrogance of raging passions and furious elements and says, " So far shalt thou go, and no farther." Who are you, that should fret and rage and bite the chains of nature? Nothing worse happens to you than does to all nations who have extensive empire, and it happens in all the forms into which empire can be thrown. In large bodies, the circulation of power must be less vigorous at the extremities. Nature has said it. The Turk cannot govern Egypt and Arabia and Curdistan, as he governs Thrace, nor has he the same dominion in Crimea and Algiers, which he has at Brusa and Smyrna. Despotism itself is obliged to truck and huckster. The Sultan gets such obedience as he can. He governs with a loose rein, that he may govern at all; and the whole of the force and vigour of his authority in his centre is derived from a prudent relaxation in all his borders. Spain, in her provinces, is perhaps not so well obeyed as you are in yours. She complies too: she submits, she watches times. This is the immutable condition, the eternal law, of extensive and detached empire.' [1]

What the British required was to review the attitude of the Americans with tolerance, perhaps even a sense of humour. ' I do not know,' said Burke, ' the method of drawing up an indictment against a whole people.' Better to let them go their own way, and to bear in mind that an extensive empire cannot be as complete a unity as a compact kingdom can be. As distinct from a single state or kingdom, ' an empire is the aggregate of many states under one common head.' [2] Now these states, situated across the Atlantic, complained that they were being taxed in a Parliament in which they were not represented. ' If you mean to please people you must give them the boon which they ask.' Burke was ' inclined to entertain the thought '—that is, of a scheme for the representation of the Colonies in the

---

[1] *Works of Burke*, ii, 190.   [2] *Ibid.*, ii, 199.

British Parliament, but, ' *Opposuit natura*; I cannot remove the eternal barriers of the creation. The thing, in that mode, I do not know to be possible. As I meddle with no theory, I do not absolutely assert the impracticability of such a representation. But I do not see my way to it.'[1] Some other way might be found ' to admit the people of our colonies into an interest in the constitution '—and this could be done by conceding to them what they had in fact until 1763, legislative independence. Great Britain should recognise the legal competency of the colony assemblies for the support of their government in peace, and for public aids in time of war.

In March 1775, when Burke made the great speech on Conciliation, the sands had not yet run out. ' I do not know,' he said, ' that the colonies have, in any general way, or in any cool hour, gone much beyond the demand of immunity in relation to taxes.' Their philosophers—like the English philosophers too—might advance theories and arguments tending towards further freedom; but ' it is besides a very great mistake to imagine that mankind follow up practically any speculative principle, either of government or freedom, as far as it will go in argument and logical illation. *We Englishmen*,' said the Irishman Burke, expressing that expansion of soul which every incomer into England feels, ' stop very short of the principle upon which we support any given part of our constitution; or even the whole of it together. . . . All Government, indeed every human benefit and enjoyment, every virtue and every prudent act, is founded upon compromise and barter. We balance inconveniences; we give and take; we remit some rights, that we may enjoy others; and we choose rather to be happy citizens, than subtle disputants.' Everybody must give up something, even some liberty, if they are to enjoy ' the communion and fellowship of a great empire.' The colonists must not, however, be expected to buy that fellowship too dear. ' None will barter away the immediate

[1] *Works of Burke*, ii, 213.

jewel of his soul.' Satisfied in their reasonable liberty, however, 'the less they (the colonists) will hazard in a vain attempt to make it more. These are *the cords of man*. Man acts from adequate motives, relative to his interest, and not on metaphysical speculations.'

It was objected by the English supporters of coercion that the power of granting supplies, if vested in the colonial assemblies, 'would dissolve the unity of the empire— truly, Mr. Speaker, I do not know what this unity means.' The empire always had parts and members, and was a diversity as well as a unity. The system which George Grenville and Lord North attempted to enforce in the empire did not secure unity, did not even secure revenue; instead of standing revenue it established a standing quarrel. Burke's plan for leaving with the colonies the power of taxation secured to the subject ' the power of *REFUSAL*— the first of all revenues '—and the power of giving. For the rest he would trust in the natural interest of America (as he collectively called the Colonies) in her old associations.

' For that service, for all service, whether of revenue, trade or empire, my trust is in her interest in the British constitution. My hold of the colonies is in the close affection which grows from common names, from kindred blood, from similar privileges, and equal protection. These are ties, which, though light as air, are strong as links of iron. Let the colonies always keep the idea of their civil rights associated with your government;—they will cling and grapple to you; and no force under heaven would be of power to tear them from their allegiance. But let it be once understood, that your government may be one thing, and their privileges another; that these two things may exist without any mutual relation; the cement is gone; the cohesion is loosened; and everything hastens to decay and dissolution. As long as you have the wisdom to keep the sovereign authority of this country as the sanctuary of liberty, the sacred temple consecrated to our common faith, wherever the chosen race and sons of England worship freedom, they will turn their faces towards you. The more they multiply, the more friends you will have; the more ardently they love liberty, the more perfect will be their obedience. Slavery they can have anywhere. It is a weed that grows in every soil. They may have it from Spain, they may have it from Prussia. But, until you become lost to all feeling of your true interest and your natural dignity, freedom they can have from none but you. This is the commodity of price, of which you have the monopoly. This is the true act of navigation which binds to you the commerce of the colonies, and through them secures to you the wealth of the world. Deny them this participation of freedom, and you break that sole bond, which originally made, and must still preserve, the unity of the empire. Do not entertain so weak an imagination, as that your registers and your bonds, your affidavits and your sufferances, your cockets and your clearances, are what form the great securities of your commerce. Do not dream that your letters of office, and your instructions, and your suspending clauses, are the things that hold together the great contexture of this mysterious whole. These things do not make your Government. Dead instruments, passive tools as they are, it is the spirit of the English communion that gives all their life and efficacy to them. It is the spirit of the English constitution, which, infused through the mighty mass, pervades, feeds, unites, invigorates, vivifies every part of the empire, even down to the minutest member.' [1]

[1] *Works of Burke*, ii, 235–236 (Conciliation with America, ad fin.).

FOR FURTHER STUDY

J. A. DOYLE, *The Colonies under the House of Hanover* (1907).

H. L. OSGOOD, *The American Colonies in the Eighteenth Century* (4 vols., New York, 1924).

W. WIRT HENRY, *Patrick Henry : Life, Correspondence, and Speeches* (1890–91).

C. H. VAN TYNE, *The Causes of the War of Independence* (1922).

G. L. BEER, *British Colonial Policy*, 1754–65 (1907).

V. L. PARRINGTON, *Main Currents of American Thought* (1927).

R. G. ADAMS, *Political Ideas of the American Revolution* (1922).

G. O. TREVELYAN, *History of the American Revolution* (5 vols., 1899–1914).

S. E. MORISON and H. S. COMMAGER, *The Growth of the American Republic* (1931).

CHAPTER XIX

ENGLAND AND THE MONARCHY

IT is a remarkable proof of the weakness of the feeling or principle of nationality in the seventeenth and eighteenth centuries that the English, as nationally-minded as any people in Europe, accepted the monarchy of foreigners over a period of nearly one hundred years. Charles II and James II were really Frenchmen; their mother was French, they were brought up, after the outbreak of the Great Rebellion, in France; when they reigned in England their manners, their policy, even their religion, tended to the French side. 'Their government was overthrown by a Dutchman; George I and George II were entirely German; and thus from 1660 to 1760, when a truly English monarch once more ascended the throne, the reign of Queen Anne appears the only exception to a foreign dominion.'

The explanation of this strange fact is that England was not democratic in the seventeenth and eighteenth centuries. Democracies are far more nationally-minded than are autocracies or aristocracies. Aristocracy is cosmopolitan; the *grande noblesse* recognises its kind in whatever country it is found. England after 1660 and down to 1760 was governed, under the king, by a small number of wealthy noble families. These families were strongly attached to certain principles—religious freedom, the Church of England, individual liberty, parliamentary government. They were sensitive too, for the honour of their country. They did not, however, consider that there was anything dishonourable or unnatural in having a Dutchman or a German

[1] Mahon, *History of England*, chap. IV.

for king, provided that England remained an independent and a free country. Nor did they object to the employment or residence of foreigners in England. At different times between 1660 and 1760 foreigners were to be found in almost every station in England—in the King's Privy Council, in high command in the Army, in the British embassies abroad, in the universities and schools, in the arts and in business.

It has been the fashion in the writing of history to be a little contemptuous of the Hanoverians. Perhaps it was Thackeray who set the fashion in *The Four Georges*. The accession of George I is regarded as a sort of mercenary bargain; as if the English wanted a Protestant king, and so were willing to put up with a foreigner; while the Hanoverian family wanted a royal crown, and so in order to obtain it were willing to give up their absolutist principles and were ready to play the part of lay figures in the scheme of constitutional monarchy.

A more generous view is probably nearer the mark. The English and Scottish peoples were overwhelmingly Protestant, and overwhelmingly in favour of limited monarchy and parliamentary government. The political chiefs who, since the Great Rebellion, had felt a sense of responsibility for maintaining these principles of religious and civil government had, all through the reign of Anne, regarded the Hanoverian family as a possible solution of the succession difficulty, if Anne died without surviving children. The Act of Settlement (1701), passed through Parliament in the last year of William III, distinctly says so :

' Be it enacted and declared . . . that the most excellent Princess Sophia Electress and Duchess Dowager of Hanover, Daughter of the most excellent Princess Elizabeth, late Queen of Bohemia, Daughter of our late Sovereign Lord King James I of happy Memory, be, and is hereby declared to be, the next in Succession in the Protestant Line to the Imperial Crown and Dignity to the said realms of England, France and Ireland, and the Dominions thereunto belonging.'

The Electress Sophia of Hanover who was expected to succeed Anne, was the daughter of an English Princess Royal. Sophia died just too soon, in the same year as Queen Anne. The Elector George, who, as Sophia's son, succeeded to the throne of Great Britain, had a natural as well as a legal claim to the throne; and, although he was a foreigner, the English, with the Stewarts out of court because of their religious and political principles, could regard George as a natural successor to the throne. That George was willing to rule as a limited, constitutional monarch shows his tact and his political sense. That he kept away from the Cabinet because he himself could not understand English is a grotesque statement. The art of interpretation was as well understood then as now. There can be little doubt that he ruled by means of the Cabinet system, because he understood this to be the way in which the English people, or the political chiefs at any rate, wished to be governed. German princes have transplanted well—the Hanoverians, Coburgs, Tecks, and Battenbergs.

The Scots and the Irish felt differently from the English with regard to the Hanoverian monarchy. George I never visited either Scotland or Ireland. There was a good deal of Jacobitism in Scotland, but apparently none in Ireland in the eighteenth century. There was current in Scotland in the reign of George I a ballad of which the refrain was: ' Wha the deil hae we gotten for a king but a wee bit German lairdie.' The ballad told how the English statesmen went over to Hanover after the death of Queen Anne, in order to ask him to be king, and how they found him ' delving in his yairdie.' The Scots, the lesser partner in the United Kingdom, were far more national in their outlook than the English.

The Jacobite Rebellion of 1715 was, probably, not very dangerous to the Hanoverian Succession. Before it took place the new *régime* had incurred some unpopularity by the impeachment of Ministers who had made the Peace of Utrecht. Bolingbroke and Ormonde lost nerve and fled. Oxford was committed to the Tower. Ormonde, who was still free, visited Oxford before fleeing to France. He urged Oxford, ineffectually, to take means of escape and flee too. ' Farewell, Oxford without a head,' said Ormonde. ' Farewell, Duke without a duchy,' said his friend. Oxford passed two years in the Tower, and was then tried and acquitted. After the suppression of the Rebellion of 1715 some twenty-six persons were executed in England—a far more moderate retribution than the Bloody Assize of James II. An important result of the Rebellion was the introduction and passing into law of the Septennial Act in 1716, partly, at any rate, to avoid the necessity of a General Election in 1717.

George I and George II were fortunate in their Ministers; on the whole George III, with Pitt, Perceval, and Lord Liverpool, may be considered fortunate too. The firm and competent administration, first of Stanhope, and then of Walpole, helped to establish the Hanoverian dynasty firmly. The Jacobite Rebellion of 1745, which was just a Highland raid on a rather large scale, could have been dangerous only to a feeble and cowardly Government. Neither the king nor the Ministry in 1745 was feeble or cowardly. The successes of Great Britain in the French War, after the elder Pitt became Secretary of State in 1757, naturally made the established system thoroughly acceptable to the people. Nothing pleases a people so much as the winning of battles.

The position of George III in the hearts of his people is difficult to estimate. They liked him at his accession, a thorough Englishman, twenty-three years old, handsome, dignified. The passage which he wrote out with his own hand for insertion in the first Speech from the Throne was singularly happy: ' Born and educated in this Country, I glory in the name of Briton, and the peculiar happiness of

my Life will ever consist, in promoting the Welfare of a
people, whose loyalty and warm affection to me, I consider,
as the greatest and most permanent security of my Throne.'
On the other hand the Peace of Paris, 1763, was held by
Chatham and by his many sympathisers to have been
inexpediently made.   The prosecution of Wilkes for issuing
Number 45 of the *North Briton*, and the use of a General
Warrant in this case, brought odium upon the Government.
George Grenville, who would have been a very good civil
servant, did not win people's confidence as Prime Minister;
nor had Grenville's predecessor, the Scotsman Bute, been
well received.   Wilkes passed through many vicissitudes
and became a popular hero; the crowd cried, ' Wilkes and
Liberty! '

Just as people are thoroughly pleased when battles are
won, so nothing depresses them more than defeats.   Between
1775 and 1783 the British lost an Empire, the American
Colonies.   The war, however (unfortunately), was not
unpopular.   Contemporary opinion in England, in spite of
the criticisms of Fox and Burke, was against the Americans.
People did not talk very much about the American War
when it was going on, but when they did refer to it (for
instance, as noted in Fanny Burney's *Memoirs*), it was not
to blame the British Government.   Therefore George's
insistence on the war did not injure him in his people's
esteem.

The attacks of Burke upon George's ' closet ' system of
Government; his intervention in politics by means of
' King's Friends '; his employment of his own friends in
parliamentary elections—in short, George's steadily maintained effort to revive the royal power, aroused a strong
feeling of protest.   In 1780 the celebrated resolution of
Dunning—' that the power of the Crown has increased, is
increasing, and ought to be diminished '—was passed in
the House of Commons.   On the other hand, Boswell
writes quite naturally, as if his readers would easily agree,
that the increase in the power of the Crown was entirely

Q

in council had power to call out the soldiers without requiring the authority of a magistrate. George immediately ordered the military to suppress the riots; within twenty-four hours peace reigned in London.

After the suppression of the riots, Fanny Burney, who was in Bath, received a letter from her sister in London telling her of ' the dreadful havoc and devastation the mob have made here in all parts of the town.' The worst elements in London had taken advantage of the collapse of authority to engage in the most outrageous behaviour. The ' genteel people ' had gone to Ranelagh to play, ' though they knew not but their houses might be on fire at the time.' There were two camps, one in St. James's, the other in Hyde Park. ' I expect we shall all have a passion for a scarlet coat now,' added Miss Burney.[1] The resoluteness of the king made a deep impression upon the country. Dr. Johnson wrote to Mrs. Thrale an account of the riots, and ascribed the breakdown of order to ' the cowardice of a commercial place.' There was, he wrote, ' a universal panic, from which the King was the first that recovered. Without the concurrence of his Ministers, or the assistance of the civil magistrates, he put the soldiers in motion, and saved the town from calamities.'[2]

In the year 1886 Lord Chichester presented to the British Museum the correspondence and state papers of the Duke of Newcastle, who was a Minister of the Crown for nearly forty years, serving under George I, George II, and, for two years, under George III. Newcastle was a busy and careful public servant, and kept very complete accounts, notes, and letters. His papers, in 500 manuscript volumes, have been for years used by historians of the eighteenth century as a quarry. It would appear that the information and conclusions to be drawn from them will never be exhausted. A very clever analysis of certain groups of them has thrown new light on middle-century

[1] *Diary and Letters of Madame D'Arblay*, sub anno 1780.
[2] Boswell's *Life of Johnson*, sub anno 1780.

politics and made necessary the alteration of some pre-conceived judgments.[1]

The opportunity for increasing, or restoring, the influence of the Crown in politics was afforded by the fact that although politics were, so to speak, divided between Whigs and Tories, there were, apparently, no party organisations, no party feuds, or discipline.[2] The Government, whether it was Tory or Whig, could never be certain that the Tories or Whigs, as the case might be, would vote for it. When division-lists of the House of Commons are analysed, it is found that members on the whole did not vote simply Whig or Tory according to their supposed party connections. On February 3, 1769, for instance, the celebrated division took place on a motion, supported by the Grafton Government, for the expulsion of John Wilkes. For the expulsion there were 218 votes; against, there were 140. The knights of the shire and members for the larger boroughs seem to have voted according to their private opinions, not according to strict party connection. They were drawn two ways, being ' divided between adherence to certain constitutional principles and dislike of the very dubious character over whom the battle was fought.' [3] The members for ' pocket ' or ' rotten ' boroughs seemed to have been most susceptible to the influence of the Government and, on the whole, to have voted with the Government in this division. Regarding the division on Wilkes and General Warrants, which fell to be taken on February 18, 1764, the Government was in the greatest anxiety. Lord Chesterfield even summoned his son, Philip Stanhope, who was a Member of Parliament, but also in the diplomatic service and absent in Germany, to come over to London and cast his vote.[4] As there was no party office, and no strict party discipline, members tended to follow the leading of some particular man, or simply to pursue their own interests. A strong-minded and

---

[1] L. B. Namier, *The Structure of Politics at the Accession of George III* (1929).
[2] *Ibid.*, p. vii.   [3] *Ibid.*, p. 190.   [4] *Ibid.*, pp. 182–183.

FOR FURTHER STUDY

F. W. MAITLAND, *The Constitutional History of England, Period IV* (1911).

J. PAUL DE CASTRO, *The Gordon Riots* (1926).

LECKY, *History of England in the Eighteenth Century.*

STANHOPE, *History of England from the Peace of Utrecht* (5th ed., 1855).

ERSKINE MAY, *Constitutional History of England* (1912).

Chapter XX

FOREIGN POLICY

STATES have to live in a society of States, just as men have to live in a society of individuals. In their relations with each other, which are generally peaceful, States tend simply to live from day to day, and to deal with each question as it arises. Nevertheless, just as individuals who are in contact with each other gradually sort themselves out according to character, temperament, and ambitions, so States form habits and adopt principles of intercourse. These habits and principles are maintained and put into action by the Foreign Offices of each country, the officials of each Foreign Office being a sort of college or corporation which retains its habits and principles for centuries. These habits and principles are the result of national temperament, experience, and thought; and, naturally, they are adapted or changed according to the demands of new situations and new eras. Thus a country's foreign relationships are directed according to definite policy, or rather policies. Every Foreign Office has a ' system,' though it is not always the same system.

The foreign policies of a Government are expressed in the instructions which it issues to its ambassadors. The French have published their instructions for the eighteenth century in a well-known series, *Recueil des Instructions données aux Ambassadeurs de France*. A selection of the English instructions for the early years of the century have been printed; the instructions for most of the eighteenth century, however, have to be sought in the manuscript material of the Public Record Office.

except that of a very great state like France, was dominated by the problem of existence. There were in the eighteenth century no international guarantees of the territorial integrity and independence of sovereign states, such as are now provided by the Covenant of the League of Nations and kindred pacts. There was a ' Law of Nations,' explained and defined in the writings of Grotius, Puffendorf, and Vattel,[1] which recognised all States as being equal, independent, and subject in their relations to each other by a ' determinable Law of Nature.' The eighteenth-century autocrats, however, recognised only State interests, *raison d'état*, as the motive and justification of their policies. Silesia was seized and Poland was suppressed, contrary to all the principles of the Law of Nations. In a Europe of monarchs who acted according to *raison d'état*, a State of only moderate strength like Great Britain had to rely on a policy of balance of power.

The balance of power could ensure the existence of the States only if it ensured the maintenance of treaties. The British Government in the eighteenth century stood firmly for the maintenance of treaties, fought for them when they were broken, and at the conclusion of each period of disturbance worked for a restoration of the treaty-system of Europe, with such modifications as seemed desirable in view of changing conditions. In general, the policy of Great Britain with regard to the continent of Europe was the maintenance of a balance of power and of the *status quo*. Particular British interests were: the mouths of the Rhine and the Scheldt, where Great Britain would not like to see any great Power in possession; and the freedom of navigation in the Danish Sound, in the Straits of Gibraltar, and in the Baltic and Mediterranean Seas.

The early years of the eighteenth century were, for the most part, years of war; and until the war was won or lost there could be little room for policy and diplomacy. The

---

[1] Grotius of Holland, 1583–1645 ; Puffendorf of Saxony, 1632–1694 ; Vattel of Switzerland, 1714–67.

War of the Spanish Succession was, on the part of the Grand Alliance, a war for the maintenance of the balance of power. Louis XIV, on his side, had a grievance. He was badly treated by the Emperor of Austria, who in 1700 refused to join in the equitable Partition Treaty concluded by England and France. On the other hand, Louis's acceptance of the whole Spanish Empire for his grandson was a breach of this treaty. His garrisoning of the Spanish Netherlands, before any threat of war had been made against him, with French troops, as well as certain other acts, showed that the Spanish Empire, under a French prince, was going to be directed by Louis himself. The phrase ' Universal Monarchy ' was in everybody's mouth at this time; and Louis XIV, if he had gathered in the whole Spanish Empire, would have been by far the most powerful sovereign in the world. The War of the Spanish Succession was undertaken by the Grand Alliance not to prevent Louis's grandson from becoming King of Spain. France and Spain were, naturally, to be prohibited from coming under the same crown; but the more immediate task was to prevent either the grandson or Louis from having the 'Belgic' Netherlands and Milan, Naples, and Sicily. These were the objects stated in the treaties of 1701-2 concluded by the English, the Dutch, the Emperor, the King of Prussia, and other sovereigns who together made up the Grand Alliance. The victories at Blenheim in 1704, Ramillies in 1706, and Oudenarde in 1708 so raised the pride of the Allies that they went quite beyond their original war aims, and demanded that Louis and his grandson should give up the whole Spanish Empire. The peace settlement of Utrecht, made (1713) after four more years of war, left the Allies with their original purposes achieved, with an added compensation for England in Gibraltar and New-foundland.

Europe thus started on the Hanoverian period with a treaty-system, established by the Congresses of Westphalia (1648) and Utrecht (1713), securing what, on the whole, was

was held at Cambrai in the years 1722–25. The British Government was represented by Lord Whitworth, an admirable diplomatist. The Congress was unable to arrange formal peace, but at any rate it prevented regular hostilities from being resorted to. As a matter of fact, the Spanish and Austrian Governments made peace by direct negotiation at Vienna in 1725, before the Congress of Cambrai came to an end.

Spain, now at peace with the Emperor, was free to make an effort to retake Gibraltar, captured by the English in 1704. Walpole, quickly but quietly, negotiated a fresh treaty of alliance with France, Prussia, the Dutch, Sweden, and Denmark (September 1725). When Spain, in 1727, opened a great attack on the Rock, the other States of Europe, owing to Walpole's alliance-system, remained passive. Meanwhile he consented that the dispute between Great Britain and Spain should be considered at a European congress. This met at Soissons in June 1728, and was rather a grand affair, being attended by Cardinal Fleury himself, the *premier ministre* of France, and by Horatio Walpole, the younger brother of the British Prime Minister. The Congress persuaded Spain to abandon the war with Great Britain, and to let the claim to Gibraltar drop. A treaty of alliance and mutual guarantee was signed (November 19, 1729) between Great Britain, France, the Dutch, and Spain. This was the result of Walpole's determination to wage only a defensive war, giving orders to the Fleet, as the poet Richard Glover later complained, 'not to fight.' In 1731 Walpole achieved another diplomatic success; the Emperor was induced to restrict the operations of a maritime company which he had founded, the Ostend Company, and which the British and Dutch merchants thought to be a very serious rival. The Treaties of Westphalia and Utrecht kept Antwerp, by nature the best port in the ' Belgic ' Netherlands, closed to seaborne commerce. The foundation of the Ostend Company by Charles VI seemed a means of circumventing the closure. Charles now agreed to limit the operations in the Indies of the Ostend Company to two ships a year. In return for this concession, Great Britain and the Dutch gave their guarantee to the Pragmatic Sanction of 1713, an Imperial law securing to Maria Theresa, the Emperor's daughter, the undivided succession to his territories (Second Treaty of Vienna, March 16, 1731).[1]

British foreign policy, directed by Stanhope down to 1721, and by Walpole afterwards, had been successful in preventing, or in helping to prevent, any fundamental alteration in the treaty-system of Europe, and any upsetting of the balance of power. Suddenly, on February 1, 1733, the ever-present danger of a general war became alarmingly acute, with the death of Augustus II of Poland, Elector of Saxony. The European Chancelleries and Foreign Offices ought to have foreseen this event and to have been prepared for it. The Crown of Poland was elective. There was always international trouble when an election had to be made. This time Austria and Russia supported one candidate (Augustus III of Saxony), France and Spain another (Stanislaus Leczynski). The election was, constitutionally, in the hands of the Polish nobles, but it was largely decided by bribery and by diplomatic pressure from the outside. Over this particular election the general war, of which Walpole was so apprehensive, broke out. He refused, however, to take part. If the French had invaded the Austrian Netherlands the British Government would almost certainly have felt itself compelled to take part in the struggle; but the French, wisely, agreed to regard the Austrian Netherlands as neutral. Hostilities lasted for about two years, and took a toll of about 100,000 lives. The preliminary treaty of peace was made in 1735, and the final peace-treaty in 1738. Augustus III of Saxony was recognised as King of Poland. A younger son of the King of Spain became King of Naples (which Austria gave up).

[1] The First Treaty of Vienna was between the Emperor and Spain, April 30, 1725.

R

Frederick of Prussia felt unsafe, and started fighting again in 1744. Great Britain won the battle of Dettingen against the French in Germany in 1743, lost the battle of Fontenoy in 1745, won Louisbourg, on Cape Breton Island, off Canada, in the same year, and lost Madras in 1746. The ding-dong struggle showed no advantage accruing to any party.

' Europe seemed to be settling down to a hopeless condition of perpetual bloodshed as in the Thirty Years War. The Austrian (Belgic) Netherlands could not be defended against French armies; Alsace was being reduced to ruins by contending Austrian and French soldiers; the Prussians were burning villages in Bohemia; the Sardinians and Austrians in alliance were fighting fiercely with Charles of Naples. A Jacobite rebellion occurred in Scotland; the Highland host invaded England. The European diplomatic system had absolutely collapsed, and the clock was set back for sixty years. The decline of Europe was never more strikingly shown than when, amid the general failure of the diplomacy of the civilised Christian Powers, the Sultan Mohammed V offered his mediation. The offer was rejected.' [1]

Pitt, himself one of the red-hot ' patriots' who had goaded Walpole into the war in 1739, wrote sadly to the Duke of Newcastle in 1747: ' This country and Europe are undone without a secure and lasting peace.' At last, in 1748, the warring Continental Powers, from sheer exhaustion, assented to come to a peace congress, which assembled at Aix-la-Chapelle in April. The final Peace Treaty of Aix-la-Chapelle was signed on October 18, 1748. Frederick of Prussia kept Silesia. A few minor territorial alterations took place in Italy; otherwise no one gained anything, but all Europe was left bleeding, suspicious, and dissatisfied.

The general war of 1740–48, usually called the Austrian

[1] Mowat, *History of European Diplomacy*, 1451–1789, pp. 232–233.

Succession War, left Great Britain in a more dangerous situation than she had been since the Revolution of 1688. The French and the British had become simply inveterate enemies. The two peoples were hopelessly antagonistic to each other in Europe, and they were even more bitterly involved against each other in India and North America. France still had some five times as many people as Great Britain, and by certain arrangements made with the Spanish Royal Family (the 'Family Compact' of 1733) could count on the firm alliance of Spain, with its Army and Navy. Great Britain had no friend. The Austrians felt that the British alliance had been of very little use in the recent struggle in Germany. The Dutch were only anxious now to remain outside of any European war and to conserve their trade and commerce. Great Britain, with no large military reserves, and threatened by a superior combination of the French and Spanish Navies, was completely isolated; and everybody knew that the general war had merely been suspended by the Peace of Aix-la-Chapelle; the causes of hostility in Europe, India, and North America were still at work.

Great Britain was now in one of the most dangerous crises of her history. The 'system' of foreign policy in which she had found security for the last sixty years—*i.e.*, since the Revolution of 1688—had broken down. She must make another system, adopt a new policy, find a fresh ally. Austria, likewise, was endeavouring to construct a new system, and Maria Theresa and Kaunitz (ambassador at Paris in 1750, Chancellor of the Empire in 1753) had formed the daring plan of constructing a French alliance. For over two hundred years the French and Austrians had been enemies. Habsburg and Valois, Habsburg and Bourbon, had fought and made peace, only to fight again another day. Now Maria Theresa approached Louis XV, and Kaunitz approached the Abbé Bernis, and they held up the glittering prize of the Austrian Netherlands. These coveted provinces, or at any rate some form of control over them, were

CHAPTER XXI

TOWARDS THE INDUSTRIAL REVOLUTION

ENGLAND is still deeply rural, a land of peaceful villages, quiet streams, wide meadows, and woodland. Among those ancient thatched cottages, with their yew-treed churchyard, and church and tower of enduring stone, time seems scarcely to have moved since the Norman Conquest. There are strange places of solitude too, not merely on Dartmoor or Exmoor or among the fells of Westmorland and Cumberland, but on wild common-land in the 'Home Counties'; indeed, no county is without them.

Yet although rural communities, and wild, unoccupied spaces of land, such as Borrow loved to visit and describe, are to be found in every county of England (and still more, perhaps, in Wales, Scotland, and Ireland), the Industrial Revolution is the most prominent feature of modern Britain. The Industrial Revolution cannot destroy, cannot even alter in many places, the enduring rural spirit of England. But in other and how many regions what a change it has made! When Tom Jones travelled out of Somerset through Bristol, Gloucester, Coventry, and St. Albans to London, he never saw anything which suggests to the reader factories or teeming cities. This was about the year 1745. But when George Eliot described a journey of some hundred years later in *Silas Marner*, she begins with rural simplicity in the valley of the Bristol Avon, but arrives in the Midlands amid the clatter of factories, and under great hovering smoke-clouds. Over large areas the face of England was being changed. Down to the end of the real eighteenth century, however—that is, down to the time of the French Revolution—the change was very slow in England, and, indeed, was scarcely perceptible.

For, from the economic point of view—although not indeed from the political—the eighteenth century stopped about 1789, and the nineteenth century began.

' The period which falls between the French Revolution of 1789 and the outbreak of the European War in 1914 [says one of the most thoughtful of economic historians] may be styled the nineteenth century. It witnessed the general application of mechanical power to manufacture, transport and mining, and was therefore a period of momentous economic change. The new inventions not merely altered all the old methods of production and distribution, but the human factor in that production and distribution, man, was powerfully affected by machinery which enlarged his capacities and potentialities, and by railways and steamships which increased his mobility. A revolution in ideas inevitably accompanied such far-reaching changes in the physical world. . . . The whole globe was knit up in a world economy of world interdependence and exchange and world rivalry. . . .

' It is thus easy to see why the nineteenth century begins (or the eighteenth century ends) in 1789. It was the starting point of the new ideas of personal freedom in continental Europe. It was also in that decade that the steam-engine, the new motive-power that was to revolutionise human capacity and mobility, came into use for other purposes than pumping water out of mines. Watt invented in 1782 the rotary movement of the steam-engine which made it possible to utilise steam to drive machinery. He had already in 1776 made steam a cheap power by his modifications of the old " fire-engine " which had been very extravagant in the use of coal, and this enabled steam to be widely used.' [1]

[1] L. C. A. Knowles, *The Industrial and Commercial Revolutions in Great Britain during the Nineteenth Century* (1924), pp. 1, 8.

The Industrial Revolution, in fact, was only just starting in 1789. When Adam Smith was writing *The Wealth of Nations*, which appeared in 1776, he did not notice any Industrial Revolution in progress, although, if the breaking of old economic and personal bonds was part of the Revolution, Adam Smith by his writing was helping to make it. In the grand and classical chapter with which *The Wealth of Nations* opens, on the ' Division of Labour,' it is clear that Adam Smith had nothing in mind but small-scale industry; and the steam-engine is not once mentioned throughout the whole book, although in an imperfect way it had been working for over seventy years. Indeed, had there been much industry of the large-scale kind the population would rapidly have increased, as it did in the nineteenth century. In the eighteenth century the population was, it is true, increasing, yet not much more rapidly than it had done in the seventeenth. In 1700 the population of England and Wales was about six millions; in 1789 it was probably about nine millions.

The Industrial Revolution, when it came, was primarily a revolution towards ' mechanisation,' that is—its basis was iron, and coal, the means of obtaining the power or heat without which iron cannot be ' worked.' Now, the use of iron is very ancient; and coal was being burned throughout the later Middle Ages. All the iron, however, produced in England before the eighteenth century had been smelted by means of charcoal; and by 1700 wood for charcoal was becoming scarce. ' Decreasing returns ' were the rule now; and by 1720 the output of bar-iron for the whole of England was only 20,000 tons.[1]

About the same time the high price of the bar-iron which had to be imported from Sweden and Russia stimulated British workers to seek out means for improving their own processes.[2]

[1] T. S. Ashton, *Iron and Steel in the Industrial Revolution* (1924), p. 13.
[2] *Ibid.*, p. 28

One of the first of the great iron-masters was Abraham Darby, who was born in 1676 at Sedgeley, near Dudley. His father was a locksmith and a small farmer, as was his grandfather also; for in those days agriculture—*la petite agriculture*—could be, and often was, combined with some domestic industry or craft. Abraham Darby was apprenticed to a maker of malt-mills at Birmingham. Small craftsmen in those days had means of saving or of borrowing a little capital. In 1699 Darby, along with two or three other men in partnership, set up small iron-works at Bristol, a progressive city which throughout its long career has quickly adapted itself to every new invention and change of trade. In the early eighteenth century Holland had a reputation in making iron pots. Darby went over there in 1704 and brought back some skilled workmen. In 1708 he took a lease of some existing furnaces at Coalbrookdale, in Shropshire. The Bristol and Coalbrookdale works were operated in conjunction.

It was at Coalbrookdale that the smelting of iron with coal and lime was first successfully accomplished,[1] probably in the year 1709.

About 1768 John Smeaton was able to make improvements upon the Coalbrookdale methods at the Carron Iron Works near Falkirk, in Stirlingshire. The Carron ' plants ' are still in operation. About 1779 Henry Cort, a Navy Agent with a forge at Fontley, near Fareham, Hampshire, so improved upon the Darby and Smeaton blast furnaces that the output of refined iron could be increased tenfold or even fifteenfold.

There was little good, however, in the production of enormous masses of refined iron if it could not be moved. The roads of the eighteenth century were really mud-tracks, only practicable for heavy goods in a dry summer, or during the short periods of hard frost in winter, and then the slipperiness was bad for the horses. The Industrial

[1] P. Mantoux, *The Industrial Revolution in the Eighteenth Century* (1927), p. 300.

Revolution would have been impossible without vastly improved means of transport. Yet the hard stone-ballasted road did not come until Macadam applied himself to the problem about 1800; and the locomotive engine did not come until Hadley's and Stephenson's inventions about 1815. Even the canal, although known since the time of the Assyrians, was not introduced into England until late in the eighteenth century. Yet, says a French observer, ' no country is more suited to a smoothly working and complete system of navigable waterways than England.' [1] It was the efficient and cheap coastal shipping transport which delayed the advent of canals. The first English canal, created through the enterprise of the Duke of Bridgewater and of his engineer James Brindley, was seven miles long, and was not completed until 1761. After this construction was rapid. By the year 1803 there were computed to be 2896 miles of canal in Great Britain. [2] In the next hundred years about one thousand more miles were added.

The ' plateway ' would have made possible the carrying (although not very swift carrying) of heavy goods, but no concerted effort was ever made for constructing plateways on a large scale; their chief importance is in leading to railways. A plateway was made by laying planks flat on the ground and end to end in two parallel lines. Loaded trucks could be drawn along this way, the wheels all the time revolving on the flat planks, without danger of sinking. Such plateways were constructed about the middle of the eighteenth century at a number of collieries. Later, in some collieries the planks were placed on edge, with a ' flange ' to prevent the wheels from slipping off. Later still the flange was put, not on the rail, but on the wheel, as it universally appears now on railway engines and wagons.

None of the plateways of the eighteenth century extended for any long distance. In any case they could only permit of slow transport until the locomotive engine was evolved ;

[1] P. Mantoux, *op. cit.*, p. 123.
[2] E. A. Pratt, *A History of Inland Transport* (1912), p. 183.

and without rapid transport for heavy goods, the Industrial Revolution could not have developed quickly—that is, it would not have been a revolution at all. It would have been a gradual adjustment of the economic, social, and political organisation of the century to the needs of large-scale industry.

The chief manufacturing industry of England at the opening of the eighteenth century was the worsted and woollen cloth industry. In the course of the next sixty or seventy years it expanded considerably, although not in the same proportion as the general trade of the country expanded. The approximate figures are as follows: [1]

	Total Exports	Exports of Worsted and Woollen Cloth
1688	£4,310,000	£2,600,000
1700	7,621,053	3,128,366
1720	6,910,899	2,960,000
1730	8,548,982	3,669,734
1750	12,699,081	4,206,762
1760	14,694,970	4,344,078

Not merely was the worsted and woollen industry growing, but it was shifting too. Since the rise of cloth-making in England, Yorkshire had been continuously of great importance in the industry. It had not, however, been supreme. Bristol, Somerset, Wilts, and Suffolk produced much more, in proportion to their size. In the eighteenth century Yorkshire rapidly gained upon the other counties. Bradford outrivalled all the East Anglian centres of the worsted industry. Although the manufacture of cloth was not increasing with marked rapidity, ' Yorkshire was developing very rapidly by appropriating to herself a larger proportion of the cloth manufacture of the nation, and was preparing for the still greater progress which the Industrial Revolution was to bring.' [2] Thus the increase

[1] H. Heaton, *The Yorkshire Woollen and Worsted Industries* (1920), p. 258.
[2] *Ibid.*, p. 259.

of population of the North as compared with the South, which was a feature of the nineteenth century, was already taking place in the eighteenth. To say that population was shifting from south to north is probably erroneous, but it was increasing more rapidly in the North.

As early as 1733 John Kay had greatly improved the method of spinning by the use of his ' flying shuttle.' Hitherto the shuttle had been thrown from hand to hand in the process of spinning. Under Kay's invention it was moved mechanically in a grooved guide or ' race-board.' Two more inventions made much later were to revolutionise the textile industry, both in woollens and cottons: these were the spinning-jenny and the water-frame. The spinning-jenny, which was successfully made in 1767, was the invention of James Hargreaves, a weaver of Standhill, near Blackburn, who, like nearly all weavers, worked at home, according to what historians call the ' domestic system.' The great idea occurred to him on observing an overturned one-thread spinning-wheel; the wheel continued to revolve, and the spindle with it. In the overturning, the spindle was thrown from a horizontal into an upright position. ' The thought occurred to him that if a number of spindles were placed upright, in a row, several threads might be spun at once.'[1] Anyone who has been through a modern mill will remember that this is the principle upon which all the spinning-machines of to-day work.

The spinning-jenny did not require any great strength to manipulate it, or any great power to drive it. It did the work of a woman—a ' spinster '—and so it was called a jenny. It could be used in a cottage, and therefore was not incompatible with the ' domestic system.' It could, however, also be used, and most economically used, in a factory, for one man could look after as many as sixty or even, it is said, 120 spindles at a time.

Hargreaves had the same trouble as all inventors of that

[1] E. Lipson, *The History of the English Woollen and Worsted Industries* (1921), p. 156.

age. Workmen rioted and broke his labour-saving machinery, and caused him to move his home; he went from Blackburn to Nottingham. Lancashire manufacturers imitated his machinery, and he had to go to law to protect his patent—unsuccessfully. He made a moderate income, however, and on dying at the age of about fifty-five in 1778 had the satisfaction of knowing that he was leaving his children comfortably provided for.

Arkwright's water-frame patented in 1769 is said to have created the factory system. Born in 1732, Richard Arkwright was a poor boy, without education. He was apprenticed to a barber in Bolton, and became highly skilled at his craft. No doubt he heard much talk about weaving and spinning among the customers of the barber's shop, for Bolton was an important place in the textile industry. He formed ideas about spinning-machinery and became friends with a clockmaker who helped him with some capital. The water-frame of 1769 was only one of his inventions or improvements, but it was the one which in time revolutionised the textile industry, for it was the application of power—first, water-power, later, steam. Its making and operation required capital and it was only worth installing if there were to be many hands and a large output and sale of textile goods. The water-frame was a machine of revolving rollers which compressed the rovings and drew them from the bobbins. It was worked by a water-wheel, and was first installed in a factory at Cromford, in Derbyshire, in the valley of the Derwent. Arkwright later became Lord of the Manor of Cromford, by purchase, in 1789.

The wealthy manufacturer, so prominent a feature in politics and society of the nineteenth century, is apparent, during the latter half of the eighteenth century, in the career of Sir Richard Arkwright. In his time, however, the wealthy manufacturer had no political power. Sir Robert Peel the Elder (father of the famous statesman) was the first to be important in politics, and this was not until after the French Revolution had begun. Arkwright, however, made a fortune, and was at least conscious of the political importance destined for ' captains of industry '; for he is said to have talked, in expansive moments, of an intention of *paying off the National Debt*. He thought and lived in the large way of the man whose resources are so great that money is no object, and who thinks time the only thing worth saving. He had ' business interests ' in all the rising industrial areas in Great Britain, and, like the modern director of great public companies, travelled swiftly from place to place, directing his powerful brain to a fresh problem in each area. A coach and four fleet horses transported him over the country. He is the creator of the factory system. In 1790 he was introducing steam-power into his mills at Nottingham. Two years later he succumbed to his old complaint, asthma, at the early age of fifty-nine.

Hargreaves' jenny and Arkwright's water-frame were the basis of the Industrial Revolution in the textile trade. Another invention, however, improved upon both of these and in time displaced them. This was Crompton's mule.

' On the one hand, it had the system of rollers which drew out and lengthened the rovings; on the other hand, it had the spindles which imparted the twist. The rovings as they were drawn out from the bobbins passed through the rollers to spindles placed on a spindle carriage. The leading feature of the mule—" the great and important invention of Crompton," as Kennedy termed it—was this spindle carriage. Instead of the spindles being stationary, as in the case of the jenny or the water-frame, they were erected on a moveable carriage or box which ran on wheels. As the rollers gave out the rovings from the bobbins, the moveable carriage—with the spindles in it rotating in order to twist the thread—receded from the rollers, drawing out and lengthening the thread. When the rollers had measured out a sufficient amount of the roving they ceased to revolve and held the roving fast, while the spindle-carriage continued to recede to a distance of 4 to 5 feet. This stretched the thread to the requisite degree of fineness and imparted the necessary twist. In order to wind the thread upon the spindles, the carriage was made to return to its original position.' [1]

In character Crompton was very different from the bold, bustling, speculative Arkwright, the barber's assistant of Bolton. Crompton was carefully brought up by anxious parents, was well educated, gentle, refined, and shy. He never could 'push' his invention, and he did not even take out patent rights. He lived with his widowed mother in an old and decayed house called ' The Hall in the Wood ' outside Bolton; and there he worked upon his mule, fearful lest at any moment the suspicious and angry operatives of Bolton would break in upon him and destroy the machine. Having at last succeeded in bringing his design to success, he sold the plan of the mule to a number of Bolton manufacturers for £106. By the year 1812 it was calculated that 70,000 spinners directly and 150,000 weavers indirectly were being employed by the Crompton mule, and that five million mule spindles were in operation.[2] The gentle, shy inventor was not penniless; he made neither much nor little, but was content with a moderate competence for his work. In 1812, however, Mr. Perceval, the Prime Minister, interested himself in obtaining a parliamentary grant for him. The sum mentioned was £20,000. Crompton was in the lobby of the House of Commons in conversation with some Ministers about it. Word came that Mr. Perceval was coming to speak to him. A few moments later a great noise and bustle arose and people were saying in horrified accents that the Prime Minister had been shot. The next Government, that of Lord Liverpool, awarded Crompton only £5000. The inventor lived on at Bolton until his death at the age of seventy-three in 1827.

The Industrial Revolution, so far as it went in the eighteenth century, was chiefly a textile revolution. The

---

[1] Lipson, *op. cit.*, p. 162.   [2] *Ibid.*, p. 161.

S

age of iron and steel really came in the nineteenth century. Down to about the year 1776 the annual increase in the output of iron, in spite of all discoveries and economies in working, is calculated to have been just 1 per cent. From 1776, however, output increased rapidly, and the application of iron to industry was enormously extended. This great increase and extension, however, was only just beginning in the years 1776-89, the period immediately preceding the great wars which ushered in the nineteenth century. It was in 1776 that James Watt brought his invention, his improvement of the steam-engine, to the stage at which it could be profitably used in commerce.

Watt had been experimenting with the steam-engine since 1762, aided by some iron-masters who supplied him with capital. Matthew Boulton, owner of the Soho Works at Birmingham, one of his supporters, wanted him to join in partnership. Accordingly Watt removed himself to Birmingham in 1774 from Glasgow, where he was a maker of mathematical instruments. It is said that the enterprising and high-minded Boulton saw more clearly than did Watt himself the great results that might flow from the improved steam-engine. A third associate was added to the fruitful partnership; this was John Wilkinson, who came of a family of iron-masters and who in 1774 was making cylinders and guns at Bradley, in Staffordshire, of a better pattern than had ever been produced before. He was not a partner in the Soho Works, but had an agreement with Boulton and Watt by which for all the machinery ordered according to the design of the Soho Works, Wilkinson should supply the cylinders. Boulton and Watt did not manufacture steam-engines for sale. They designed engines for firms who were setting up mills; the firms could order the parts of the machinery from any foundry or works they pleased, as long as they ordered the cylinders from Wilkinson's. Boulton and Watt would erect the machinery and act as consultants to the firm who had ordered the designing. In the same way, Wilkinson, when firms ordered his specialities from him, referred the firms to Boulton and Watt for such parts of the work as they were able to undertake.[1] The works of Boulton and Watt were not enormous, but machinery according to their design was ordered by practically every progressive manufacturer not merely in the British Isles but also, in the short period that intervened before the Revolution broke out, in France.

It is possible that historians of economics, beginning with Arnold Toynbee, have overestimated the social effects of the Industrial Revolution. It is true, as Toynbee wrote, that ' the essence of the Industrial Revolution is the substitution of competition for the mediæval regulations which had previously controlled the production and distribution of wealth.'[2] The change in population, however, in their numbers and in their geographical position and density, was not altogether, not perhaps even chiefly, caused by the great inventions of the eighteenth century. The progress of the Industrial Revolution was not so rapid but that very many of the labourers under the older systems could have adapted themselves to the new. Nor was the Industrial Revolution the cause of poverty, for with great output of low-priced goods, and with the effective demand of consumers strong, all workers would have been employed, and at wages really, if not nominally, good.

Unemployment, and low purchasing-power of money (and therefore of wages), under-consumption and over-production of goods, were all chiefly due to one thing, war. The Industrial Revolution made it necessary for England to be, more than ever before, an exporting country; but the recurring wars of the eighteenth century and the great Napoleonic war enormously curtailed trade with the Continent, and diminished the purchasing-power of all the European peoples, including the English themselves. The price of food, and, indeed, of practically everything, rose greatly, and taxation became crushingly high. War had the most disastrous

---

[1] Ashton, *op. cit.*, pp. 65–66.
[2] *Lectures on the Industrial Revolution* (1925 ed.), p. 64.

effect on the textile trades, which so largely depended upon export. Only the iron trade received some stimulus from orders for cannon, but this source of increase has never proved wholesome to the iron industry itself; for it directs the industry into channels not permanently and continuously prosperous. Even during the wars the iron industry did not continuously make gains; for the outbreak of every war was immediately followed by a commercial crisis, from which every trade suffered; and when the iron industry was at the height of its unwholesome war development peace might suddenly come and leave it bloated in one direction, starved in another.

FOR FURTHER STUDY

W. CUNNINGHAM. See under chap. IX.

SIR W. ASHLEY, *The Economic Organisation of England* (1923).

WITT BOWDEN, *Industrial Society in England towards the end of the Eighteenth Century* (New York, 1925).

J. L. and B. HAMMOND, *The Skilled Labourer* (1919).

J. LORD, *Capital and Steam Power*, 1750–1800 (1923).

G. W. DANIELS, *The Early English Cotton Industry* (1920).

E. LIPSON, *The Economic History of England*, vols. ii–iii, ' The Age of Mercantilism ' (1931).

INDEX